FENG SHUI

FOR

2019

己亥

年運程下卷

Feng Shui for 2019

JOEY YAP RESEARCH GROUP SDN BHD (944330-D)
19-3, The Boulevard, Mid Valley City,
59200 Kuala Lumpur, Malaysia.
Tel   : +603-2284 8080
Fax   : +603-2284 1218
Email   : info@masteryacademy.com
Website   : www.masteryacademy.com

INDEX

PREFACE

With the recent wave of Feng Shui Renaissance, we found ourselves once again drenched in a newfound interest and respect for the historic art and science of Classical Feng Shui.

If you're a careful observer, you can certainly observe what this new wave of Feng Shui pushed in: an era of accessibility where F-I-Y or "Feng Shui-It Yourself" methods emerge ubiquitously left, right and centre. Everywhere, Feng Shui enthusiasts and amateurs can be seen dipping their hands and proclaiming the methods and applications to Feng Shui in ways never seen before. As a master trainer, consultant and practitioner of this field, I am of course more than glad to see this escalating trend and interests in the field of Feng Shui and its complementary studies, Chinese Astrology, Yi Jing and Face Reading taking off.

This book is produced as my call to answer the pressing demand from the masses seeking accessible Feng Shui information and knowledge, and as well as to provide an avenue of learning for those who for reasons of the time, or perhaps distance, are unable to attend my annual Feng Shui and Astrology seminars. Just treat this annual publication as your trusty go-to guidebook to foster a new layer of understanding on the Qi that will influence properties in 2019, and the correct know-how on how to best deploy these energies in your home and workplace to your advantage. The book you're holding also clarifies and draws a comprehensive overview for the year based on the Flying Stars chart and the Afflictions for 2019.

Together with the monthly Flying Stars outlook based on the Main Door and Bedroom locations for all Twelve Months of 2019, the section on the Flying Stars for all 8 Houses for 2019 presents a clean and solid foundation to enable you to gain a more direct and encompassing insights on how the Qi in 2019 will affect you and your family, or your business.

If you're unfamiliar with the methods of plotting a Flying Stars chart, don't worry, I'll make it more convenient for you. Just go to the link as indicated on Page 12 to obtain your individual access code and generate your own results with the online Flying Stars calculator there.

Those with a more thorough understanding of Chinese Metaphysics studies would know that luck is divided into Man Luck, Earth Luck and Heaven Luck - all collectively known as the Cosmic Trinity. Notably, Feng Shui makes up only one single component of the

Cosmic Trinity, so don't be exceedingly concerned if there is a presence of negative stars in your property. Remember, any view in Feng Shui is incomplete without taking into consideration the proportion and the bigger picture of the situations or structures. Hence, the full impact of the stars must also be viewed in light of the landforms in the surrounding area, which will trigger or activate the stars' negative or positive energies.

If you're interested and would like to know more about how to do simple assessments of forms, you may want to look into my Feng Shui for Homebuyers series.

Every once in a while, I would give some "words of wisdom" to my clients to let them view things in a bigger picture. Giving in to your fear and paranoia will succumb you to a state of inaction and thus, making you incapable of accepting changes. It is important for you to note that in Chinese Metaphysics, nothing is completely bad or purely good. For every Yin, there's a Yang, and vice versa. Worrying is essentially useless; the most important thing you need to do is to understand what the Feng Shui influences are, prioritise your actions and make informed decisions.

I hope you'll find this book supportive, practical and most importantly, informative. To wrap it up, I wish you a smooth sailing year ahead in the Year of the Earth Pig!

Warmest regards,

Dato' Joey Yap
July 2018

Connect with us:

www.joeyyap.com   JOEYYAP TV www.youtube/joeyyap

@DatoJoeyYap   @RealJoeyYap   @JoeyYap

Academy website:
 www.masteryacademy.com | jya.masteryacademy.com | www.baziprofiling.com

己亥年

The Year of the Earth Pig

Exclusive content available for download with your purchase of the Feng Shui for 2019 book.

Claim your FREE ONLINE ACCESS now at:
www.masteryacademy.com/bookbonus2019

BONUS CONTENT

FREE DOWNLOAD

FSR92AC7

Expires
31st December 2019

Introduction

Introduction

In order to fully utilise the information and material in this book, you need to have a basic understanding of how to derive certain information - for example, the location of your Main Door, the various directional sectors in your home and your personal Gua Number.

How to ascertain the Location of your Main Door

In order to tap into the beneficial Qi of the year and the kind of Qi that will influence your home in 2019, it is important to be able to identify the various directional sectors of your home and also determine which sector your Main Door is located. This knowledge is particularly important for those who wish to make use of the information contained in the Eight Houses for 2019 chapter, which is based on the directional sector in where your house or office's Main Door is found.

The first step is to divide your house into Nine Grids. To do this, you just need a simple scout's compass and the plan of your house. On the plan of your house, draw the Nine Grids as illustrated in Step 1 and Step 2.

Step 1

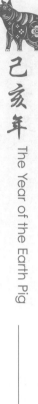

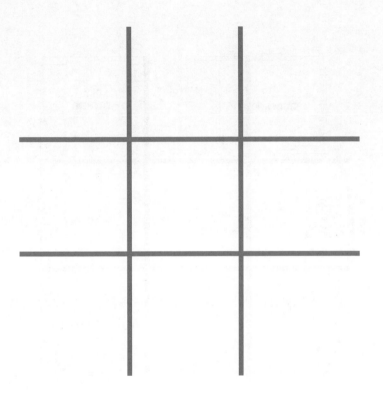

Step 2

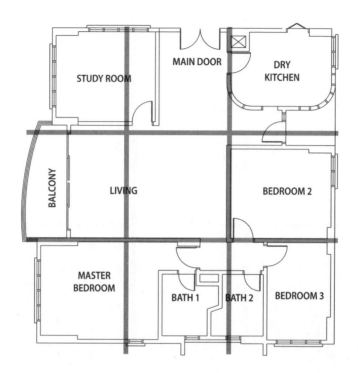

Next, stand at the center point of your house and establish the North direction using the compass. On the plan of your house, mark out the sector in that direction as North and then identify all the other directions according to the directions of the compass.

Step 3

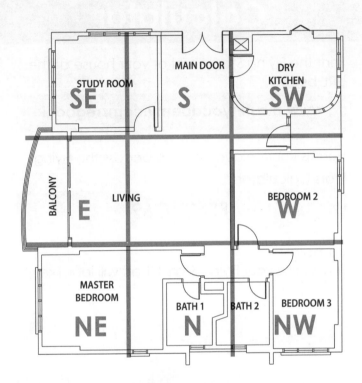

Using this simple Nine Grids, you will be able to identify the favourable and unfavourable sectors of your home and make less or more use of the corresponding rooms. You will also be able to ascertain the location of your Main Door and determine what kind of energies will influence your home in 2019.

Flying Stars Feng Shui Calculator

Print the Flying Stars chart of your house at the URL below:

www.masteryacademy.com/regbook

Here is your unique code to access the Flying Stars Calculator:

FS12VC69

Sample:
This is how your Flying Stars Chart will look like:

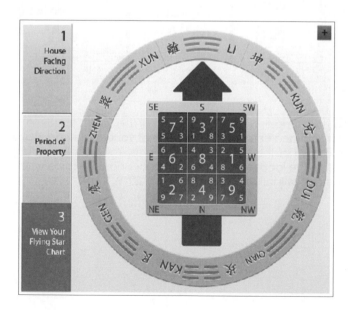

Find Your Gua Number and Animal Sign

Gua Numbers for Years 1912 - 2007

年 The Year of the Earth Pig

Year of Birth		Male	Female	Year of Birth		Male	Female	Year of Birth		Male	Female	Year of Birth		Male	Female
1912 壬子 Ren Zi	Water Rat	7	8	1936 丙子 Bing Zi	Fire Rat	1	8	1960 庚子 Geng Zi	Metal Rat	4	2	1984 甲子 Jia Zi	Wood Rat	7	8
1913 癸丑 Gui Chou	Water Ox	6	9	1937 丁丑 Ding Chou	Fire Ox	9	6	1961 辛丑 Xin Chou	Metal Ox	3	3	1985 乙丑 Yi Chou	Wood Ox	6	9
1914 甲寅 Jia Yin	Wood Tiger	2	1	1938 戊寅 Wu Yin	Earth Tiger	8	7	1962 壬寅 Ren Yin	Water Tiger	2	4	1986 丙寅 Bing Yin	Fire Tiger	2	1
1915 乙卯 Yi Mao	Wood Rabbit	4	2	1939 己卯 Ji Mao	Earth Rabbit	7	8	1963 癸卯 Gui Mao	Water Rabbit	1	8	1987 丁卯 Ding Mao	Fire Rabbit	4	2
1916 丙辰 Bing Chen	Fire Dragon	3	3	1940 庚辰 Geng Chen	Metal Dragon	6	9	1964 甲辰 Jia Chen	Wood Dragon	9	6	1988 戊辰 Wu Chen	Earth Dragon	3	3
1917 丁巳 Ding Si	Fire Snake	2	4	1941 辛巳 Xin Si	Metal Snake	2	1	1965 乙巳 Yi Si	Wood Snake	8	7	1989 己巳 Ji Si	Earth Snake	2	4
1918 戊午 Wu Wu	Earth Horse	1	8	1942 壬午 Ren Wu	Water Horse	4	2	1966 丙午 Bing Wu	Fire Horse	7	8	1990 庚午 Geng Wu	Metal Horse	1	8
1919 己未 Ji Wei	Earth Goat	9	6	1943 癸未 Gui Wei	Water Goat	3	3	1967 丁未 Ding Wei	Fire Goat	6	9	1991 辛未 Xin Wei	Metal Goat	9	6
1920 庚申 Geng Shen	Metal Monkey	8	7	1944 甲申 Jia Shen	Wood Monkey	2	4	1968 戊申 Wu Shen	Earth Monkey	2	1	1992 壬申 Ren Shen	Water Monkey	8	7
1921 辛酉 Xin You	Metal Rooster	7	8	1945 乙酉 Yi You	Wood Rooster	1	8	1969 己酉 Ji You	Earth Rooster	4	2	1993 癸酉 Gui You	Water Rooster	7	8
1922 壬戌 Ren Xu	Water Dog	6	9	1946 丙戌 Bing Xu	Fire Dog	9	6	1970 庚戌 Geng Xu	Metal Dog	3	3	1994 甲戌 Jia Xu	Wood Dog	6	9
1923 癸亥 Gui Hai	Water Pig	2	1	1947 丁亥 Ding Hai	Fire Pig	8	7	1971 辛亥 Xin Hai	Metal Pig	2	4	1995 乙亥 Yi Hai	Wood Pig	2	1
1924 甲子 Jia Zi	Wood Rat	4	2	1948 戊子 Wu Zi	Earth Rat	7	8	1972 壬子 Ren Zi	Water Rat	1	8	1996 丙子 Bing Zi	Fire Rat	4	2
1925 乙丑 Yi Chou	Wood Ox	3	3	1949 己丑 Ji Chou	Earth Ox	6	9	1973 癸丑 Gui Chou	Water Ox	9	6	1997 丁丑 Ding Chou	Fire Ox	3	3
1926 丙寅 Bing Yin	Fire Tiger	2	4	1950 庚寅 Geng Yin	Metal Tiger	2	1	1974 甲寅 Jia Yin	Wood Tiger	8	7	1998 戊寅 Wu Yin	Earth Tiger	2	4
1927 丁卯 Ding Mao	Fire Rabbit	1	8	1951 辛卯 Xin Mao	Metal Rabbit	4	2	1975 乙卯 Yi Mao	Wood Rabbit	7	8	1999 己卯 Ji Mao	Earth Rabbit	1	8
1928 戊辰 Wu Chen	Earth Dragon	9	6	1952 壬辰 Ren Chen	Water Dragon	3	3	1976 丙辰 Bing Chen	Fire Dragon	6	9	2000 庚辰 Geng Chen	Metal Dragon	9	6
1929 己巳 Ji Si	Earth Snake	8	7	1953 癸巳 Gui Si	Water Snake	2	4	1977 丁巳 Ding Si	Fire Snake	2	1	2001 辛巳 Xin Si	Metal Snake	8	7
1930 庚午 Geng Wu	Metal Horse	7	8	1954 甲午 Jia Wu	Wood Horse	1	8	1978 戊午 Wu Wu	Earth Horse	4	2	2002 壬午 Ren Wu	Water Horse	7	8
1931 辛未 Xin Wei	Metal Goat	6	9	1955 乙未 Yi Wei	Wood Goat	9	6	1979 己未 Ji Wei	Earth Goat	3	3	2003 癸未 Gui Wei	Water Goat	6	9
1932 壬申 Ren Shen	Water Monkey	2	1	1956 丙申 Bing Shen	Fire Monkey	8	7	1980 庚申 Geng Shen	Metal Monkey	2	4	2004 甲申 Jia Shen	Wood Monkey	2	1
1933 癸酉 Gui You	Water Rooster	4	2	1957 丁酉 Ding You	Fire Rooster	7	8	1981 辛酉 Xin You	Metal Rooster	1	8	2005 乙酉 Yi You	Wood Rooster	4	2
1934 甲戌 Jia Xu	Wood Dog	3	3	1958 戊戌 Wu Xu	Earth Dog	6	9	1982 壬戌 Ren Xu	Water Dog	9	6	2006 丙戌 Bing Xu	Wood Dog	3	3
1935 乙亥 Yi Hai	Wood Pig	2	4	1959 己亥 Ji Hai	Earth Pig	2	1	1983 癸亥 Gui Hai	Water Pig	8	7	2007 丁亥 Ding Hai	Fire Pig	2	4

• Please note that the date for the Chinese Solar Year starts on Feb 4. This means that if you were born in Feb 2 of 2002, you belong to the previous year of 2001.

Gua Numbers for Years 2008 - 2103

Year of Birth			Gua (M)	Gua (F)	Year of Birth			Gua (M)	Gua (F)	Year of Birth			Gua (M)	Gua (F)	Year of Birth			Gua (M)	Gua (F)
2008	戊子 Wu Zi	Earth Rat	1	8	2032	壬子 Ren Zi	Water Rat	4	2	2056	丙子 Bing Zi	Fire Rat	7	8	2080	庚子 Geng Zi	Metal Rat	1	8
2009	己丑 Ji Chou	Earth Ox	9	6	2033	癸丑 Gui Chou	Water Ox	3	3	2057	丁丑 Ding Chou	Fire Ox	6	9	2081	辛丑 Xin Chou	Metal Ox	9	6
2010	庚寅 Geng Yin	Metal Tiger	8	7	2034	甲寅 Jia Yin	Wood Tiger	2	4	2058	戊寅 Wu Yin	Earth Tiger	2	1	2082	壬寅 Ren Yin	Water Tiger	8	7
2011	辛卯 Xin Mao	Metal Rabbit	7	8	2035	乙卯 Yi Mao	Wood Rabbit	1	8	2059	己卯 Ji Mao	Earth Rabbit	4	2	2083	癸卯 Gui Mao	Water Rabbit	7	8
2012	壬辰 Ren Chen	Water Dragon	6	9	2036	丙辰 Bing Chen	Fire Dragon	9	6	2060	庚辰 Geng Chen	Metal Dragon	3	3	2084	甲辰 Jia Chen	Wood Dragon	6	9
2013	癸巳 Gui Si	Water Snake	2	1	2037	丁巳 Ding Si	Fire Snake	8	7	2061	辛巳 Xin Si	Metal Snake	2	4	2085	乙巳 Yi Si	Wood Snake	2	1
2014	甲午 Jia Wu	Wood Horse	4	2	2038	戊午 Wu Wu	Earth Horse	7	8	2062	壬午 Ren Wu	Water Horse	1	8	2086	丙午 Bing Wu	Fire Horse	4	2
2015	乙未 Yi Wei	Wood Goat	3	3	2039	己未 Ji Wei	Earth Goat	6	9	2063	癸未 Gui Wei	Water Goat	9	6	2087	丁未 Ding Wei	Fire Goat	3	3
2016	丙申 Bing Shen	Fire Monkey	2	4	2040	庚申 Geng Shen	Metal Monkey	2	1	2064	甲申 Jia Shen	Wood Monkey	8	7	2088	戊申 Wu Shen	Earth Monkey	2	4
2017	丁酉 Ding You	Fire Rooster	1	8	2041	辛酉 Xin You	Metal Rooster	4	2	2065	乙酉 Yi You	Wood Rooster	7	8	2089	己酉 Ji You	Earth Rooster	1	8
2018	戊戌 Wu Xu	Earth Dog	9	6	2042	壬戌 Ren Xu	Water Dog	3	3	2066	丙戌 Bing Xu	Fire Dog	6	9	2090	庚戌 Geng Xu	Metal Dog	9	6
2019	己亥 Ji Hai	Earth Pig	8	7	2043	癸亥 Gui Hai	Water Pig	2	4	2067	丁亥 Ding Hai	Fire Pig	2	1	2091	辛亥 Xin Hai	Metal Pig	8	7
2020	庚子 Geng Zi	Metal Rat	7	8	2044	甲子 Jia Zi	Wood Rat	1	8	2068	戊子 Wu Zi	Earth Rat	4	2	2092	壬子 Ren Zi	Water Rat	7	8
2021	辛丑 Xin Chou	Metal Ox	6	9	2045	乙丑 Yi Chou	Wood Ox	9	6	2069	己丑 Ji Chou	Earth Ox	3	3	2093	癸丑 Gui Chou	Water Ox	6	9
2022	壬寅 Ren Yin	Water Tiger	2	1	2046	丙寅 Bing Yin	Fire Tiger	8	7	2070	庚寅 Geng Yin	Metal Tiger	2	4	2094	甲寅 Jia Yin	Wood Tiger	2	1
2023	癸卯 Gui Mao	Water Rabbit	4	2	2047	丁卯 Ding Mao	Fire Rabbit	7	8	2071	辛卯 Xin Mao	Metal Rabbit	1	8	2095	乙卯 Yi Mao	Wood Rabbit	4	2
2024	甲辰 Jia Chen	Wood Dragon	3	3	2048	戊辰 Wu Chen	Earth Dragon	6	9	2072	壬辰 Ren Chen	Water Dragon	9	6	2096	丙辰 Bing Chen	Fire Dragon	3	3
2025	乙巳 Yi Si	Wood Snake	2	4	2049	己巳 Ji Si	Earth Snake	2	1	2073	癸巳 Gui Si	Water Snake	8	7	2097	丁巳 Ding Si	Fire Snake	2	4
2026	丙午 Bing Wu	Fire Horse	1	8	2050	庚午 Geng Wu	Metal Horse	4	2	2074	甲午 Jia Wu	Wood Horse	7	8	2098	戊午 Wu Wu	Earth Horse	1	8
2027	丁未 Ding Wei	Fire Goat	9	6	2051	辛未 Xin Wei	Metal Goat	3	3	2075	乙未 Yi Wei	Wood Goat	6	9	2099	己未 Ji Wei	Earth Goat	9	6
2028	戊申 Wu Shen	Earth Monkey	8	7	2052	壬申 Ren Shen	Water Monkey	2	4	2076	丙申 Bing Shen	Fire Monkey	2	1	2100	庚申 Geng Shen	Metal Monkey	8	7
2029	己酉 Ji You	Earth Rooster	7	8	2053	癸酉 Gui You	Water Rooster	1	8	2077	丁酉 Ding You	Fire Rooster	4	2	2101	辛酉 Xin You	Metal Rooster	7	8
2030	庚戌 Geng Xu	Metal Dog	6	9	2054	甲戌 Jia Xu	Wood Dog	9	6	2078	戊戌 Wu Xu	Earth Dog	3	3	2102	壬戌 Ren Xu	Water Dog	6	9
2031	辛亥 Xin Hai	Metal Pig	2	1	2055	乙亥 Yi Hai	Wood Pig	8	7	2079	己亥 Ji Hai	Earth Pig	2	4	2103	癸亥 Gui Hai	Water Pig	2	1

• Please note that the date for the Chinese Solar Year starts on Feb 4. This means that if you were born in Feb 2 of 2002, you belong to the previous year of 2001.

Using the 12-Month Outlook based on Bedroom Location Section

To use this section, you must know the location of your property's Main Door and the location of your bedroom. Note that your bedroom may be located on the Ground Floor or 1st or 2nd floor.

1. Identify the location of your Main Door.

In the example below, the Main Door is located in the West. So turn to page 153, for the section on the 12-month outlook for all 8 bedrooms for a West Sector Main Door.

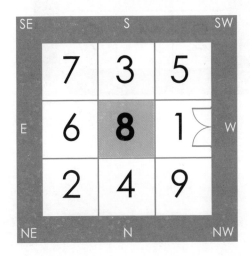

2. Identify the location of your bedroom.

In the example below, the bedroom is located in the South. So turn to page 162 and you will find the 12-month outlook for your bedroom, located in a West Sector Main Door.

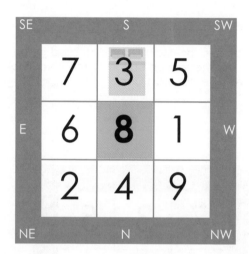

2019 Feng Shui Afflictions

2019 Feng Shui Afflictions

The Three Killings (三煞) – WEST 247.6° - 292.5°

| 庚 酉 辛 | **WEST** |
| Geng You Xin | **Three Killings** 三煞 |

As 2019 rolls around, the West sector of the house should be treated with caution as the Three Killings star occupies this space. It would be advisable to ensure no activity goes on in this side of your living quarters and leave it undisturbed. This would make sure that the negative effects would not manifest.

This particular star can be activated through any substantial changes to the immediate environment. This includes renovations, breaking of walls and ground-breaking ceremonies. Such activities would disrupt your everyday life and you might find it difficult to find some peace of mind. In worst-case scenarios, you might have to deal with the loss of material possession, compromised health, accidents and robbery if this star is in effect.

The Five Yellow (五黄) – SOUTHWEST 202.6° - 247.5°

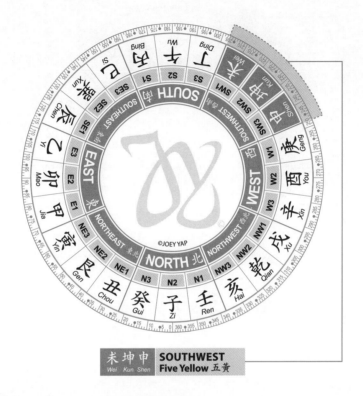

未 坤 申	SOUTHWEST
Wei Kun Shen	Five Yellow 五黄

The Southwest sector is another area to be avoided this year as it becomes the host for the Five Yellow. To avoid any unwanted events from happening, there shouldn't be any activity here whatsoever. This includes seemingly inconsequential labour such as nailing or drilling the wall. Any plans to remodel or refurbish the sector should be postponed to a later date.

If it just so happens that there are inhabitants in this direction, perhaps a study room or a bedroom, it should be relocated elsewhere for the entirety of the year. Trouble becomes your friend if this sector continues to be used and this is one friend that would stick with you throughout the year. Leave the Five Yellow alone and 2019 will be smooth sailing for you.

The Year Breaker (歲破) – SOUTHEAST 3 142.6° - 157.5°

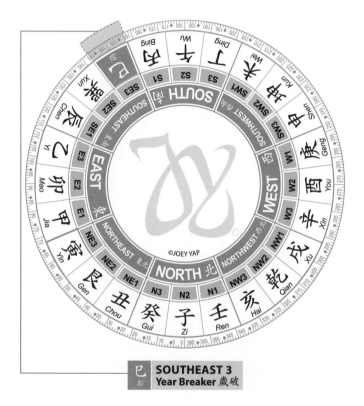

巳
Si
SOUTHEAST 3
Year Breaker 歲破

Wherever the Grand Duke arrives in any year, the opposite direction becomes the "Wrath of the Grand Duke". For 2019, the Year Breaker would be in Southeast 3. As you might have guessed from the name alone, this sector is another no-go zone.

Activating the Year Breaker is a bad idea in general, even more so compared to activating the Grand Duke negatively. If you have any prior arrangements or plans to make changes in this area, they'll have to wait. Save it for another time as it would require less effort to avoid potential problems than to handle it.

The Grand Duke (太歲) – NORTHWEST 3 322.6° - 337.5°

| 亥 | **NORTHWEST 3** |
| Hai | **Grand Duke** 太歲 |

As this is the year of the Earth Pig, it is Northwest 3's turn to become the Grand Duke. While there are negative effects if this corner is negatively triggered, it can be avoided altogether by refraining from performing any activities here. It would save you time and resources to not do anything in the Northwest 3 sector.

It is important to note that these directions don't just apply to where you live, but where you spend most of your time in as well. This means you should be mindful of where you are in your office or places where you do work. It is unfavourable not only to reside here, but to face this direction as well. However, it can be beneficial for you if you put your back facing the Grand Duke. This would allow you to have more control in your workplace and exercise authority better.

Flying Stars
Feng Shui for
2019

Flying Stars Feng Shui for 2019

Overview

Wealth Sectors : Northwest

Academic Sectors: North, West

Negative Sectors : Southwest, Northeast

2019 Flying Stars by Sectors

Direction/ Location	Annual Star	Forecast
東南 Southeast	七赤 7 Red	Things were going well in this sector last year, but it's time to move out. Where it was previously the Wealth sector is now where the Seven Red lies. Those who continue to inhabit the Southeast sector would find their physical and emotional well-being to be in jeopardy. If they happen to be married to one another as well, frequent quarrelling would be prevalent throughout the year. As if that's not bad enough, additional negative effects are in place should the Main Door be in this sector. If this is the case, the likelihood for robbery and theft for this house and its occupants would increase.
南 South	三碧 3 Jade	The Three Jade is a star that should be avoided as it may cause troublesome disagreements. With the star settling itself in the South sector, the effects it can cause include arguments and conflicts. It may also be possible to be met with lawsuits and legal complications. These issues may give you undue stress on your emotional and mental well-being. However, the effects mentioned can be mitigated by placing oil lamps or bright red items here for the duration of the year.

2019 Flying Stars by Sectors

Direction/ Location	Annual Star	Forecast
西南 Southwest	五黃 5 Yellow	The Southwest sector is a place to look out for as Five Yellow can be found here this year. Because it is one of the more inauspicious stars, it would be in your best interest to keep this part of your living quarters dormant. Any refurbishment, renovation or modification plans for this place should be postponed. Additionally, the negative effects of this sector can be suppressed by having heavy metal objects here. They can be made out of copper, brass, iron or even pewter.
西 West	一白 1 White	The West sector is the place to be in this year if you're keen on self-improvement. Make this a place to do your work or study, as the presence of One White would allow you to communicate with others better and improve your literary skills. As these are crucial skills to have, the benefits of improving them can be seen in multiple facets of your life besides academic pursuits. You may even enjoy career advancement, wealth accumulation, likelihood to travel and more. Better communication skills also translate to better relationships, so those looking to tie the knot would find this sector useful.

2019 Flying Stars by Sectors

Direction/ Location	Annual Star	Forecast
西北 Northwest	九紫 9 Purple	In 2019, the Northwest direction becomes the Wealth sector this year as the Nine Purple resides in this location. If you'd like to see an increase in your earnings, particularly if it's permanent and long-term in nature like a steady job, the energy of this sector would make that happen. With growth in profit and fruitful investments, it would bring you fame and recognition. Overall, this would contribute to your general happiness and success in your career. While the going is good, you might even want to plan for a marriage or start a family.
北 North	四綠 4 Green	If you are in the academic or artistic field, you will find Four Green to be beneficial for you. Intellectuals and literary type of people who make the North sector their bedroom or study room will find their endeavours to be successful and this includes students. The boost of creativity and inspiration can also be enjoyed by artistic people. If your Main Door is located in this sector, you may be blessed by favourable results from travelling as well as strengthening your romantic relationship.

2019 Flying Stars by Sectors

Direction/ Location	Annual Star	Forecast
東北 Northeast	二黑 2 Black	If your constitution is poor, you might want to consider avoiding this sector for the year as Two Black is now in the Northeast. The trouble associated with this star would be health-related issues and whatever problem that you might have now could potentially be aggravated. Pregnant ladies should be particularly mindful of this sector as it could put their baby in harm's way. If this sector absolutely cannot be avoided, the negative effects can be minimized by placing metal items here. The items can be made out of brass, copper, bronze or pewter. On the flip side, you can expect good returns from property-related investments out of this sector.
東 East	六白 6 White	If you have been a busy bee at work, your efforts would be rewarded with recognition and career progression thanks to the Six White. Expect good things related to this aspect of your life such as an increment of salary, promotion or being in your superior's good grace. Should your office's Main Door be situated in the East sector, your professional prestige and influence would be far more outreaching. The Six White however is not entirely a good thing, because there are consequences if it is negatively activated. Unwelcomed and abrupt changes in your working environment and health issues related to the legs or kidney would be the result.

The Eight Types of Houses in 2019

North Sector Main Door

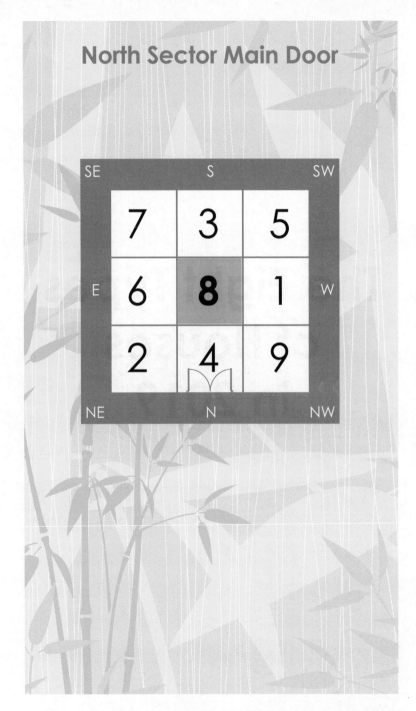

SE	S	SW
7	3	5
6 (E)	**8**	1 (W)
2	4	9
NE	N	NW

Overview

The North sector is a favourable one for you in 2019 if you happen to be involved in artistic or academic pursuits. When it comes to these two industries, creativity and ingenuity is required in order to succeed. The presence of Four Green will become your muse, inspiring you and getting your creative juices flowing.

If you're a student, it is especially auspicious to have your Main Door located in the North sector. If this area becomes your designated study room, you will find that whatever you're studying is easily understood and remembered. Working adults may benefit from this sector as well, if you're currently trying to learn or pick up a new skill. By studying here, examinations will produce positive results.

For writers seeking to overcome that pesky writer's block, this sector would be ideal and it doesn't matter what sort of writer you are. As long as the task at hand requires imagination, creativity or ingenuity, you'll get your work done in no time. If you are in the literary or writing industry, doing your work at home in this area will make it seem like a walk in the park.

Whether it's a hobby that you dabble in from time to time or something you do for a living, crafters can also enjoy the effects of the Four Green. Any craftsmanship that you create yourself such as assembling model kits, painting, carving or drawing would be best done here. The handiwork that you produce would be just as you envisioned, if not entirely flawless.

If your Main Door is here, you can expect additional positive effects in store for you this year. This particular combination would allow you to have more opportunities to travel and see the world. If you had dreamt to go on a vacation abroad or visit a place you have never been to, now could be the year to do so. The cherry on top here would be that your relationships would be strengthened as your bonds with others is now stronger than ever before.

Northwest Sector Main Door

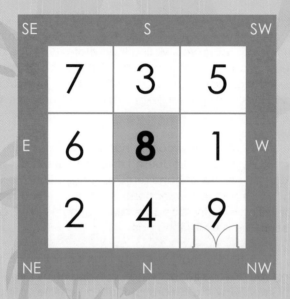

	SE	S	SW	
E	7	3	5	W
	6	**8**	1	
	2	4	9	
	NE	N	NW	

Overview

It's a joyous occasion to be in the in the Northwest sector this year in terms of love and wealth thanks to the Nine Purple. When this sector is activated, one can see improvements to their wealth luck, financial standing and social relationships with other people throughout the year. Whether it's starting a new job or a new relationship, this is a sector you will definitely want to use for your efforts to be fruitful.

While this star is particularly useful for those who have steady and permanent jobs as it would increase their salary, overall it would be a boost to your wealth luck. As such, if you're thinking of changing jobs or starting a new business venture, living here would give you outcomes that you want if not better than what you would expect.

Artistic occupants of this sector can also benefit from the Nine Purple as they would find themselves to be more expressive with what they have to offer. These individuals would be able to demonstrate their talents and in turn produce tangible results that would bring in recognition for their efforts. If you are in the creative industry, you'll shine like a star.

When it comes to love and relationships, your endeavours will become favourable. If you're single and looking, in a relationship and want to make it official, or married and want to start a family, this is the place to be in. Even if romance is not in your mind, the positive effects also extends to platonic relationships so you can enjoy your friendships better with this sector.

West Sector Main Door

SE	S	SW
7	3	5
E 6	**8**	1 W
2	4	9
NE	N	NW

Overview

The One White, residing in the West sector this year, is also known as the Nobleman star. If your Main Door is in this sector, occupants of this house will find that they'll never be without help this year. The noble assistance received can come in many forms such as mentors who can foster your growth or help in your pursuit of wealth and career.

If you live here, dealing with people in general will be a breeze. If you need any help from your superiors, they'll be more than happy to assist you. Colleagues will have no problems in helping you achieve your tasks. These effects in tandem with one another translates to career advancement, recognition and acknowledgment. Once you're successful, do remember to give credit and show your appreciation to those who helped you along the way.

Having your Main Door in this sector would also improve your likelihood to travel and accumulate wealth. While there are plenty of opportunities to improve your financial status, most of these would have been hidden if not for the One White. While you may not see the potential in each and every opportunity, there will be people with valuable insights that can advice you. As such, listen to what they have to say and you'll be well on your way to riches.

This is also a favourable star to have if you'd like to start your own family. To fully take advantage of the One White however requires this sector to be supported by good landforms. A visible mountain or hill in the vicinity would indicate noble help from an authoritative figure. There shouldn't be any water bodies or highways near the Main Door. If such influence exists, emotional issues such as psychological complications and depression might be affect the occupants this year.

Southwest Sector Main Door

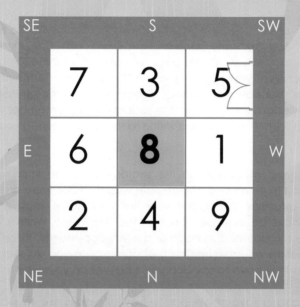

SE	S	SW
7	3	5
6 (E)	**8**	1 (W)
2	4	9
NE	N	NW

Overview

Be mindful of the Southwest sector this year as it is where the Five Yellow star now resides in. If your Main Door happens to be here, you don't need to press that panic button just yet. The inauspicious Qi can remain dormant if you keep this sector quiet and inactive throughout the year. There are also ways to circumvent around the Five Yellow.

In this sector, there should be no activities that might trigger the star. Renovation and construction that involves drilling and hammering are the sort of things that should be avoided in this sector. Any excessive noise might accidentally activate the unfavourable effects of the star which would cause unwanted problems. Suffice to say, it's an area that should be avoided.

Should this star become active, the occupants might be subject to bad luck throughout the year. They would also have to deal with constant arguments and conflict both at work and home. This undue stress may even aggravate health issues if not properly handled. Ultimately, it's best to save yourself the trouble and just keep the Southwest sector quiet.

You would be in luck if you have two Main Doors in your property. This way, you have the option to enter your house from the other door instead. If your property only has the Southwest Main Door, you may ease the negative energies by placing metal objects in this sector. Anything that is made out of iron, copper or brass may reduce the negativity and thus allow you to use this sector with less worry; albeit with caution nonetheless.

South Sector Main Door

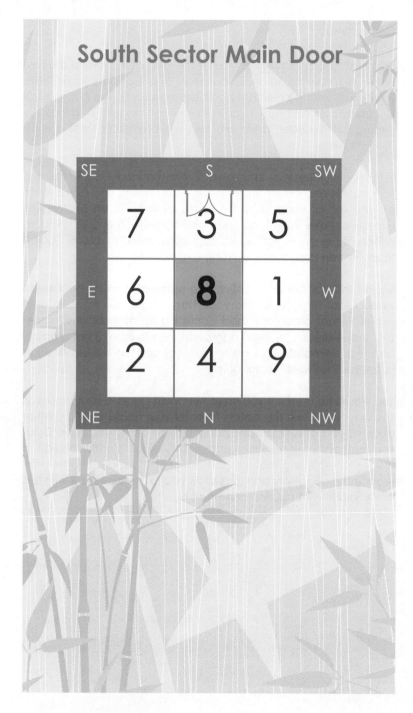

SE	S	SW
7	3	5
E 6	**8**	1 W
2	4	9
NE	N	NW

Overview

The South sector is not really harmful per se this year, but it can be rather annoying no thanks to the Three Jade star. This particular star is known to cause arguments and disagreements. This is something you probably wouldn't want to have in your relationships with other people.

The Three Jade star has the ability to disrupt the harmony of the relationships you have with others. Arguments, disagreements and quarrels would manifest itself in your social circle. Whether it's a minor or major issue, you would find yourself embroiled in unnecessary drama. One can expect to be constantly misunderstood or falsely accused. With this knowledge, at the very least, you'd know what to expect so you may handle this better.

While the effects of this star can range from mildly annoying for most people to somewhat serious if the issues it causes grows worse, if you draw the short end of the stick, you might find yourself in hot soup. There is a possibility for some people to be tangled with legal problems. It could appear in their life as a lawsuit where they are involved directly or indirectly.

If your Main Door is located in the South sector, you don't have to worry just yet. The effects of the Three Jade can be subsided by placing an oil or bright red lamp in this sector to minimize the negative influence. Ideally, this sector should be left alone to keep the integrity of your relationships.

Southeast Sector Main Door

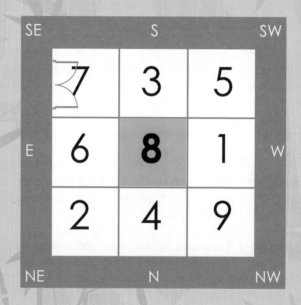

SE	S	SW
7	3	5
E 6	**8**	1 W
2	4	9
NE	N	NW

Overview

Extra vigilance and caution should be taken by occupants of the Southeast sector this year as they have to deal with the Seven Red star. This star is inauspicious for relationships in general as it would be detrimental to communication. As such, those living here would be susceptible to misunderstandings especially if their bedroom is located here.

Burglaries and theft may also become an issue this year, particularly if the Main Door is located in the Southeast sector. If this is applicable to you, it would be worth it to add security measures to your property. With ample surveillance and diligence, you may keep your personal belongings safe this year.

For those who have pre-existing health issues, staying in this sector may aggravate those conditions. Aside from more frequent trips to the clinic, in worst case scenarios you might have to go through surgery. It would be advisable for you to keep your health in top shape so even if it gets compromised, it's something you'll be able to take on with stride.

If there is a presence of lamp posts or sharp roof corners pointing to this sector, you should be particularly wary. It may result in unfortunate events that would cause harm to your well-being or career. There is a silver lining to be seen here if there exist any hills in the vicinity of this direction. It would denote a positive effect where noble people will always be there to help you out in your time of need.

East Sector Main Door

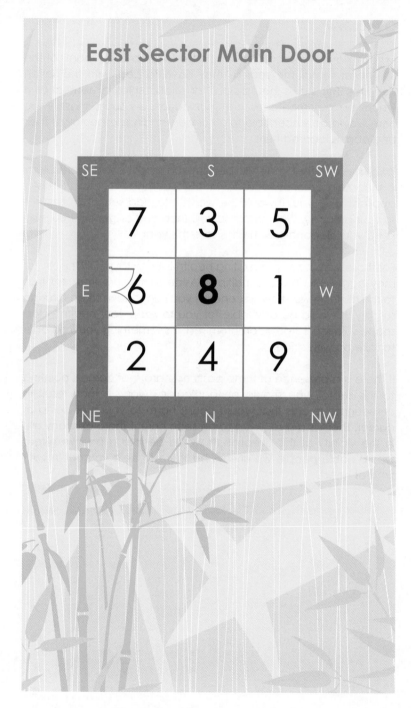

Overview

Good news for those in the East sector this year as the Power and Authority star is in your corner this year. The Six White would be beneficial for the occupants in this area as the effects would be advantageous to them. The positivity would be amplified if the Main Door is in this location as well.

If you're looking to gain authority and success in your career, you should definitely look to have this sector activated. Having the Main Door in the East sector would bring you many opportunities to let your talents be acknowledged and capture the attention of your superiors. If you have longed to get yourself promoted, this might just be the year for that to happen. Your boss would be more than willing to listen to what you have to say and offer. This star is especially auspicious if you are in the military, academic or sports industry.

Having the Main Door in the East this year is also beneficial to managers and leaders. If such condition applies to your office, it will solidify the authority and leadership of those in top positions. Their strengths will be made known and respect would naturally follow. Use this Main Door often enough and their professional status and reputation would rise. Those who stand to gain the most out of Six White would be the tourism, printing and freight-related businesses.

Take note however that there may be some unwanted side-effects should there exist any negative features in this sector. If there are any pylons or sharp corners outside of the Main Door, then disruption may occur in the office. Additionally, health complications may also be possible; particularly if it involves the legs or kidneys.

Northeast Sector Main Door

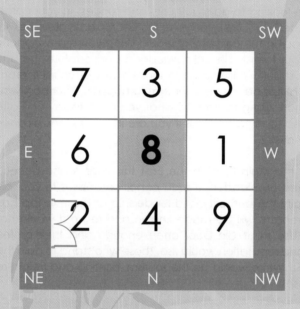

SE	S	SW
7	3	5
E 6	**8**	1 W
2	4	9
NE	N	NW

Overview

In general, the Northeast sector is a place to avoid in 2019 due to the presence of the Two Black. Also known as the Sickness star, it is known to be detrimental to the health of the occupants of this house throughout the year. Should the Main Door be located in this sector, you might want to consider staying in a different house.

The negative effects that can be expected of the Two Black related to the occupants would be susceptibility to illness. Those living here might have to take better care of their health, especially in regards to their skin and stomach. As the saying goes, prevention is better than cure; these issues can be avoided if one were to take better care of their diet and exercise regularly. Routine medical check ups and ample rest would also allow you to remain in good health. Pregnant women should avoid this sector altogether, however.

The Two Black doesn't only cause health issues, it can also make pre-existing conditions worse. As such, you should immediately seek medical attention if you notice any symptoms cropping up. Take all the necessary precautions such as your medications being readily available, keeping your loved ones close by in case of any emergencies and getting professional opinion on how to handle your well-being better. The negative effects of this star can also be minimized by placing metal items in this sector that is made out of iron, bronze, copper, pewter or brass.

While this star isn't a good one to have for one's health, it can be considered auspicious for those in real estate and investments. One of the advantages Two Black has to offer is that it can help in increasing financial gains through those endeavours. If you have a Bright Hall outside of your Main Door that is free from any negative features, you can reap the benefits and collect the positive Qi. If you're already in those lines of work and your health is as great as it is, this could play out in your favour.

12-Month Room-by-Room Analysis for the Eight Types of Houses

INDEX

Using the 12-Month Outlook Based on Bedroom Location Section

To use this section, you must know the location of your property's Main Door, and the location of your bedroom. Note that your bedroom may be located on the Ground Floor or 1st or 2nd floor.

1. Identify the location of your Main Door.

In the example below, the Main Door is located in the West. So, turn to page 153 for the section on the 12-month outlook for all eight bedrooms for a West Sector Main Door.

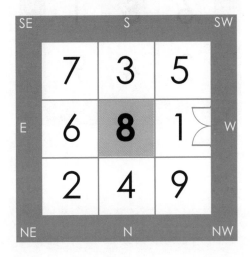

2. Identify the location of your bedroom.

In the example below, the Bedroom is located in the South. So turn to page 162, and you will find the 12-month outlook for your bedroom, located in a West Sector Main Door House.

Note: Instead of the bedroom, you can also use the same analysis for your office or study room located in that sector.

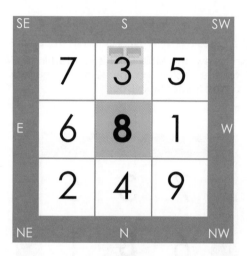

North Sector
Main Door

This section contains the monthly outlook for all 12 months of the year for different bedroom sectors, in a property with a North Sector Main Door.

Ground Floor

First Floor

農曆正月 (February 4th - March 5th) 丙寅

This will be a good month to get studious! All that is related to academics and scholarly activities will enjoy favourable luck, so if you're sitting for important examinations, writing theses, or any other activities relevant to academia then you would do well to use this room. Writers and literary types who want to put out new work and receive a favourable response will find this the ideal month to look around for publishers and agents. Travel activities will also prove to be beneficial, as it will be a good time to expand your business or forge new alliances and partnerships.

農曆二月 (March 6th - April 4th) 丁卯

Couples who use this room will find that the air is heavy with tension and discord this month. Strained relations could lead to frequent disagreements or arguments. One way to deal with it would be to go travelling together as it will help to alleviate some of the stress. Those who are in the financial and literary fields will find that they would be able to bring results from deals that are based abroad. There is a possibility of kidney and lung ailments though, so keep an eye out for any irregularities.

農曆三月 (April 5th - May 5th) 戊辰

This month, for those in the forestry and dairy farming industries, there might be a noticeable spike of interest for your products and you'll be able to take advantage of that demand. Entrepreneurs and business people will find that their company enjoys the effects of good team morale, as employees will go out of their way for the benefit of the company. However, you will do well to avoid any form gambling and financially-speculative activities this month, because the chances for sustaining huge losses are remarkably high.

農曆四月 (May 6th - June 5th) 己巳

Married couples using this room might find themselves walking on eggshells this month, as the likelihood of the female partner being argumentative is high. Those of you who need to embark on any travel trips should take the necessary precautions and invest in good insurance. Fire hazards are possible this month, so be careful when using electrical appliances and items – exercise wisdom and caution by checking the electrical wiring in your home this month, especially if it's prone to being faulty.

Main Door	North	Bedroom Sector	North

農曆五月 (June 6th - July 6th) 庚午

It's a good month for relationship ties in general, and those using this room will find it especially beneficial to consolidate both personal and professional relationships. If it's the latter, don't hesitate to strike up deals or negotiate pacts that will merge both parties closer together as this will only work in your favour. Where personal long-term relationships are concerned, it will be a good time tie to the knot. At the very least, it's also a good time to plan for marriage. You'll also find that opportunities to travel actually boost your reputation and reputation this month, putting your name in bright lights in whatever industry or field you're in!

農曆六月 (July 7th - August 7th) 辛未

Among other things, couples using this room this month would need more room both figuratively and literally. Do that and you'll find your relationship improving by leaps and bounds. You'll be inclined to be more tolerant of each other and accepting of each other's quirks and flaws when there is more breathing room between the partners. Where finances are concerned, however, huge financial losses are likely if you decide to dabble in gambling and speculative investments. This might be a time to keep your wallets firmly in your bags and pockets!

農曆七月 (August 8th - September 7th) 壬申

It's a good time to pack your bags and take off on a jet-setting trip around the world – or at the very least get yourself elsewhere! This month bodes well for your travel activities, so if you've been itching to go on a holiday or on a trip, this is the right month to do so. Your travel trips are likely to go well, and you're bound to gain quite a bit from it as well. It's a month of growth and happiness for couples who use this room. This effect also extends to couples in long-term relationships as they will find their ties growing warmer, closer, and more intimate. However, pregnant women are better off not using this room for the duration of this month.

農曆八月 (September 8th - October 7th) 癸酉

Most squabbles and tension are likely to arise on the domestic front so your home won't be a safe haven and refuge from the troubles of the world this month. There will be a lot of family disputes and issues arising that are likely to trouble you and cause some upheaval in your ties with others. In particular, these disagreements are likely to affect the female occupants more than the others. Relations between married couples are also likely to be strained this month, so you will do well to exercise lots of forbearance and patience.

農曆九月 (October 8th - November 7th) 甲戌

This will be a good month to focus on self-cultivation, as this room bodes well for such pursuits. If you intend on pursuing a course in self-improvement and development such as physical fitness regimes or motivational seminars and talks, then this would be the ideal room to use in order to enjoy favourable results. If you were to travel about this month, then it would be best for you to consider investing in some travel insurance. You might run into a few problems while on the move, as such it would be best to deal with these issues with some form of protection in place.

農曆十月 (November 8th - December 6th) 乙亥

If you're involved in public office or politics in any way, you might find it a good idea to move around more and get in there among the grassroots while on your travels. This will enable you to score popularity points and cement your reputation while simultaneously advancing your career. It will only work in your favour to put yourself out in the public eye at this point in time. People already in committed, long-term relationships might find this the perfect month to seal the deal, so to speak – so it's a good time to get married, if you've been thinking about it!

農曆十一月 (December 7th 2019 - January 5th 2020) 丙子

If you're involved in athletics, sports, or journalism, you'll find yourself enjoying a fairly good month in terms of your work and productivity. However, it will be your reputation that will enjoy a good boost during this period of time. If you're patient, you'll get all the just rewards that are you deserve. Elderly people using the room in this sector during this time will face an increased risk in strokes. They may also have to deal with potential arterial blockages and blood-circulation problems and complications.

農曆十二月 (January 6th - February 3rd 2020) 丁丑

All forms of gambling and speculative activities should be avoided this month, unless you wish to sustain huge financial losses! Certainly, property deals are a big no-no. Women in particular may be afflicted with gynecological issues so it would be recommended to go for regular medical check-ups.

農曆正月 (February 4th - March 5th) 丙寅

If last month wasn't good for you to invest your cash, this month will prove to be quite the opposite. It will be a good time to invest your money in the financial markets, because you're likely to make quite a killing on the investment circuit! Don't be afraid to proceed and let nothing hold you back. This room will also improve relationship ties for couples, in addition to benefiting students who will be sitting for examinations anytime soon.

農曆二月 (March 6th - April 4th) 丁卯

If you're looking to have children, then this is the room you should use. Your efforts are likely to bear the right kind of fruit! The only way you're likely to see income this month is through travel. Rather than seeing this in a negative light, you should consider the benefits to be reaped! There are plenty of gains to be made through your travels, so don't hesitate to grab the opportunity when it comes knocking. Be careful when signing legal documents. Don't be negligent about the fine print.

農曆三月 (April 5th - May 5th) 戊辰

You've got an eye for beauty, and while that may not be a bad thing, don't let it be the only thing you seek. As your luck in romance is fairly good this month, make sure that your potential partner is not just an attractive package, but has all the inner qualities that you're looking for, too. Interestingly enough, people using this room might be afflicted with eye trouble at this point of time! If you're dabbling in the equities market or speculative financial ventures, you're likely to see some considerable gains this month.

農曆四月 (May 6th - June 5th) 己巳

People using this room will find that their levels of recognition increase at the workplace, and with it the opportunity to receive some form of career advancement. However, you will need to bear in mind that the promotion is only the first step – as greater power and prestige comes with its fair share of added responsibility. If you've been developing a proposal or waiting to apply for a grant, then this is the month to do it. It's a good time to promote your ideas and at the same time consider selling them as well. The outcome is favourable for you to receive financial backing for your plans. Professional and personal relationships proceed quite well this month, and you will be able to enjoy an improvement in your ties with others.

| Main Door | North | Bedroom Sector | Northwest |

農曆五月 (June 6th - July 6th) 庚午

If you're keen to dip your toes into the waters of spiritual or religious pursuits, then this is the room you'd want to use. Similarly, activities like meditation and others along those lines will bode well for you this month. If you work in media and marketing, or are involved in consultancy, then you'll have new avenues and opportunities opening up for you. If you're looking for capital to help you fund a project or deal, then you're likely to receive the offers you need!

農曆六月 (July 7th - August 7th) 辛未

Bear in mind that the presence of negative external landforms outside this sector will increase the risk of fires. You will also find yourself gaining some form of positive publicity by the media this month, and it will be good for you to use this in a beneficial way to further your professional and business interests. However, if you're in transport and travel, then you should be on guard against competition and rivalry. You should be aware that possible hostile takeover bids are likely, so you can't relax and let down your guard now. Remain watchful, and always try to be one step ahead of your competitors.

農曆七月 (August 8th - September 7th) 壬申

Your hard work may enable you to get transferred to another department or division within your workplace. This, however, will be a transfer on your favourable terms, as the perks and benefits of this new position will benefit you greatly. This will be in due recognition for all your efforts. If you're feeling under the weather, don't neglect the symptoms and hope it goes away. Get it checked out, as otherwise you might exacerbate the situation into something serious. Speculative investments in finance and equities markets will result in favourable outcomes for you this month. But don't put all your eggs into one basket and pour your hard-earned wealth into every possible portfolio.

農曆八月 (September 8th - October 7th) 癸酉

If you own a business, you might be at the risk of fraud. In order to circumvent the problem, it will be better for you to do some financial spring-cleaning and conduct audit checks in order to lessen the risks. If you have a vast web of contacts, utilise them well and find ways to enable them to increase your profits. If you're a student, avoid using this room for your studies and revision, especially if you're due to sit for an examination soon. And where your relationships are concerned, both personal and professional, it would be wise to hold your tongue in most matters and maintain a low profile.

農曆九月 (October 8th - November 7th) 甲戌

If you let work stress get the best of you, it will! Don't succumb to work pressure easily, as you should exercise more control over your time to attain peace of mind. It will be extremely important for you to manage your time well and achieve proper balance between your work demands and your personal needs. Pregnant women are advised against using this room this month, as it could cause complications that could result in a miscarriage. Don't get involved in any financially unsound or speculative schemes this month, such as gambling, as the possibility to incur massive financial losses is high.

農曆十月 (November 8th - December 6th) 乙亥

After working hard to earn your cash, it's understandable if you're a little reluctant to part with it. However, if any month was a good month to do it – this would be it! Consider doing your research and investing your money in the financial markets, as you're likely to see viable returns, and maybe even some profits! Using this room can also improve your romantic relationship. Both of you are likely to be in better harmony and agreement.

農曆十一月 (December 7th 2019 - January 5th 2020) 丙子

Couples keen to start a family should use this bedroom for the month as your chances of conceiving will be higher. You'll have to do a bit of travelling to and fro before you can start to see any financial gains. If you put up with a little discomfort, the benefits are tremendous. Where legal documents and contracts are concerned, scrutinise it carefully before putting pen to paper – being negligent in this matter and signing what you don't carefully observe could land you in legal hot soup later on.

農曆十二月 (January 6th - February 3rd 2020) 丁丑

Romance Luck may well be on your side this month. At the same time, take care so as not to be too blinded by the beauty or charms of your potential partner as you may overlook the more important virtues of this person. Additionally, eye and one's vision could pose problems for those using this room this month! Nevertheless, those involved in speculative property investments and in the equities market will enjoy considerable gains on their ventures.

North Sector Main Door

Main Door	North	Bedroom Sector	West

農曆正月 (February 4th - March 5th) 丙寅

Drinking and driving is always a bad idea, but it's an especially bad idea this month as you are more likely to get into an accident this month if you were to do so. This room doesn't bode well for relationships this month either, as the likelihood of these ties ending badly and causing a dent to your reputation is quite strong. At work, you'll have some personal battles as well – colleagues who are jealous of your success and envious of you will not hide their need to compete. Don't play into their hand, or else you'll get sucked into a vicious game that will leave no winners.

農曆二月 (March 6th - April 4th) 丁卯

Go all out in striking foreign deals this month, because the outcome will be profitable. Don't stick to your usual network of connections this month; consider expanding to include people from abroad as well in order to incur some benefits. Go all out there and be visible – this is not the time to be a wallflower! Politicians will find that they enjoy a favourable month, leading to good support from the grassroots that can propel their careers forward.

農曆三月 (April 5th - May 5th) 戊辰

If you own a business or enterprise of any sort, you might find this month a little tough going. You'll find it hard to make any progress, so it will best not to waste your energy trying too hard. Instead, just keep a low profile and secure your position at where it is. Where your physical health is concerned, you will need to be careful of potential head injuries this month. Also, lung infections or lung-related troubles might crop up. Avoid all forms of speculative investment, or you'll only end up losing your money.

農曆四月 (May 6th - June 5th) 己巳

For this month, this room bodes well for academic luck. If you're a student using this room for studies, you'll find that it will benefit you if you have to sit for any examinations this month. Any deals located abroad or in other countries will need to be concluded and closed this month, especially if it involves some form of asset acquisition. This room also bodes well to further your romantic ties, and it will also be useful for furthering relationship ties – however, this will only work if there are no natural water in this sector.

Main Door	North	Bedroom Sector	West

農曆五月 (June 6th - July 6th) 庚午

Couples who use this room might run into a spot of romantic trouble this month. If your relationship is strained and tense, don't give in to your temptation to be short with your words and hurtful with your actions. Instead, it would be better for you to be more tolerant and understanding of each other. If you're involved in the furniture business, you will find that profits will pour in! Generally, those using this room should be careful with their behaviour and speech; there is a good chance that lawsuits might dog you and people will talk about you behind your back. Don't give them fodder for gossip and keep a low profile.

農曆六月 (July 7th - August 7th) 辛未

Expectant women should avoid using this room for the month, as miscarriages or complications might occur. In general, if you're in poor health or feeling unwell and frail, avoid this room altogether as otherwise you will be prone to illnesses. Marital tension is rife for couples using this room. Be more tolerant of each other, as no one is perfect and every person comes bundled with a package of flaws. The more you strive to understand each other, the stronger your relationship will be – and the chances of being bothered by trivial differences will lessen.

農曆七月 (August 8th - September 7th) 壬申

Generally, this will be a favourable month for most. Relationships and career aspects of your life is looking to be smooth sailing. All that you need to succeed and make inroads at work is already in you; use your knowledge, wisdom, and unique talents to be ahead of the curve. Be proactive in doing this, take the initiative and the results will be in your favour! This is an especially good month for Gua 6 people to highlight and showcase their own talents.

農曆八月 (September 8th - October 7th) 癸酉

This month continues much in the same vein as before where work is concerned. Don't be too modest or shy to show off your abilities and talents at work, as this where you'll gain true recognition! Doing so will enable your superiors and bosses to notice you and value your contribution, leading to a much-deserved promotion for you. Married couples using this room will notice an increased improvement in relationship ties. If you're in the midst of negotiating or closing new deals, make an effort to seal the deal this month as the results are likely to be in your favour.

農曆九月 (October 8th - November 7th) 甲戌

If you're involved in the real estate industry, then this would be a good month for you to consider some sound investment opportunities. If you're single and looking for some romance this month, then this would indeed be the room to use! If you're into professional sports and athletics or work with machinery, it will be good for you to take advantage of the opportunities at your disposal.

農曆十月 (November 8th - December 6th) 乙亥

Where work is concerned, this is a highly competitive month. You'll find rivalries have intensified to a boiling point. As such, office politics and drama will be played out with concentration. It would be best, and safest for you to remain as the detached, impassioned observer. If you get involved, you're likely to be beaten down by your rivals. Those of you entering the career workforce for the first time should be extra vigilant, as there is a strong likelihood that you will be manipulated or exploited. Don't trust anyone too easily and maintain a healthy sense of skepticism.

農曆十一月 (December 7th 2019 - January 5th 2020) 丙子

If you're involved in politics and public service, then you're likely to enjoy a favourable month. You'll enjoy the benefits of strong support from the public which could help you rise in ranks and attain more respectable positions in the political parties to which you feel affiliation. Foreign connections and networking will bring favourable results for you and professional partnerships with someone who lives abroad would also count! Make this your month of being a professional social butterfly as it will be a good time for you to forge new connections and build relationships from scratch.

農曆十二月 (January 6th - February 3rd 2020) 丁丑

Speculative investments – especially equity investments and gambling – should be avoided at all costs this month, as there is a risk of significant loss of wealth. Health-wise, you need to look out for lung and head injuries this month. Business owners will find it hard to make progress in anything this month so if you're one of them, lie low and consolidate your position at this point.

| Main Door | North | Bedroom Sector | Southwest |

農曆正月 (February 4th - March 5th) 丙寅

High risk investment deals are a no-no for this month. The results could be bad, and this is especially true where property deals are concerned. It would be best to stake your bets on this another time. If you own a business, don't think about expansion at this point. Instead, seek to consolidate your position and use it to leverage new connections. There will be a time in the future to magnify your assets and until then, have patience.

農曆二月 (March 6th - April 4th) 丁卯

Couples will be having problems in their relationship, more so than usual. Your best bet is to prevent these from becoming serious full-fledged arguments. Be objective in evaluating each problem, and don't let your emotions take the reign. If it seems like solving certain issues in your life feels like you're beating your head against the wall, then take a step back and relax. Not every problem needs to be solved immediately. Some solutions will come to you with patience, in time.

農曆三月 (April 5th - May 5th) 戊辰

If you own or run a company or a corporation, a key problem that you'll face this month is your employees' lack of motivation. It is imperative that you boost their morale, or the repercussions could be severe in the coming months. This concern should override any financial or strategic directives you seek to implement at this point in time. Those of you using this room will also sense a chill descending upon your romantic relationships. It might be better to consider using another room in the meantime. Health-wise, pay attention to potential kidney and eye problems that could develop into something worse.

農曆四月 (May 6th - June 5th) 己巳

Any health issues this month, even seemingly minor ones, should be thoroughly checked out. Don't put off going to the doctor if you see any symptom, or you'll have to pay for your oversights later on – and the consequences could be serious. Better to be safe than sorry. Pregnant women should avoid using this room for the month as complications could arise. There is also a possibility for you to lose when it comes to property dealings, so if something seems too risky then it's better to avoid it altogether.

Main Door	North	Bedroom Sector	Southwest

農曆五月 (June 6th - July 6th) 庚午

Financial losses are still quite possible for this month, so it's best to toe the line and avoid risking anything. That means speculative financial investments are to be avoided like a plague! Gambling is another high-risk activity that you'll do best to refrain from. You'll find yourself having to beat down tough competition this month, which will leave you feeling drained of energy. Try not to drown your sorrows in alcohol, if you can help it, as drinking too much this month could result in negative outcomes for your relationships! So be on guard and try to be on your best behaviour to ride out the stress of this month.

農曆六月 (July 7th - August 7th) 辛未

There is trouble in paradise this month for those of you who are happily ensconced in relationships and marriages. Be careful that small arguments and disputes don't turn into something nasty and serious. Lay low if you have to. You'll find that your employees, if you run a business or corporation, to be less than helpful this month. So if need be, avoid scheduling major projects and tasks that require their serious collaboration and input. For the time being, it's best for you to fly solo and take on the work alone.

農曆七月 (August 8th - September 7th) 壬申

This would be another month to avoid risky transactions. This is especially true if property deals are involved. You are more likely to lose money rather than gaining it. You might also want to avoid diving into anything new this month, as the chances of it enjoying success are slim to none. It would also be a good idea to avoid this room if you're feeling generally listless and poor of health, as the energies present here could exacerbate the issue. This is particularly true if you're having gastrointestinal issues.

農曆八月 (September 8th - October 7th) 癸酉

Couples using this room for this month will find their relationship ties somewhat strained, and testy at points. Even seemingly normal and ordinary arguments could get blown out of proportion. If using another room is unlikely, then bear this mind and avoid getting into any serious discussions this month. Those of you who are business owners and managers in the tourism, travel, and media industries will also find it hard-going. You'll have some trouble meeting your sales targets. Health-wise, bladder and kidney problems should be anticipated.

農曆九月 (October 8th - November 7th) 甲戌

Be on a lookout for fire hazards this month and check out all the electrical wiring in your home. If you run a company, try not to focus so much on creating profits and boosting your financial standing. You have more important things to look into, and that includes ensuring that your employees are satisfied. Focus on building team morale. If that is an issue, no amount of planning can take your company further.

農曆十月 (November 8th - December 6th) 乙亥

Certain health problems will present themselves to people using this room this month. These will mostly be in the form of injuries like ligament, muscle, and tendon injuries. Be particularly careful if you lead an athletic lifestyle, play sports, or workout. If you're newlyweds using this room, then you should be prepared for the honeymoon period to definitely be over as tension and strife will feature prominently. Be cautious when dealing with these problems and be gentle when dealing with each other. Sleeping in this room will also cause some mental stress and emotional instability. Think of ways you can de-stress and relax, otherwise the pressure will get to you.

農曆十一月 (December 7th 2019 - January 5th 2020) 丙子

Further misunderstandings and disagreements will plague couples this month, so you will have to guard against these becoming full-fledged problems. Try to approach each problem calmly, and don't over-react or the repercussions could be unfavourable. Most of you using this room will find that problems are hard to solve this month. It will be challenging to get to the root of the matter. Don't try too hard; just let it go, and the situation will improve in time. Certain serious health issues may possibly come up, like throat and mouth cancer, so get yourself a thorough check-up if something doesn't seem right.

農曆十二月 (January 6th - February 3rd 2020) 丁丑

If you're a manager or employer, this will be a tough month. There will be a tendency amongst your employees or subordinates to be disloyal this month. Look out accordingly for any potential signs of disgruntlement or trouble. You may find yourself feeling disgruntled and very out-of-sorts. This is not an ideal time to finalize any deals, so wait until a better opportunity appear to make your move.

North Sector Main Door

SE	S	SW
7	3	5
E 6	**8**	1 W
2	4	9
NE	N	NW

農曆正月 (February 4th - March 5th) 丙寅

Clarity of thought will favour those who need to make important decisions this month, so those of you facing big decisions needn't be overly worried! Just be calm and consider your options without too much of an emotional to-do, and you're likely to reach a conclusion easily. If you're involved in business, hostile takeovers from rivals and enemies are possible; you need to be prepared with some counter-attack plans. Be ready for some fierce competition and be ready to fight back! Romantic interludes should be avoided this month, as it will only bring about trouble and heartache.

農曆二月 (March 6th - April 4th) 丁卯

Hold your tongue, and you may just save yourself a world of potential trouble by doing so. This is not the month to fly off the handle and give in to your emotional outbursts! See if you can delay or postpone any major business decisions to a more favourable period, because otherwise they're all likely to go wrong. If you're feeling sick and unwell, then using this room will only make your condition worse – so see if there's a chance for you to move into another room temporarily.

農曆三月 (April 5th - May 5th) 戊辰

If your health situation is frail and weak to begin with, this is not the month to push your body further. Don't be reckless and negligent; your body has served you well throughout the years, so now you should give it the proper care it deserves! Otherwise, internal injuries are possible. Fraud and theft could plague people using this room, resulting in a loss of finances. However, speculative financial investments are likely to yield some good profits.

農曆四月 (May 6th - June 5th) 己巳

Recognition and praise could come your way at work, with bouquets instead of brickbats thrown at you! With this recognition there exists a chance to get promoted, and to have your status and authority at the workplace also strengthened. Don't be too modest – you've done your work and you deserve your time to shine, so step forward accordingly. Parents might have to deal with difficult, rebellious sons if their sons are using this room. A change of rooms might restore peace to the household and calm their rebellious natures.

Main Door	North	Bedroom Sector	South

農曆五月 (June 6th - July 6th) 庚午

It would be best to avoid important business decisions this month if you sleep in this room, because disputes are possible – particularly those born in the Year of the Goat. Along with this comes the possibility of slander as well. Those in business should toe a conservative line this month as there is a possible demotion if they step out of line! It will be best for you to play by the rules and consider attempting any risks only in the future. Couples using this bedroom this month must be patient and tolerant with each other, especially so since both of you will be listening to others instead of each other.

農曆六月 (July 7th - August 7th) 辛未

If you own or run a business, be super vigilant of rivals posing as allies as this will result in losses for your enterprise. Wolf dressed as sheep clothing will be heading your way this month, so exercise skepticism and be on guard. Couples should make an effort in their relationships this month. Neglecting your other half could result in poachers honing in on your territory! In other words, don't neglect to pay attention to your partner, or you might find others are more than willing to step into your shoes. Newfound fame and enhanced reputation will bring an increase in wealth for those in the literary and creative arts field.

農曆七月 (August 8th - September 7th) 壬申

Those in the analytical, research, statistical, or scientific fields will benefit from the good energies of this sector and find breakthroughs in their line of work. What seemed mired in uncertainty before will now seem crystal clear! If you're in the mining and construction industries, then you will find this a good month to make inroads into your competitors' markets. If you're reluctant to implement the changes that are required in your line of work, you'll find this an immensely challenging month indeed. It's best to adapt to the new requirements and stretch your creative-thinking muscles.

農曆八月 (September 8th - October 7th) 癸酉

Speculative investments, especially in the futures market, will return favourable profits. This is a month where you can afford to play around with your money! If you're in merchant banking or equity dealing, you'll be able to negotiate some favourable deals and strike a good profit. Couples using this bedroom will need to be discreet and tolerant of each other, as disputes and arguments will be prominent this month. If there's nothing nice to say, then you're better off not saying anything! You may suffer a loss of income through legal issues caused by financial problems this month, so you will need to be on guard and be careful.

農曆九月 (October 8th - November 7th) 甲戌

If you're in the legal field, you will do well financially this month. However, bear in mind that you won't be seeing the money and rewards for your efforts immediately. These can only be claimed at a later date. There is a heightened increase in risk of robberies and theft this month. Those who want to change careers or who want to start new businesses should do so this month, because you'll find that the opportunities to do are available and the results are likely to be good.

農曆十月 (November 8th - December 6th) 乙亥

This month, those using this room will have clarity of thought at its peak, and logical thinking and clear-headedness prevails. This is the month when you will want to put strategic thinking and planning into action, because the results that come out of it will be positive. But if you're offered investment deals that sound too good to be true, it probably is. Don't be swayed by the sweet-talking of conmen, as you'll not only end up losing your money but become mired in legal troubles as well. Children who use this room will likely benefit from the good energies to do well in academics.

農曆十一月 (December 7th 2019 - January 5th 2020) 丙子

Those of you in the restaurant or food and beverage industry will find it a good month to consider expansion. If you're required to travel to conclude the deals or negotiation, all the better for you, as the outcome is likely to be in your favour. If you run or operate a business and will need to do some leveraging in order to float your company, you'll find that the hard work this month is its own blessing in disguise. The month is auspicious for just such activities, and your efforts will not go unrewarded. Possible health problems that could crop up from using this room will be related to the eyes.

農曆十二月 (January 6th - February 3rd 2020) 丁丑

If you're a professional in the engineering and technical field, you will find your skills duly recognized by your superiors, resulting in a possible promotion and salary increment. Therefore, make the most of this month. However, as an employer, don't be surprised or disheartened if you find your employees seemingly working against each other. Perhaps they just lack clear direction and a sense of purpose and you will need to provide direction. Emotional problems may hound you, so don't delay in seeking professional help to prevent yourself from slipping into a state of depression.

| Main Door | North | Bedroom Sector | Southeast |

農曆正月 (February 4th - March 5th) 丙寅

You'll have to guard against jealousy creeping into relationship this month, or it could result in a lot of painful arguments. If you're able to put things into perspective and exercise a lot more patience, things will go smoothly for you. You should avoid using this room to study, as there could be sudden disruptions that might cause your examination results to go in entirely a different direction than you hoped. Possible gossip or rumours might plague the people using this room, resulting in a loss of reputation or credibility. Endeavour to keep your head above water and avoid doing anything that will cause further speculation.

農曆二月 (March 6th - April 4th) 丁卯

Stress and turbulent emotions might be the hallmarks of this month. At the same time, travelling about this month will help you enhance your reputation. Your public image will receive a much-welcomed boost. If you're working in a legal capacity, or in a legal advisory of any sort, your services will be sought after this month! Business will be booming for you.

農曆三月 (April 5th - May 5th) 戊辰

This month, the fires of romance will be easily snuffed out and there is a high chance of short-lived relationships. However, in terms of finances, this is a fairly favourable month. Property investments that you may have dabbled in at some point in the past will start to show returns this month. At the same time, salaried workers and employees who are working for someone else will find this a good month to make some cash on the side. Explore all possibilities for freelance and side income – if it's based upon your interests and passions, it's a double bonus!

農曆四月 (May 6th - June 5th) 己巳

Health issues are of primary importance this month, so try to make your own wellbeing a priority. The possibility of limb injuries is high, and you may also experience some food poisoning issues. Also, get your blood checked to make sure nothing is amiss. Where work is concerned, those of you in the travel and communication industries will find this a bumper month in terms of increased status. You'll enjoy enhanced status and recognition in your field and will likely also see promotions and advancements in your career.

| Main Door | North | Bedroom Sector | Southeast |

農曆五月 (June 6th - July 6th) 庚午

As much as possible, you need to reign in the party animal in you this month and spend some quiet time at home. Too much time spent at bars and nightclubs will only invite unwanted trouble into your life at this point. However, you do require the center stage spot at this point in time – where your career is concerned. Any publicity you get as a result of the work you do will result in strong career advancement, so don't shy away from the limelight where your job's concerned! Females using this room who invest in enterprises and businesses located abroad will profit well from it, enough to make some sustainable financial gains.

農曆六月 (July 7th - August 7th) 辛未

Financial boon is possible this month, perhaps by opportunities made and realised through real estate. However, it doesn't come easy as misunderstandings and quarrels are likely to plague you before you're able to see the gains. Where your work or business is concerned, you're able to make some profits by attracting new clientele and customers to your enterprise. But, you need to be ambitious and strong as the only way to attract new people is to take on your competitors headfirst. Children and young people using this room will do well in their studies, as the sudden changes brought upon them in their work will benefit them and help them to obtain the results they want in their examinations.

農曆七月 (August 8th - September 7th) 壬申

They say if you've got it, flaunt it, but you're better off keeping your extra wealth under wraps this month! There is a risk of robbery and theft for those using this room, so it's best to keep a low profile where money matters are concerned. Your relationships are rife with emotional undertones this month, so it would be best to have a clear head about matters at hand. Separate reason from emotion and don't confuse your feelings with the issue at hand.

農曆八月 (September 8th - October 7th) 癸酉

People in the legal and judicial fields will do well this month and see some recognition and advancement at the workplace. Others will find that this is a somewhat challenging month, as rivalries intensify and competition becomes strong. This will affect both employers and employees, putting a damper on the morale somewhat. It will be important to keep an eye on the future and see the bigger picture. The green-eyed monster rules the roost in the domestic sphere this month, and as a result, you're likely to be knee-deep in fights and quarrels as a result. Keep your relationship free of suspicion and finger-pointing as much as possible.

農曆九月 (October 8th - November 7th) 甲戌

Words said and words misunderstood will be the general theme this month as misunderstandings are rife and relationships are likely to be a little tense as a result. This applies to both personal and professional ties, so you might want to be a little careful with what you say and how you convey your message. Negative forms or features located outside this particular sector and room will negatively affect any of your business dealings, as legal tussles are likely to be the result of it. But, in general, you will need to be sensitive and attuned to all the legal details in all of your business deals this month, because otherwise you're liable to face some problematic issues in the future.

農曆十月 (November 8th - December 6th) 乙亥

If you're in the publishing or media industries, then you can gear up for a pretty spectacular month. You'll be able to make sizeable investments that can ring in quite a hefty chunk of profits – however, you'll need to be sure that you're not taking any shortcuts. Keep all the legal strings tied and all issues in place, and you're likely to do well. In fact, this month may bring about sudden and unexpected highly-charged problems. If you're not careful, it could necessitate the involvement of lawyers. Be patient and calm through it all. Couples who use this room will also find themselves at opposite ends of the spectrum, as misunderstandings are common. Keep the lines of communication open to prevent emotional distance.

農曆十一月 (December 7th 2019 - January 5th 2020) 丙子

If you're looking anew in the romance department, then there's no better place to scope out prospective mates than among your own circle of friends and acquaintances! Think about the awkward getting-to-know-you phase you can skip; plus you'll already have an idea of your prospective partner's good and bad points. You'll be able to make some quick investment gains this month, but don't attempt it alone. In order to move things forward, you'll need to rely on the advice of people in the know. If you're in the business of leisure and entertainment – specifically adventure and theme parks and games – you'll see the financial aspects of your business doing well this month.

農曆十二月 (January 6th - February 3rd 2020) 丁丑

You will want to use this room this month if you plan on starting a family soon. This will increase your chances of conceiving! Relationships will be harmonious and thriving this month, so why not use this opportunity to foster even closer ties with your loved ones? Indeed, this is a fairly favourable month where good financial returns can also be expected of any property investments made earlier.

North Sector Main Door

農曆正月 (February 4th - March 5th) 丙寅

There will be a heightened risk of family discords and tension for this month. Try not to let your emotions be blown about by every wind, or you'll risk saying the wrong thing and offending people. Negative structures outside this room during the month indicate a high possibility of the son in the family turning against the father or having some intense disagreements. Where work is concerned, you will find that there is a lot of internal fighting going on, leading to heightened office politics. It would be best to keep your head down and stay out of it. Health-wise, older men using this room should pay attention to any health problems that arise out of blood and lung disease or complications.

農曆二月 (March 6th - April 4th) 丁卯

There are some good news for investment and merchant bankers as you'll be able to conclude certain deals in the share and equity markets that will bring you good profits. Those of you who work a salaried job will finally gain long-awaited respect and accolades from your superiors – which could happily lead to a pay raise or even a promotion. If you're using this room this month, chances are your emotional landscape is a little dotted with anxiety. You may be feeling somewhat fragile emotionally, and prone to suffering from excessive loneliness. It would be the best time not to retreat from friends and loved ones, try to spend more time with them to assuage the isolation you feel.

農曆三月 (April 5th - May 5th) 戊辰

This will be a bumper month for you if you're in the legal industry, as there will be a strong demand for your skills and expertise. Your time will be spent constructively. But you do need to be wary of gossip, as this might plague you and cause a slight dent to your reputation. As such, it might be preferable for you to take a backseat this month and keep a low profile. Because jealousy and rivalry will be intense, even small missteps can result in possible legal tangles. You'll also find that relationships begun this month will be passionate but short-term flings, rather than long-term partnerships with a potential future.

農曆四月 (May 6th - June 5th) 己巳

If you've been a hardworking, faithful employee in your company thus far, you'll find that you get your just rewards and benefits this month! Your efforts will not go unrecognised. Those of you who run or manage a company should take it easy on your staff and employees this month, especially if you need to achieve your goals urgently. They will respond better, and produce better work, if you take the pressure off of them. If you're a professional sports player, you will find yourself outshining your competitors this month.

| Main Door | North | Bedroom Sector | East |

農曆五月 (June 6th - July 6th) 庚午

If you're using this room this month, you will find that most of your efforts go unnoticed by your boss or superiors. A certain feeling of invisibility might creep in! You will have to work doubly harder to obtain even the simplest form of acknowledgement. Don't bend over backwards to receive recognition – just roll with it and bear in mind that this time will pass soon. You might want to make an effort to invest in property transactions this month, as there is a chance of making good financial gains. People who use this bedroom this month will find that anxiety, stress and mental pressure will start to take its toll. Make an effort to learn how to distress and relax, as otherwise the repercussions will only affect you.

農曆六月 (July 7th - August 7th) 辛未

If you dabble in speculative investments in equities and stocks, you'll find that this a good month to make some profits of it and enjoy some financial gains. But resist the urge to shout about your profits to all and sundry, as it will be better for you to conceal this windfall. If you're an academic or involved in the literary field, this will be a great month for bouts of new inspiration and ideas; better still, these are likely to lead to good financial gains as well. Newly-weds who are using this bedroom will find this month to be a conducive one for enhancing growth and development.

農曆七月 (August 8th - September 7th) 壬申

Be extra careful when you're driving and on the road this month. The risk of accidents is particularly high. Don't cut corners and be cautious. Adolescents using this room this month will be particularly fractious and rebellious, they will continue to test the boundaries set by their parents. Parents will have to be particularly patient and unyielding at the same time! If you work in the engineering industry, you'll find yourself on the good side of your bosses and superiors. In fact, a pay raise is entirely possible this month!

農曆八月 (September 8th - October 7th) 癸酉

If you're in the real estate industry, then make the most of the positive energies of this month! Consider investing in some worthy property deals, as you're likely to receive good profits in return. If you're working in the insurance field, you are also likely to expand your business. Business will be good and you'll benefit tremendously from it all. You'll also find yourself battling bouts of depression and dealing with tumultuous emotions and feelings.

農曆九月 **(October 8th - November 7th)** 甲戌

If you're in the literary and academic fields, this is a good month for you to receive recognition and rewards that can lead to both fame and advancement! This is most definitely a beneficial month for you. Analysts will find this an exciting month, as your career will take off as a result of your smart and strategic positioning in the equities market. Partnerships and alliances do well this month, especially for those who invest in their future together.

農曆十月 **(November 8th - December 6th)** 乙亥

Couples using this room this month will have a happier and more contented time of it, and both of you are also doing well in your respective careers. As such, satisfaction is high in both personal and professional aspects. Try your best not to situate any children in this bedroom this month, as they are likely to become rebellious and difficult to control. The common word parents will be hearing is "No!" Employers should be careful with how you deal with interpersonal relations with your employees, as they will be somewhat disgruntled and prone to defiance. They are likely to challenge authority, and you will have a harder time managing this.

農曆十一月 **(December 7th 2019 - January 5th 2020)** 丙子

A change of sorts awaits you in your career this month, be it a pay raise or career advancement in the guise of a promotion. This is particularly true for people who are Gua 1. Investment and merchant bankers who engage in stock and corporate deals will make good financial profits. All deals that you strike at this point in time are favourable. If you're a couple using this room this month, you're likely to receive some good news that will put a smile on both your faces!

農曆十二月 **(January 6th - February 3rd 2020)** 丁丑

Business partners may well find themselves disagreeing with each other, over who gets what and who controls what. In any case, it is very likely that the older or more experienced partner will prevail at the end of the day. Similarly, couples using this room will also squabble and bicker endlessly. See if you can take some time away from your home and go on a vacation together to iron things out. Elderly folk, in particular, should also look out for ailments affecting their kidneys this month.

North Sector Main Door

SE	S	SW
7	3	5
6	**8**	1
2	4	9
NE	N	NW

農曆正月 (February 4th - March 5th) 丙寅

If you're in real estate and property development, you're likely to find this a good month to make beneficial property investments. The gains to be derived are likely to be profitable. If you've been gunning for a promotion or seeking to be elevated to a higher position in society, then this could be a very fulfilling month for you. You'll be able to attain and realise your expectations and goals. Those of you with heart and eye problems will find that these problems will aggravate you this month.

農曆二月 (March 6th - April 4th) 丁卯

If there are elderly ladies using this room in your house this month, they will have to pay very close attention to their health. This is particularly because they are susceptible to gastrointestinal ailments and illnesses that can lead to more serious and major problems if left untreated. If you're living with your in-laws, this is a month for you to maintain your distance. Even if you don't live in the same household, try to minimise your contact with them as your interactions will be frosty.

農曆三月 (April 5th - May 5th) 戊辰

As a salaried employee, you will find it hard to make money this month, no matter how high you jump or how flexible your backbending is! The best solution is to give up trying so hard and pay more attention to yourself, without compromising the quality of your work. If you're in the legal field, your judicious and fair skills will be in demand! Your current clients just can't stay away from you, and new ones will come flocking as well. Make the most of it and use this opportunity to gain new business.

農曆四月 (May 6th - June 5th) 己巳

This is a difficult month for those of you in merchant banking, shares, and stock trading as your deals will sometimes fall flat. Your profits will start to dwindle as a result and cause some serious losses. In general, this is not a good month for you to get involved in the financial markets at all, as sustaining heavy losses might be the only result that arises out of this. Women who use this room should be careful of illnesses and accidents, which could lead to some grave consequences.

| Main Door | North | Bedroom Sector | Northeast |

農曆五月 (June 6th - July 6th) 庚午

If you're working in the media and consulting industries or in marketing, you'll find that investing in property will actually lead to profits. Make the most of this favourable time to do so. If by chance, you find yourself having to spend more time with your in-laws this month, you will face an increased risk of arguments and tension. To prevent unwanted conflicts, it might be better to just take a holiday or use alternative accommodation. Where health is concerned, women are more likely to suffer from gastrointestinal problems. Don't ignore these problems and hope that it will go away, as it will only likely become worse with time.

農曆六月 (July 7th - August 7th) 辛未

If your work involves logistics or strategy and deduction in any way, you will find this month to be quite a challenge. As such, if you're looking to hire fresh minds, it might be best to defer this to a more favourable time in the future. Hiring new people now could result in getting the stubborn and less-intelligent (even idle) employees who could only cause you more loss than gain. If you're single and on the lookout, then this is the month when romance could strike from Cupid's bow! Make an effort to expand your social circle and meet new people.

農曆七月 (August 8th - September 7th) 壬申

If you find yourself of weak and poor health of late, don't just hope for the symptoms to go away. It would be better for you in the long run to get it checked out sooner rather than later. If you're thinking of making some additional income through investment ventures, you can do no better than going into real estate this month. You're likely to see some good profits as a result. If you're a married woman, however, it will behoove you to have your guard up! There are sweet-talking wealthy men about who would only want to use you for their own gains, so don't be swayed.

農曆八月 (September 8th - October 7th) 癸酉

Domestic disharmony might be the theme for the month, because you'll find yourself mired in arguments with your family members more frequently. You'll need to exercise greater patience and tolerance. Try not to dwell only on the negative side of things and see the positivity of everyone even when in the midst of an argument. If you're a student using this room and you're writing examinations this month, your results might not be favourable – you might want to consider temporarily using another room. In general, confusion reigns for this period of time and so you'll find it difficult to make important decisions.

農曆九月 (October 8th - November 7th) 甲戌

Those of you embarking in new relationships this month should not take things seriously, as you may be putting in more hope than is necessary. Things may not be what they seem, and after awhile the real situation will shine through. The females in this house might tend to be stubborn and foolish, which means that no important decisions should be made this month. Otherwise, you risk looking back on these decisions later and wondering why on earth you made them!

農曆十月 (November 8th - December 6th) 乙亥

At work, you will need to protect and act in your own best interests. Otherwise, you will find that rivals who appear in the guise of friendly colleagues will be looking to undermine you this month. Be careful about how much you reveal to others, especially if it's your ideas about new developments and projects. However, your personal and professional relationships are positive and smooth this month. In terms of finances, this might be a good month to consider changing homes if it's something you've wanted to do for a while.

農曆十一月 (December 7th 2019 - January 5th 2020) 丙子

If you work as a judge, or in the legal field, or are a doctor – you'll find this a month when your services are really needed. People will come to you for your counsel and help, especially when times seem particularly hard. It will be a good time to give the best service you possibly can to cement your reputation. This will not be the ideal bedroom to use if you're looking to start a family, so it would be best to avoid it if you're serious about doing so.

農曆十二月 (January 6th - February 3rd 2020) 丁丑

Settle all outstanding traffic fines, summonses and taxes at once, unless you wish the long arm of the law to eventually catch up with you. And if you're one half of a couple using this bedroom, you may find yourself arguing and quarrelling with your partner or spouse more frequently than usual, this month. Indeed, the energies of this sector tend to bring about disagreements, misunderstandings and disputes. In some serious cases in your professional relationships, it could lead to legal complications.

East Sector
Main Door

Main Door	East	Bedroom Sector	East

This section contains the monthly outlook for all 12 months of the year for different bedroom sectors in a property with an East Main Door.

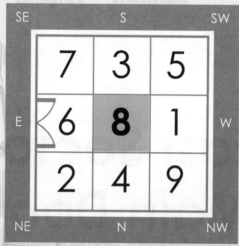

Ground Floor

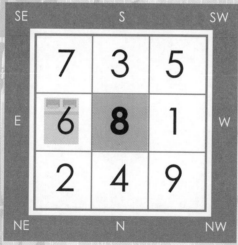

First Floor

農曆正月 (February 4th - March 5th) 丙寅

Elderly males using this room should be careful of certain health problems, particularly if you are susceptible to diseases or ailments affecting your lungs and blood circulation system. Those of you who hold a position of authority and power at work will have to be prepared for possible defiance from your subordinates. Parents will face a similar situation at home with your children. People who dabble in the share market will stand to make some good financial gains this month.

農曆二月 (March 6th - April 4th) 丁卯

You will find that your success at work will increase for reasons that you are not exactly clear about. However, there is no need to be worried – just enjoy it! Those among you in the real estate and property businesses will find that you profit from a lot of your dealings this month. Salaried employees who are looking for ways to increase your pay and gain greater benefits will stand a chance of fulfilling your ambitions this month.

農曆三月 (April 5th - May 5th) 戊辰

People involved in the logistics, courier, and tourism businesses will enjoy increased profits this month. You will be able to make quite a comfortable income from those gains. For those among you whose jobs at work involve strategic thinking or analysis, there will be a chance for you to advance your career and create quite a name for yourself this month. In general, the outlook for health and relationships is stable – so you don't need to worry about anything, as there will be very few problems.

農曆四月 (May 6th - June 5th) 己巳

Some of you who use this room will find yourselves more susceptible to flu, cold or any illnesses that attack your respiratory systems. Therefore, you should maintain a healthy lifestyle and change your daily habits so that your immune system is strengthened. If a particular illness, even though minor, takes a long time to cure, be sure to get professional medical treatment. Additionally, it's a good time to make an appointment with your boss to discuss possible salary increments or promotions. Beware that there are jealous, resentful individuals keen to bring you down, though.

Main Door	East	Bedroom Sector	East

農曆五月 (June 6th - July 6th) 庚午

Newly-weds will find this a good month, as their relationship will be harmonious and intimate with many happy moments enjoyed together. Salaried employees who have been patiently waiting for a promotion and further recognition will find their wishes being granted this month. In general, it's a favourable month for property and gilt investments. So, don't be afraid to make a bold move, as the gains are likely to be very good.

農曆六月 (July 7th - August 7th) 辛未

A favourable month is in store for you, especially if you're in the field of academics or sitting for a major examination. You're likely to pass all tests with flying colours! For those of you required to travel for work and business purposes, you will find that your trip yields immensely successful outcomes. People who are in steady, committed relationships will find that ties are more harmonious than ever; your partner is as-equally sincere and committed as you are.

農曆七月 (August 8th - September 7th) 壬申

Those among you who are involved in professional and competitive sports will find this a good month, as you'll be able to obtain good results in all your tournaments and competitions. Faithful employees will find that your efforts will be rewarded this month with more than just a pat on the back, so expect some financial gains to come your way! Elderly members of the household should be treated with care and understanding, as they might become somewhat stubborn when it comes to health issues this month. Bear in mind that they might be more afraid than anything else.

農曆八月 (September 8th - October 7th) 癸酉

If you're keen on increasing your profits, this will be the month to do it. However, try not to be too hasty or careless when it comes to signing any legal contracts or documents as you may succumb to the fraudulent manipulations of some unscrupulous people. Or, you might also end up getting much less than what you expected. This is not a good room for couples that are looking to start a family. Where health is concerned, occupants could suffer from kidney or head-related ailments and injuries.

農曆九月 (October 8th - November 7th) 甲戌

Couples using this room will have a better month, as there are improved communication ties. You will be able to enjoy a smoother, more intimate relationship that will leave you both feeling fulfilled. Those among you working in the marketing and consulting fields, or in research and development, will find that business starts to pick up this month. There is also a very good chance of promotion among the more senior female employees. Travel bodes well for you this month as you'll be able to close lucrative property deals while you're abroad.

農曆十月 (November 8th - December 6th) 乙亥

Males will run into health problems this month, which will largely present itself as stomach ailments. Take extra care of your health and don't neglect any existing medical conditions. It would be best to stay away from all speculative investments this month. If you're in the engineering business, however, it is the right time to go all out and find new clients. Parents will find that children using this bedroom will be prone to being more defiant and stubborn than usual! Move them to another room if the situation becomes uncontrollable.

農曆十一月 (December 7th 2019 - January 5th 2020) 丙子

Unfortunately, people using this bedroom will be plagued by mental and emotional instability. If some of you are already prone to depression or mental illness, you might want to consider using another room. Those among you who value financial stability will find this a generally good month that is free of troubles. It's also a good month for speculative investments in the defense industries, as it will produce good profits. Ensure that you do all the research and groundwork beforehand.

農曆十二月 (January 6th - February 3rd 2020) 丁丑

This month spells intense business rivalry, accompanied by backstabbing and jealousy at work. Given the negative situation you are in, a confrontation or argument of any sort could well blow-up into epic proportions. As such, keep your emotions under control and be tactful. Politicians will, however, find their policies and stances popular amongst the masses this month. You might also want to monitor your health closely and keep an eye open for kidney-related trouble.

農曆正月 (February 4th - March 5th) 丙寅

This is a very good month to make large investments in property and real estate as the returns will be extremely good. Therefore, if you've long had an eye on one, don't hesitate to acquire it at this point in time. Those among you in the upper-social circles of society will find that this month brings with it plenty of opportunities to rub shoulders with the rich and famous; you will be able to be introduced to the crème-de-la-crème of society. However, those of you who are married should be careful that your spouse is not seduced by a rich and powerful person who is only out to have a good time.

農曆二月 (March 6th - April 4th) 丁卯

Those of you who are married should minimise the amount of contact you have with your in-laws. If you do so, you'll be able to eliminate quite a bit of troubles and conflicts that will serve to increase you stress. In general, however, this is a good room to use. Ensure that you manage all your work-related stress well, as otherwise it could start to affect your health. This could appear in the form of stomach ulcers and digestive-tract issues. Take it easy and give yourself plenty of rest.

農曆三月 (April 5th - May 5th) 戊辰

You'll be able to gain some beneficial results through real estate ventures. But, bear in mind that it will inevitably lead to some stress and pressure. Even when you're working hard for financial gain, you have to ensure that you get a proper amount of rest so as to not over-exert yourself. Mental and emotional problems are prevalent this month; so, for those of you already prone to these issues, extra care should be taken to prevent the issue from worsening.

農曆四月 (May 6th - June 5th) 己巳

Pregnant women should avoid using this room this month, as it could lead to complications – or in the worst-case scenario, a miscarriage. Likewise, students and scholars should also avoid this room if you're sitting for important examinations. Try to use another room if possible, as this room will likely bring about poor results. It's a good month for you to invest in property and real estate, so make an effort to select the best type of property that gives you maximum returns.

| Main Door | East | Bedroom Sector | Northeast |

農曆五月 (June 6th - July 6th) 庚午

This month, you'll have to be a lot more skeptical than usual as certain people will make an effort to come off as something they're not! Remember, if something or someone seems too good to be true, it probably is. Be careful of the papers and documents you are required to sign and check it through several times to ensure that you don't misinterpret the fine print. Students and scholars should avoid using this bedroom for their studies and revision. The energies here are not conducive for such work. Avoid making any major decisions this month, as well.

農曆六月 (July 7th - August 7th) 辛未

This is a good bedroom to use if you're looking to become involved in spiritual issues or if you wish to develop your spiritual cultivation. Those of you who work as salaried employees should be careful of falling into arguments and disputes at the workplace this month. This is because if it gets particularly nasty or serious, it could end in legal issues. Those among you who are involved in romantic relationships will find yourself also embroiled in quarrels and arguments.

農曆七月 (August 8th - September 7th) 壬申

There are plenty of good opportunities and openings this month that enable you to make more money. However, don't be too excited or greedy and become carried away as the constant pursuit for more will only lead to more stress and discontent. If you're single, you'll be happy to know that Cupid seems to be on your side this month! There will be opportunities to meet your ideal partner. At the same time, do closely observe the operations of your business if you have one.

農曆八月 (September 8th - October 7th) 癸酉

Couples, either those married or in long-term relationships, will face arguments and disharmony this month. Both parties need to remain calm and tolerant, as otherwise the situation is likely to deteriorate into a tense one. If you're close to cutting a deal this month, you should not be deceived by appearances. Probe deeply into each one and evaluate them objectively. Otherwise, you risk spending quite a bit of money. In general, you need to be careful of all business deals this month – as rivals and competitors are out to deceive you.

農曆九月 (October 8th - November 7th) 甲戌

If you are interested in spiritual or metaphysical knowledge and practices, you may want to use this bedroom. But do ensure that you check outside this sector to ensure that there are no negative features or structures outside. Otherwise, the opposite effects are likely to happen and you will run into obstacles and problems. Real estate agents, as well as those looking to sell their houses, should make their best offer to prospective buyers. This enables you to reap good financial benefits.

農曆十月 (November 8th - December 6th) 乙亥

This month, females who use this room have to be careful of potentially illicit relationships. These relationships could very well end in disaster, especially if there is water located outside of this sector. Health-wise, you need to be careful of potential head injuries and brain problems this month. In general, however, most people will find that opportunities crop up quite a bit, resulting in profits and maybe even a substantial increase in income.

農曆十一月 (December 7th 2019 - January 5th 2020) 丙子

Those among you who work as surgeons will find that there is an increase in demand for your services, most likely through word of mouth for your skills. At the workplace, there will be increased competition and rivalry, and this is largely caused by the female figures. As such, there could be plenty of arguments and disputes taking place and you will do well to stay out of it. Those of you who are parents should not become overly involved in your careers to the point of neglecting your children, as it will only bring a significant amount of troubles.

農曆十二月 (January 6th - February 3rd 2020) 丁丑

Your real estate and property deals will net you handsome gains. On the downside though, you might find your relationship with your partner rather strained and tense this month, so be sensitive and tactful in dealing with him or her. Drive safely this month, as there's a risk of getting involved in a traffic accident due to reckless driving.

Main Door	East	Bedroom Sector	North

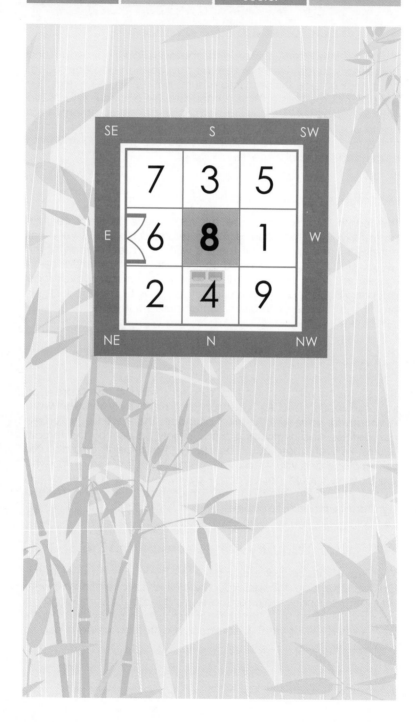

農曆正月 (February 4th - March 5th) 丙寅

Couples and newlyweds will want to avoid using this room to sidestep any unnecessary tension and conflicts that could arise. If this isn't possible, prepare yourself for arguments. Be tactful and tolerant when dealing with your loved one. Furniture manufacturers and shop-owners will find this a favorable month. However, it is always advisable to carefully go over all legal documents before signing. Otherwise, you risk inviting unnecessary future complications. You'll want to use this bedroom for all meditative, religious or spiritual pursuits if you're so inclined. The energies present here will allow your mind to be at peace and allow you to reach a greater sense of spiritual fulfillment.

農曆二月 (March 6th - April 4th) 丁卯

Those of you in the financial and banking industries might need to travel abroad to conclude deals. Grab the opportunities, because these overseas ventures will yield many profits. This is also a good month for people involved in professional and competitive sports as your reputation stands to gain a good boost. However, you'll need to be prepared that the financial benefits won't be as quick to arrive. Where health is concerned, lung or kidney problems are likely for people who use this bedroom. This is particularly prominent if there are negative features located outside. It would be safer to avoid using this sector for the duration of the month.

農曆三月 (April 5th - May 5th) 戊辰

People working in the agriculture, forestry or dairy farming will have a good month and should use it to further your name in your industry. They may want to consider expanding and acquiring new farms. Marital problems are likely to affect couples using this sector so spouses should try to travel more to give one another more space as absent makes the heart grows fonder. This can lead to greater intimacy between the two of you in the long run. The elderly people using this room will face the risk of stroke or arterial blockage related to circulation this month; they will need to exercise extra caution.

農曆四月 (May 6th - June 5th) 己巳

Expectant mothers should avoid using this bedroom this month, as you otherwise risk having pregnancy complications or a possible miscarriage. Females who are ready to enter the world of romance and dating again should be careful of the people they choose. There is a strong risk that you may fall for someone with a shady personality or one who is not who he seems. Those of you who make a living from your artistic or creative talents, you may need to travel this month to earn your keep. It will, however, be ultimately worth your while and prove to be immensely beneficial.

| Main Door | East | Bedroom Sector | North |

農曆五月 (June 6th - July 6th) 庚午

People who are seeking new romantic involvements will find yourself struck by Cupid's arrow this month and will have favourable luck meeting new partners. Artistic and creative people will also benefit from using this sector, particularly if you are seeking to market their skills abroad. Those of you who are parents may find that your children seem to be more prone to picking fights with others. You might want to consider relocating them to another bedroom. You certainly don't need them to be continuously engaged in some form of unfriendly or unhealthy rivalry!

農曆六月 (July 7th - August 7th) 辛未

This month, you will need to tread carefully as hidden agendas and ulterior motives may affect your business affairs. Make sure that you fully understand what you're in for before you finalise any important deals. Pay attention to the small details so that you don't miss out on anything. On the domestic front, you could well experience some trouble arising from a misunderstanding between the ladies in your household; particularly between mothers and daughters-in-law. Be fair and tactful in handling any such situation as you might risk making it worse. Health-wise, keep a look-out for ailments affecting your abdominal region, or even possible stomach and pancreatic troubles.

農曆七月 (August 8th - September 7th) 壬申

You'll want to use this bedroom if you're sitting for a major examination soon or happen to dabble in the academic, literary or media fields. The energies here are conducive for just such endeavours. Newly-weds and couples in a committed relationship will also find this room to be an ideal bedroom for romance and cultivating solid, loving ties. However, do be careful of any significant water forms or features outside this sector; these would instead indicate the possibility of scandals or infidelity with the possibility of betrayal.

農曆八月 (September 8th - October 7th) 癸酉

Your fine negotiation skills will be able to net you substantial financial gains from your investments, so go ahead and seize every opportunity that presents itself. This is also an ideal month to establish a joint-venture or partnership with another party; more so if you're looking to expand your business or capitalise on a larger portion of equity ownership. Mergers and expansions will bode well for you at this point. Those among you in a steady, committed relationship and wish to take your relationship to the next level will find this month ideal to do it. Perhaps it can be discussed over the course of a romantic dinner or weekend getaway.

農曆九月 (October 8th - November 7th) 甲戌

On the domestic front, problems with the in-laws may plague those who share a home. Therefore, it is best to avoid contact or even move away for the month to prevent any major disagreements and quarrels. Those of you working in metaphysics and alternate therapies industries should use the media to promote and market your business, as you will find it very fruitful and beneficial. However, most of you in general have to be careful of female subordinates or superiors causing problems at work by making sudden unexpected changes this month.

農曆十月 (November 8th - December 6th) 乙亥

It will be a good month for married couples and newly-weds who use this bedroom, as their relationships become more intimate and harmonious. Those among you involved in the literary field should look for publishers in order to put out new work this month, as it could very well result in fame and fortune for you. This is not the time to be shy and retiring about your talents! Scholars and students approaching important examinations this month should use this room to sleep in or to study, in order to benefit from the good energies that are present here.

農曆十一月 (December 7th 2019 - January 5th 2020) 丙子

Your good reputation and honour will be enhanced this month so you should use this time to promote yourself aggressively, but not too aggressively that you turn people off! A modicum of good grace will always help, especially when you know that your talents and abilities will then do the larger work of speaking for itself. If you are expecting to conclude deals in the entertainment industry this month, you should take advantage of this as the outcomes will move in your favour. Those in a committed relationship will find this a good month to formalise your partnership. If you've long wanted to pop the question and ask about marriage, this would be the ideal time to do it.

農曆十二月 (January 6th - February 3rd 2020) 丁丑

Not a very good month for most, if not all, endeavors unfortunately. Marital bliss won't exactly be there for married couples to enjoy, so give each other some breathing space this month and be patient. Keep a sharp eye open for any negative features in the North that result in negative Qi. These indicate the risk of acquiring an infection or worse still, liver or breast cancer. Hold on to your money as well, and do not invest in real estate or property at least for the duration of the month because you'll only stand to suffer losses from such investments.

Main Door	East	Bedroom Sector	Northwest

農曆正月 (February 4th - March 5th) 丙寅

Students due to sit for important examinations soon should use this bedroom to study and sleep in if possible, as the energies present here will be very favourable for creating good results. Beware of the presence of any significant body of water within or beyond this sector, however, as it might not bode well for romantic relationships. Partners may stray and betray one another or be tempted by and external party and succumb to an affair.

農曆二月 (March 6th - April 4th) 丁卯

Make an effort to use this bedroom more frequently this month. Chances are, you stand to benefit from this endeavour as your abilities and skills will be recognised by others; this is particularly true for those in positions of authority. Those involved in the travel, tourism or engineering industries will find this month to be a relatively profitable one. Therefore, go all out in cultivating all the opportunities that come your way and don't allow yourself to rest on your laurels too much this month.

農曆三月 (April 5th - May 5th) 戊辰

Business owners who are looking to expand or are interested in diversifying your area of commercial operations should definitely use this room to enjoy favourable results. If you work hard and expand your network of contacts, you should be able to enjoy the results of your hard work. But, you shouldn't be afraid of putting in the necessary legwork to achieve the results you want. In addition, make an effort to travel this month, as it will bring about some wealth luck as well!

農曆四月 (May 6th - June 5th) 己巳

The energies present in this room for this month augurs very well for academic luck, so children or students whose exams are just around the corner should use this bedroom to sleep in to enjoy maximum results. In addition, they should strive to use this room in which to perform their studies and revision. If you are in sales and marketing, you will want to double your efforts this month and pursue every business opportunity that comes your way. Success and financial gains are likely to swiftly follow. You may also want to use this room for meditative or spiritual pursuits.

| Main Door | East | Bedroom Sector | Northwest |

農曆五月 (June 6th - July 6th) 庚午

It's a good month for all relationship endeavours for people using this room. Those of you who have long been involved in committed relationships and wish to make it official should do so this month. Couples who wish to start a family will also benefit from using this room. Business partnerships and joint ventures also fare well this month. If you are almost nearing the end of a deal or negotiation, this would be a very good time to gun for a spectacular closing!

農曆六月 (July 7th - August 7th) 辛未

Wealth luck will be particularly favorable for those of you who depend on your network of contact and business allies to secure revenue. But you need to remember that moderation is always the key to success and a well-balanced life. You will only be doing yourself a disfavor by overworking or neglecting your health as you could well end up suffering from fatigue, stress, cardiac problems or even eye ailments. It would also be advisable to spare some time to hire a qualified electrician to check the wiring and electrical system of your home or workplace to minimize the risk of a fire hazard.

農曆七月 (August 8th - September 7th) 壬申

Bear in mind that you should drive carefully this month and ensure that the necessary insurance policies are up-to-date, as there's a possibility of a travel-related accident. In general, be extra cautious when you're on the road. Your earlier investments will yield substantial gains this month, so now's the time to cash in on them. If you are a boss or employer, you can expect employees to be a little more defiant this month and they will be tempted to question your authority. Make an effort to understand the grievances of your staff before you decide to take any action.

農曆八月 (September 8th - October 7th) 癸酉

This is not the month to embark on anything major. Avoid concluding that all-so-important business deal or making any important investments this month. These may cause more losses than gain. Instead, wait for the right opportunity to make your move. The presence of any negative features or structures outside this sector of your home or office poses the threat of food-poisoning to those who use this sector frequently throughout the month.

農曆九月 (October 8th - November 7th) 甲戌

Females who work in the marketing, public relations and sales industries will find this to be a most rewarding month. However, pay attention to your marriage and relationship as otherwise your spouse may end up feeling neglected. In general, most of you will find that your diligence and commitment to your job earns you the recognition of your superiors and colleagues. You will be able to use this to your advantage by expanding your network of contacts to bring you financial and monetary rewards.

農曆十月 (November 8th - December 6th) 乙亥

If your employer has recently undergone a financially-challenging time, be understanding of the situation. You may need to be a little more patient in expecting any extra benefits, increments, or advancements. This is likely to affect everyone in the company, across the board, so it will be best not to expect too much. However, this room is likely to be beneficial for students and scholars. Your exam results will be good if you use this room for your revision and learning throughout the month.

農曆十一月 (December 7th 2019 - January 5th 2020) 丙子

Matters of the heart enjoy a significant boost from use of this room this month. This is especially true if you're already in a committed, loving relationship. Make an effort to cultivate closer ties, and you'll start to see results in your partnership. In general, it would be good for people to use this room more frequently this month. If you do, you stand to benefit from receiving acclaim and recognition from others for your talents and efforts.

農曆十二月 (January 6th - February 3rd 2020) 丁丑

Looking to expand your business or diversify your area of commercial operations? Then use this bedroom. With hard work and expanding your network of contacts, you should be able to enjoy the rewards of your labors in due time. What's more, do take every opportunity to travel as much as possible, as those who do so will enjoy favorable wealth luck this month. Look out, though, for any sharp or negative features outside this sector. The presence of such features only increases the risk of heart disease or eye problems.

Main Door	East	Bedroom Sector	West

	SE	S	SW	
E	7	3	5	W
	6	**8**	1	
	2	4	9	
	NE	N	NW	

農曆正月 (February 4th - March 5th) 丙寅

A fairly competitive month is in store for you at work, with office politics at their height. You need to avoid getting involved with your rivals, as you are sure to end up on the losing side. Avoid also taking sides in any feuds that seem to be taking place, especially the subtle ones! This month, romance is best left alone. Not only are things likely to end badly, but it might also tarnish your reputation. In terms of personal safety, avoid driving while under the influence of alcohol this month as there is a good chance that you will get caught and have to pay a heavy fine. It goes without saying that drinking and driving is dangerous to begin with.

農曆二月 (March 6th - April 4th) 丁卯

Politicians and public servants will have a good month enjoying excellent public support and may even find themselves rising up the ranks in government or in their parties. You will be able to receive plenty of help from people this month; they will help you break past some of the more persistent barriers and overcome those pesky obstacles. Still, be wise and discerning about whom you choose to trust as there are plenty of wolves dressed in sheep's clothing out to take you for a little spin. If there was ever a time you need to put on your skeptic's cloak, this month will be it.

農曆三月 (April 5th - May 5th) 戊辰

This is a tough month for business owners. All your attempts at progress and moving forward will be stymied, so those of you who own your own enterprise need to think in less ambitious terms this month. Instead of planning how to grow and expand and move forward, consider consolidating your position instead. Any sustained efforts in the former will only lead to setbacks anyway, so you might as well use this period of time in a more constructive way.

農曆四月 (May 6th - June 5th) 己巳

This is a good room for children and scholars to use as a study, especially if they are facing important examinations this month. It generally bodes well for academics and exam preparations, resulting in favourable results in tests. Those involved in ports and transportation will do well financially this month, as deals increase and profits also start to multiply accordingly! Couples are likely to benefit from the good energies of this room for the month, particularly if there is a well-situated mountain outside.

農曆五月 (June 6th - July 6th) 庚午

Business booms for those in the furniture or publishing industry this month, so do your best to try to attract more customers – because it will result in greater profits. Look for overseas and offshore business opportunities in particular, as those will enhance the bottom line even more. Couples using this room may experience some marital discord this month. Patience and tolerance will be needed in liberal amounts so as to not further aggravate the tension in the relationship.

農曆六月 (July 7th - August 7th) 辛未

This will be the ideal month for you to offload property from your property portfolio, as it will result in good financial gains. Think about what you need to do and then proceed to act on it shrewdly! If you are pregnant, it would be best to avoid this room this month. Otherwise, you risk some complications or even a possible miscarriage. Do not accept remarks or information at face value from anyone this month as you are surrounded by people who are only out to look after their own interests. You won't be getting the most accurate answer; you may even have the wool pulled over your eyes.

農曆七月 (August 8th - September 7th) 壬申

This is a good month for those in the creative industries as there is a chance for you to make a name for yourself and get into the limelight. Good financial profits are set to follow, so what are you waiting for? Those in committed relationships should be careful of temptation this month, as this will lead to tension with your partner. Avoid inciting their jealousy or suspicion by getting too flirtatious with someone else, even if you think it's only harmless. There are many mentors and helpful people around you this month, so go ahead and embark on your most ambitious endeavours – you are likely to get all the support and assistance you need.

農曆八月 (September 8th - October 7th) 癸酉

Relationships should be good this month so if you wish to take it to a new level, you should do so and don't let your fear or inhibitions hold you back. Remember, fortune – and romantic luck – favour the brave! Let your intelligence and innate wisdom flower, as it will lead to opportunities that bring about a promotion or a greater sense of authority at the workplace. This is the month to show the boss what you are made of, so don't hold back! It is time to gain the rewards for your hard work. Health-wise, be careful of eye and heart problems if there are negative formations outside of this sector.

農曆九月 (October 8th - November 7th) 甲戌

This is a good month for employees who are hoping for a career promotion, as the results are likely to be quite spectacular this month. Business owners will make money if they are in the oil and gas industries or the mining industry this month. Travelling can bring about positive benefits at this time, and this includes investors with new venture possibilities.

農曆十月 (November 8th - December 6th) 乙亥

The good news: romance is on the cards this month for people using this room! However, you should expect short-term passionate flings rather than anything lasting and concrete. If you keep this mind your expectations low, you should be able to enjoy it for what it's worth. There should be an improvement in interpersonal relationships amongst family members and friends at this point in time, so use this time to strengthen your ties and solidify strong bonds. In general, this is a month to mind your own business. If you meddle in other people's affairs, you're likely to incite anger and resentment rather than garner any form of gratitude.

農曆十一月 (December 7th 2019 - January 5th 2020) 丙子

Those among you involved in professional and competitive sports will find this a very favourable month for your respective fields and disciplines. You'll be able to augment your reputation and garner some acclaim. In a sense, it's all about putting your name out there this month! The presence of a Nobleman star allows most of you to derive help from others in order to fulfill your goals and ambitions, leading to much success. However, be careful of those who try to use you to fulfill their own gains.

農曆十二月 (January 6th - February 3rd 2020) 丁丑

Business owners will find it hard to make progress in anything. As such, if you own a business, you need to keep a back seat and consolidate your position instead. Couples using this bedroom will find that jealousy may cause discord this month so it's best they should avoid this room. Pregnant women in particular may take this advice to heart as using this room might lead result in susceptibility to complications.

Main Door	East	Bedroom Sector	Southwest

農曆正月 (February 4th - March 5th) 丙寅

Things are not looking so bright for people using this room this month. You find yourself unable to communicate and see eye-to-eye with both your co-workers at work and loved ones at home. Tempers are easily frayed, and seemingly minor disputes escalate into major quarrels. You will have to exercise greater effort in being patient and forgiving. Avoid any long-distance travel this month as there is a high risk of accidents and obstacles.

農曆二月 (March 6th - April 4th) 丁卯

You should try to avoid using this room as much as possible for the duration of this month. Otherwise, emotional problems may affect your peace of mind and your relationship with others. Things get even worse when you have difficulty finding the underlying sources of the problem. It might be necessary for you to talk to people or seek help in order to get the load off of your chest. Psychological problems are nothing to be ashamed of; sometimes we are unable to overcome them on our own no matter how hard we try.

農曆三月 (April 5th - May 5th) 戊辰

It's a tough and difficult month in store for lawyers as you will have trouble putting your case across. Hence, winning cases also become marginally harder. Communication is at an all-time low this month, so couples using this bedroom should be careful about what is said and done; this could exacerbate any strains and tensions and prolong it for an indefinite length of time. Miscommunications will be a problem this month and those in the cell phone and IT industry will find that losses may be incurred.

農曆四月 (May 6th - June 5th) 己巳

Where health is concerned this month, you would be better off taking care of your own body and seeking immediate treatment from your doctor at the first sign of an illness. Don't neglect or put off attending to obvious warning signs. Do not engage in any high-risk ventures this month, especially where property and real estate are concerned. The chances of incurring huge amounts of losses are very high! And by 'high-risk' ventures, it also includes gambling, games of chance and speculative investments. Leave the lottery and numbers game for another time, when the chances of winning are higher!

Main Door	East	Bedroom Sector	Southwest

農曆五月 (June 6th - July 6th) 庚午

Those of you who are involved in the tourism, travel and/or media business, this might be a challenging month for you. As such, refrain from making any major decisions this month. Chances are, you would already be in a confused and irritable state of mind and this doesn't augur well for your sense of reasoning and judgment. Expectant mothers should not use this bedroom, as this will only result in pregnancy complications. Where possible, move into another bedroom for the time-being.

農曆六月 (July 7th - August 7th) 辛未

Health problems affect the people using this bedroom this month and you might run into complications with your kidneys or blood circulatory system. Where relationships are concerned, your relationship with your partner will also be affected due to a possible interference by a third party. This could lead to some pretty tense arguments. If you're working in the tourism, courier and logistics industries, you'll find yourself having to double your efforts this month. Help or support from friends, superiors and mentors will not be forthcoming, but don't give up easily as perseverance will pay off.

農曆七月 (August 8th - September 7th) 壬申

Those of you involved in professional and competitive sports should watch how you go about in practice and competition. This is to prevent against injuring your tendons, ligaments or bones. Keep an eagle eye on the property market this month and seize any good deals that come your way! Should you encounter any hostile competition that threatens to derail your investment plans in the property concerned, pull out of the deal immediately. You might also want to be on the lookout for malicious, petty-minded people who will be out to backstab you and spread rumours and gossip.

農曆八月 (September 8th - October 7th) 癸酉

This is not a month to get involved in any major decisions or business deals, as these will not end up as good investments and may even result in some losses. There is a possibility of concluding property deals this month. But, as soon as there are any hints of volatile and argumentative bargaining involved in securing the investment, you need to withdraw from the deal. It will definitely not be worth the fight. Gastrointestinal problems will plague elderly females using this room, so they will need to take greater care of their health.

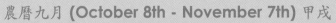

農曆九月 (October 8th - November 7th) 甲戌

Business partners should be aware of possible fallout from tension and stress this month, as this will result in loss of wealth. You will need to take some time out and relax, or risk having to lose your finances. In general, this will be a difficult month for business owners and managers, as sales targets will be difficult to meet. This is especially true for those in the tourism, travel and media business industries. Academics and scholars will find an increase in reputation this month especially if they decide to publish their research and papers in their fields of expertise.

農曆十月 (November 8th - December 6th) 乙亥

Fire hazards will pose a serious problem this month and electrical wiring should be checked where it is old and in need of replacement. Don't forget to also double-check all your gas and stove outlets. This month, those of you who own or manage a company should delay all investment deals and focus on employee motivation instead. Distraction by monetary issues could result in financial ruin. Your mentors and superiors are not around this month and as a result, you may find your business contracts and prospects lessening or drying up. You will need to make more of an effort to keep yourself visible.

農曆十一月 (December 7th 2019 - January 5th 2020) 丙子

Conservative property deals will bring financial gains this month, but you need to ensure that extreme caution needs are exercised throughout the deals. Relationships don't fare very well, and those using this bedroom should be extra patient with their loved ones and exercise a greater a sense of tolerance. This month, cutting words will have long-lasting hurtful effects on others. Younger children in the home may have health problems this month in the form of muscle and tendon injuries, so parents may need to keep a watchful eye.

農曆十二月 (January 6th - February 3rd 2020) 丁丑

Those in the entertainment business, operator of a pub, disco or bistro might want to keep a closer eye on your finances this month, especially when it comes to dealing with third parties. Your relationships will also be stormy and troubled. Health-wise, you'll find yourself prone to leg injuries, liver ailments and/or other forms of illnesses.

East Sector Main Door

	SE	S	SW	
	7	3	5	
E	6	**8**	1	W
	2	4	9	
	NE	N	NW	

East Sector Main Door

農曆正月 (February 4th - March 5th) 丙寅

Accidents and mishaps may plague you this month, so be careful when you're out travelling... even if this means venturing out your front door! However, this particularly applies to road-related mishaps – so be careful when on the road or when driving. If you have children, you will find that your teenage daughters are apt to be more rebellious than usual this month. Open the channels of communication to find out exactly what's wrong, instead of reacting with emotional anger.

農曆二月 (March 6th - April 4th) 丁卯

Avoid investing in high-risk portfolios this month, because you'll only stand to lose – not gain! In general, it's a month to keep an eye out on all your financial expenditures. It's easy for your money to trickle out of your fingers at this point, and you don't want to see that happen after all the effort you've put in. Be especially vigilant, as there is a heightened risk of armed robberies and thefts. In terms of health, do consider relocating to another bedroom if that's possible; otherwise, you're at risk of suffering from ulcers, gallstones, and gastrointestinal issues.

農曆三月 (April 5th - May 5th) 戊辰

Deals that you are able to make with partners overseas can lead to surprising windfall gains! Therefore, work on your international alliances because it will likely result in good things for you. Where your health is concerned, this month brings with it its fair share of ligament tears and tendon injuries. Be especially careful when you do exercise or any form of sports. Theft and fraud are problems this month, especially by close friends and family members – you'll have to be extra cautious and put specific financial controls in place.

農曆四月 (May 6th - June 5th) 己巳

Be careful when you're travelling and out and about, as there is an increased risk of accidents. This could be caused by your own negligence, so don't let yourself get distracted when you're travelling on the road. But in general, your professional life is set to receive a boost as there are great opportunities for career advancement. This will lead to more power and authority at the workplace. Parents may find that their male teenage children using this room will be more rebellious than usual, so they should consider using another room if it becomes too much to handle.

| Main Door | East | Bedroom Sector | South |

農曆五月 (June 6th - July 6th) 庚午

There are some health problems that will come to the fore this month. This will manifest itself primarily in the form of liver trouble. Profits might come your way in the form of smart property investments, so strike a deal if it feels particularly right. There is a continued threat of robbery and theft for people using this room this month, so for those of you who have just come into some money – ensure that you share this information with only the people you trust the most. Others might use it in a devious way.

農曆六月 (July 7th - August 7th) 辛未

For students and scholars sitting for important examinations this month, this would be the room to use. It bodes well for your studies and revision. People involved in the media and marketing industries will find this month bringing with it achievements and honour, so get ready to enjoy your moment in the spotlight! Your past efforts and labours will finally get its due. In general, however, people using this room might have to battle some emotional volatility and psychological problems. With that in mind, take extra care if you're already prone to depression and mental instability.

農曆七月 (August 8th - September 7th) 壬申

This month, put on your strategic thinking hat and plan ahead carefully. Having a solid arrangement will allow you grasp every opportunity that comes your way, and with proper timing and calculated efforts, significant financial rewards will simply fall into your lap! In general, this month bodes well for all thinking and intellectual activities; you can be sure that whatever your carefully and deliberately think through will benefit you tremendously. Students will benefit from the energies of this room for their academic and educational activities. The results are likely to be seen in their examinations!

農曆八月 (September 8th - October 7th) 癸酉

It will be a rewarding month for people involved in the academic, creative, and literary fields. You will find your career moving ahead by leaps and bounds. But, do keep in mind that what's success to you is reason for envy for someone else. As such, be prepared for jealous, petty people keen to speak ill of you when your back is turned. However, don't let them get you down; you will do well simply to ignore their shallow actions. Young children using this room might be at risk of being injured by sharp objects and metal implements.

農曆九月 (October 8th - November 7th) 甲戌

Those among you who make a living as counsellors, life coaches, and trainers will find this to be a bumper month – as you will literally be inundated with new clients seeking your help and assistance. If you work as senior personnel in your corporation, you should be vigilant against third parties who are out to extort large sums of money from you. Keep your friends close but keep your enemies closer! If you've long been involved in a tumultuous and unsettled personal or professional relationship, you'll find this to be the month that puts it all to an end.

農曆十月 (November 8th - December 6th) 乙亥

It will be a good month to gain some profits this month from the metals and equities markets, but it will help that you have past knowledge and expertise on your side. It wouldn't hurt to probe the minds of experts in this field to gain some perspective. In general, this is a month of heavy competition, so you need to be prepared for bids for hostile takeovers. Plenty of conmen and sweet-talkers are out to weasel things out of you, so be on guard when conducting your business activities and never trust a person who seems to be too good to be true!

農曆十一月 (December 7th 2019 - January 5th 2020) 丙子

Those among you who work in fashion and garment retailing will find this month bringing in excellent gains. If you are in the real estate and property industry, you will find that you're able to close better deals than usual. This has the ability to greatly increase your turnover rate, bringing in more profits and a newer clientele as well. For most of you, however, be careful of envious older colleagues or superiors who will be out to make you tumble. It can be expected of them to try to keep you down any way possible out of resentment to your success.

農曆十二月 (January 6th - February 3rd 2020) 丁丑

It's always wise to listen to good, sound financial advice. As such, lend others your ears and listen very carefully as they dispense positive tips on how you can make your money work for you. This however does not mean that you can afford to let your guard down, unless you wish to fall victim to conmen or fraudsters. Additionally, don't feel too bad if you find yourself feeling a bit down this month. It's quite natural to feel depressed or sad once in a while. If the symptoms persist, though, seek professional advice.

農曆正月 (February 4th - March 5th) 丙寅

Those of you who have steadily been working hard and putting in extra labour will find your efforts being recognised and perhaps even rewarded this month. Continue to do the good work – even when it seems that you're plugging away alone, someone is always observing! If you work as a politician or civil servant, you need to keep a low profile this month in order to avoid unnecessary scandals and gossip. If you invest in properties, you're likely to see good profits this month – but you'll need to travel to meet with quality buyers and close your deals.

農曆二月 (March 6th - April 4th) 丁卯

Elderly ladies using this room should be aware of potential health troubles in store. There will be signs of illnesses and even if these seem minor, you need to get them checked out to ensure that it isn't anything serious. Students who will be sitting for examinations soon should avoid using this room this month as it will not be conducive for your learning and studies. There is some female trouble to be expected at work and at home. So, if there are messy fights or conflicts involving females (regardless if it's personal or professional relationships), steer clear out of it!

農曆三月 (April 5th - May 5th) 戊辰

The threat for expectant ladies is present when using this room, so it might be best for them to consider using another room altogether for the duration of their pregnancy. Elderly females using this bedroom will also be at risk for health problems, this will appear in the form of stomach and abdomen troubles. It will be a profitable month for doctors in general due to people recognising your expertise and wanting to be treated by only the best medical practitioner – you!

農曆四月 (May 6th - June 5th) 己巳

Fire hazards are a serious threat this month. Protect yourself by double-checking all your electrical wiring and systems, preferably by an experienced professional. Don't just limit this to your home – if you own a business, get your office and work space checked out too, especially if you sleep in this room. Decisions are best left to another time; both for professional and personal ones. Injuries are also a risk this month, and it's possible that you might suffer from a broken limb if you engage in risky contact sports or extreme physical activities.

| Main Door | East | Bedroom Sector | Southeast |

農曆五月 (June 6th - July 6th) 庚午

In matters of the heart, single people should avoid expecting a serious relationship out of anything that has just begin. The outlook for long-term relationships is dim, but that doesn't mean that you can't enjoy a few casual relationships and gain some valuable dating experience! If you've been huddled away in your lab or workspace, busily crafting something new and ingenious – this is the time to share your inventions with the world! There will be good publicity and word-of-mouth that can help propel your career forward. Negative structures located outside this sector can lead to an increased risk of fire hazards.

農曆六月 (July 7th - August 7th) 辛未

Certain niggling health troubles crop up for people using this room this month. Although they are by no means serious, it can still be somewhat troublesome. Pay attention to any throat ailments, or to toothaches and gum infections. Get it checked out as soon as possible instead of avoiding it and hoping it goes away! Communication is at an all-time low this month, so you're likely to get entangled in miscommunication and misunderstandings with the people closest to you. It's not a month for love either, as your new infatuation or romance is likely to lead to scandal and not great happiness!

農曆七月 (August 8th - September 7th) 壬申

Ah, the sweet young female with the silver tongue and the face of an angel – the bane of red-blooded men everywhere. This month, men have to be careful of just this sort of temptation, as otherwise you'll only find yourself entangled in a compromising and embarrassing situation! Guard against frivolous temptation. Be careful as well with your personal safety this month, for there is a risk of robbery and theft. If you run a business, avoid embarking on any new ventures. Instead, seek to eliminate internal fraud committed by dishonest employees.

農曆八月 (September 8th - October 7th) 癸酉

It's a volatile month for relationships, as disagreements caused by jealousy and suspicion are likely to cause some gloom in love ties. You'll have to make more of an effort to keep the relationship on an even keel. People working in the legal and judicial fields will do well this month, because you're bound to be inundated by requests for your services. Elderly women using this room and prone to stomach ailments might want to consider temporarily moving into another room for the month.

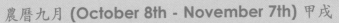

農曆九月 (October 8th - November 7th) 甲戌

Communication in general will suffer from a temporary collapse this month so don't rely on word-of-mouth deals and agreements. Get everything down in black and white. Likewise, don't count on people delivering the right message to others this month, as the threat of lawsuits is high. Where possible, have a written message prepared instead. Romance also takes a backseat to bickering this month. As miscommunication is rife, it would drive a wedge between partners. In that same vein, be prepared for arguments and conflicts at the workplace. Understand that this is a temporary glitch and avoid overreacting to explosive situations.

農曆十月 (November 8th - December 6th) 乙亥

Pregnant ladies should consider moving out to another room where possible. Try to make alternative arrangements where possible as otherwise you will suffer the risk of complications or a chance of miscarriage. People working in the communications industry will find this a good month to make some sound financial investments. If you're an academic, a teacher or educator, you are likely to gain recognition for your hard work thus far if you use this bedroom.

農曆十一月 (December 7th 2019 - January 5th 2020) 丙子

If you own a business, you can relax a little this month because you look set to expect an increase in customers and clientele. This is largely through referrals and word of mouth, so give yourself a pat on the back and carry on doing what you-re doing. Whatever it is, it is proving to be good! It will be fine to dabble in quick investments, as you are likely to see some gains. But, be careful as there is also an increased risk of fraud and theft. Your relationship boat is being rocked hard by tumultuous waves this month, so consider docking at an island somewhere far away so the both of you can have some much-needed peace and time alone together!

農曆十二月 (January 6th - February 3rd 2020) 丁丑

This month might leave you smiling in satisfaction, as it will generally be a very smooth and productive one. This will be true both in a professional or personal sense. In addition, newly-married couples who have just embarked on an exciting new life should use this bedroom for its positive energies. Property investors should be bold this month and invest in the properties of their choice, as it will likely lead to good results. However, ensure that you read the fine print of all documents before committing to anything.

Northeast Sector Main Door

Main Door	Northeast	Bedroom Sector	Northeast

This section contains the monthly outlook for all 12 months of the year for different bedroom sectors in a property with a Northeast Main Door.

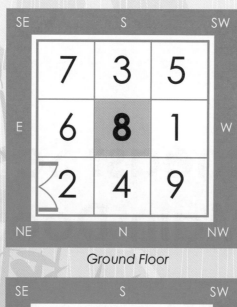

Ground Floor

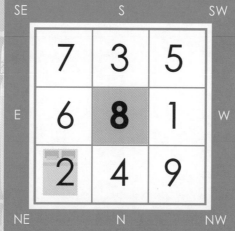

First Floor

農曆正月 (February 4th - March 5th) 丙寅

Reign in any temptations that might lead you to engage in speculative investments, or high-risk ventures. You will probably end up with a lot less than you expected. This is not the right time for you to commit to major deals. Otherwise, all you will gain are losses. Elderly women using this room should consult their doctor at the first sign of abdominal troubles. Otherwise, this could risk becoming something very serious with long-term consequences.

農曆二月 (March 6th - April 4th) 丁卯

Married females using this room should be careful of running into troubles with their mothers-in-law, especially if they live under the same room. Try not to get into any arguments, if possible, and hold your tongue where possible. Otherwise, things will only be bad for you. At the same time, this will be a good room to use for those writing important exams soon. It will also work well for people involved in the real estate and property industries. You will be able to strike good deals and make quite a bit of money this month, so it will be an ideal time to take your career to the next level.

農曆三月 (April 5th - May 5th) 戊辰

There is a possibility of mental and emotional strain for people using this room, which may cause stress or even hallucinations for you this month. Try not to let stress get to you too much or your mental health will suffer. Schedule some regular time out from work and don't let your work take priority over your wellbeing. Make sure that any deals concluded this month does not rely on capital, as this may end in losses that could be potentially serious. Employees will find that no matter how hard they work this month, they will find it difficult to make money. Just lay low and consolidate your position for now.

農曆四月 (May 6th - June 5th) 己巳

You stand a good chance of generating substantial financial gains by investing in real estate or property, as long as you remember to vet through each and every deal carefully before committing yourself to it. Do note that if there are water features located outside this sector, there are significant losses in store for you instead. Females using this bedroom will tend to behave in a more domineering and assertive manner this month. At the same time, they should also mind their health as they are particularly susceptible to stomach-related ailments.

Northeast Sector Main Door

農曆五月 (June 6th - July 6th) 庚午

Pregnant ladies should avoid using this bedroom right now, as there's a very high possibility of miscarriage or premature delivery. There could be other complications in store as well. It will be best to postpone that real estate deal you've been eyeing until the month is over. As of current, rushing into such a deal will only incur losses for you. On the domestic front, there will be plenty of squabbles to keep you busy. You will have to play mediator for relatives who are in the midst of tussles.

農曆六月 (July 7th - August 7th) 辛未

Any dealings pertaining to real estate or properties would probably result in losses for you this month; avoid investing in real estate at this point in time. At home, you might find the elder ladies in your household behaving in a more stubborn manner. You will need to be patient and seek to understand their viewpoint and disgruntlement by sitting down and talking to them where possible. Where health is concerned, watch out for potential eye afflictions this month. Consult your physician at the first indication of trouble.

農曆七月 (August 8th - September 7th) 壬申

If you happen to be suffering from a chronic illness of any sort, you need to take extra care of your health this month. Try to implement healthier daily routines that will keep your illnesses at bay. Be mindful of any negative landform features located outside of this sector, as these are possible indicators of trouble involving older females. However, any property or real estate dealings you embark on this month will probably land you substantial financial gains.

農曆八月 (September 8th - October 7th) 癸酉

Do bear in mind that confusion may come into the decision-making process if you are using the bedroom this month, so it is preferable to refrain from making any key decisions at this point. If this can't be avoided, seek the help of trusted confidants who can be objective about your situation. Pregnant women should be careful if they are using this room this month, as there is a risk of miscarriage or untimely delivery. Ensure that you take the proper precautions. If you're a student, you should avoid this sector for study or revision if you are facing important examinations this month.

農曆九月 (October 8th - November 7th) 甲戌

Those of you who run a company and need to employ more staff members this month, it will be best to postpone this to a more favourable time. Otherwise, you risk selecting people who are the skim of the cream as opposed to the cream of the crop! If there are negative formations outside this sector this month, it could cause deteriorating vision or even blindness for the people using this room. However, don't worry unnecessarily and just take the proper preventive measures.

農曆十月 (November 8th - December 6th) 乙亥

There is a good chance that any romantic escapades you embark on this month will do better than you expected, but you should be careful nonetheless of jealous individuals spreading gossip about you. In terms of health, if you've been in poor health of late, be extra careful as there is a chance of recurring illness this month. Real estate ventures will be successful and bring great financial success. At the same time, you should make sure that all the legal issues are covered as there could be problems later on.

農曆十一月 (December 7th 2019 - January 5th 2020) 丙子

Elderly ladies using this room should be careful of potential injuries this month, especially ones that result from the use of sharp metal objects and implements. In general, you will also have to be careful of fire hazards this month. This will be particularly exacerbated if there are any negative features located outside this sector. Those of you involved in athletics or competitive sports will do well if you use this bedroom this month.

農曆十二月 (January 6th - February 3rd 2020) 丁丑

To avoid substantial losses as outcome of sealing deals, don't rely on capital for the duration of this month. If you're a salaried employee, you will have a difficult month. You will find that no matter how hard you work and how much of extra time you put in, commensurate financial remuneration is not forthcoming. There is a possibility of mental and emotional strain which may cause stress or even hallucinations for you this month. Try not to let stress get to you too much or your mental health will suffer.

| Main Door | Northeast | Bedroom Sector | North |

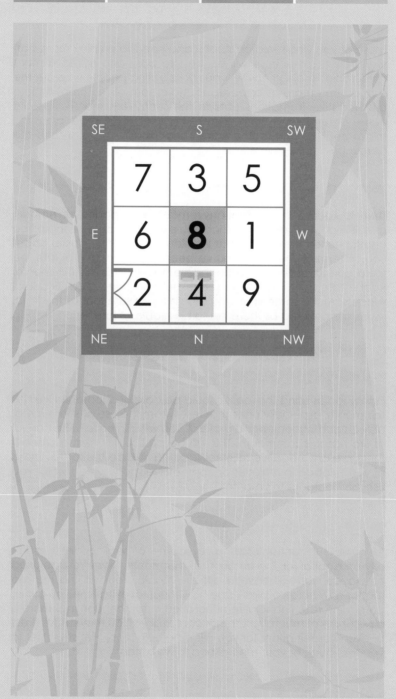

農曆正月 (February 4th - March 5th) 丙寅

It's a good time to go on a vacation you've always dreamed about, as you've earned this time off and should rightfully claim it! Chances are, as you might also be able to embark on a little fling while you're abroad – but bear in mind that these are likely to be short-term ones rather than anything lasting. Professionals in the marketing and consultation businesses should consider going ahead and publishing that research paper that you've been working on long enough.

農曆二月 (March 6th - April 4th) 丁卯

This month, keep a strong watch on your back and what you say. Malicious people are out to get you in any way possible, so don't give them ammunition to launch any attacks. Where your health is concerned, pay close attention to head or brain-related injuries. In any case, seek professional medical treatment if possible instead of letting your symptoms on its own. Those among you involved in the artistic and creative fields will enjoy success this month, although you might have to travel to earn your income. But this can be a positive thing, as being in a new place with fresh sights and sounds can serve as fodder for your hungry muse!

農曆三月 (April 5th - May 5th) 戊辰

If you're always someone ready to pack your bags and go away at a moment's notice, you'll find that travelling this month bodes well for you. Where your work and business are concerned, it brings about the likelihood of greater profits and returns. Travelling to close deals on property acquisitions is also a good thing as your returns are likely to be much higher. Those among you involved in the forestry or dairy farming industries will an increase in the demand for your products. Elderly females using this room need to be careful of strokes and migraines.

農曆四月 (May 6th - June 5th) 己巳

Couples who want to find that loving feeling again should consider using this room, as it will keep their passion for one another burning! However, be careful of any significant water features located outside this sector as that could lead to one of the partners straying or becoming involved in an affair. Specialists in the media and consultation industries will be able to enjoy much fame and publicity this month, so let your talents and capabilities shine! This room will also benefit academics, scholars, and researchers, as well as students.

| Main Door | Northeast | Bedroom Sector | North |

農曆五月 (June 6th - July 6th) 庚午

This is not a month for female employees, as you will not find support or encouragement from your superiors to be forthcoming or readily-available this month. However, don't let this get you down too much. If you plan your goals and workload accordingly it will reduce the effects of any sudden hiccups and at the same time allowing you to be in control. This is not a month to use this bedroom for students and scholars sitting for important examinations, as your results will be worse than you expected. Additionally, there are good outcomes from any joint-venture projects you undertake in the financial world.

農曆六月 (July 7th - August 7th) 辛未

Romantic relationships come under strain this month, and couples using this bedroom will find that their relationships are a little tenser than usual and mired with petty quarrels. Consider going off on a trip together to strengthen ties or perhaps doing some activity and hobby together that can remove you from your daily cares, at least for a little while. If you're involved in management and consulting, this will be a good month to expand your business. Professionals in the literary and media fields will also do quite well this month, as inspiration just seems to flood you!

農曆七月 (August 8th - September 7th) 壬申

This month, you'll have to be careful of the legal documents that you sign. Make sure that you read the fine print. If you're not sure what's going on, enlist the help of a legal professional to ensure that everything is above-board. It's also a month to be careful of your words and how you present yourself; it might be something you said in jest or anger will come back to haunt you! Those of you who have been feeling upset and unappreciated by your bosses and superiors this month need to lay low and avoid drawing attention to your concerns, as this is not the time for it. It might only backfire on you.

農曆八月 (September 8th - October 7th) 癸酉

People with an artistic and creative bent will find the energies of this room benefiting them this month, especially if you pursue commercial opportunities abroad. You'll be able to garner both mass attention and critical acclaim. At the workplace, you'll need to tread carefully, as office politics are at an all-time high. It could become unhealthy and out of control, so try not to get involved. Parents of children using this room may need to be more patient than necessary, as their children are liable to be influenced by peer pressure and be more rebellious than usual.

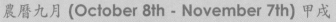

農曆九月 (October 8th - November 7th) 甲戌

Those of you in relationships should give your partner some breathing space this month, especially if you find that both of you are more quarrelsome than ever lately. It would also be advisable for you to keep an eye open for health issues, particularly breast cancer or liver ailments if you happen to be using this bedroom. It will also prove to be a volatile, unstable month to indulge in the stock market. It would be much better for you to hold on to your money just a little longer.

農曆十月 (November 8th - December 6th) 乙亥

This room bodes well for scholarly activities and examinations, as students who use this bedroom for their studies and revision will greatly benefit from the energies present. You will be able to enjoy a clarity of mind and intense concentration that will be a boon to your revision process. In general, this is a good month for most of you to engage in a full-blown expansion of your business or to consider forming alliances with partners abroad. Those single and looking for love might be able to find some temporary distractions, but nothing long-term will come out of it.

農曆十一月 (December 7th 2019 - January 5th 2020) 丙子

Females need to be on guard if they use this room this month, as potential squabbles and petty disagreements will plague you and destroy your peace of mind. Where possible, try to remain removed from all of it. If you're in the midst of concluding financial investments, you will find that this is a good month for you – with negotiations likely to end well! In general, it's a good month for joint ventures in finances. It's also the right time to build upon your current partnerships and alliances.

農曆十二月 (January 6th - February 3rd 2020) 丁丑

This is a good month for property acquisitions, but these will produce even better financial rewards if you are required to travel to conclude the deal. Travel can bring about greater profits, so consider doing it if possible. Those of you in forestry and dairy farming will find that business demands increase the need for your products. Bear in mind, however, that older women might have problems with strokes and migraines if they're using this room.

Northeast Sector Main Door

農曆正月 (February 4th - March 5th) 丙寅

Those among you who have been more spiritually inclined these days will find this room to be beneficial for your pursuits. Things bode well for you in terms of improving your knowledge. You might want to consider embarking on a spiritual or meditative retreat to cleanse your thoughts and purify your mind. It will be very good for you to get away from the heavy worries of your daily life. Fire hazards are possible this month, so be extra careful with your daily routines and check through all your wiring and gas outlets.

農曆二月 (March 6th - April 4th) 丁卯

Where things on the domestic front are concerned, happy occasions and events and celebrations are likely. Surrender to the moment, pack your cares away in a hard-to-reach place and enjoy the pleasure for what it is. There will be plenty of opportunities to reconnect with your loved ones and enjoy closer, more intimate ties with your family members. Budding entrepreneurs looking to establish a joint-venture or partnership with another party should also seize the opportunity to do so this month, as the outcomes look very good.

農曆三月 (April 5th - May 5th) 戊辰

Lately, your friends might have commented that you're starting to seem more and more easily irritable. And it might very well be that you're easily annoyed and somewhat more hostile than ever lately. You'll need to keep your emotions from bubbling over the surface, however, as you might scald others and land yourself in hot soup! You'll have to make more of an effort to remain calm to prevent others from becoming hurt or offended by your words and behaviour.

農曆四月 (May 6th - June 5th) 己巳

Your relationship and health luck are both looking good this month. Make the best of your luck prospects and milk the most out of every opportunity that comes your way! Remember that sometimes the same opportunity doesn't knock on your door twice. There are fires burning a-plenty at your workplace this month, and you shouldn't add fuel to the already explosive office politics and issues. Try to put out the fires, instead, by attempting to solve the problems before it gets out of hand. Those of you dabbling in futures, equities and stock trading should go all out with the chances that crop up.

Main Door	Northeast	Bedroom Sector	Northwest

農曆五月 (June 6th - July 6th) 庚午

Those of you in romantic relationships and using this bedroom will have to be extra-sensitive to your partner's feelings this month. There is a chance that both of you will be crabby, moody and prone to feeling things more profoundly than usual. Try to be a bit more understanding and a lot more tactful, instead of saying the first thing that pops into your mind. Where business interests are concerned, it's not the right time to make any investment deals because these are unlikely to generate profits. Watch out for any negative formations or structures located outside this sector, as food poisoning is likely.

農曆六月 (July 7th - August 7th) 辛未

This is not an ideal month to place elderly folk or those weak in health in this bedroom, as the energies present there would only further aggravate their health problems. Liver problems in particular would be a significant worry. If you happen to be involved in the education business, look out for competition from industrial rivals. The good news is that you stand to profit from your endeavours so long as you execute your business plans with care and shrewdness. Females in the public relations and marketing industries using this room will find tremendous benefits coming to them at work.

農曆七月 (August 8th - September 7th) 壬申

At this point in time, fortune favors the wise and prudent. As such, invest carefully and only after much deliberation. This month would also bring domestic and family-related problems; do your best to try to solve them quickly and swiftly to prevent things from festering into a more serious situation. If you happen to counsel or provide others psychiatric or psychological treatment, you will be pleased to know that your beneficiaries will appreciate the wisdom, advice and knowledge you share with them.

農曆八月 (September 8th - October 7th) 癸酉

If you happen to be in a serious, committed relationship, it goes without saying that unsavory nightclubs, entertainment areas and places of ill-repute should be avoided at all costs this month – as there are temptations in store that could risk jeopardising your relationship! Those who dabble in metaphysics will be able to use the good energies of this room to broaden their knowledge. On a similar note, employees in the marketing, sales and consultation industries who have been toiling at their jobs will probably reap the fruits of their labour soon enough. So, keep your chin up!

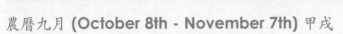
農曆九月 (October 8th - November 7th) 甲戌

Go ahead and pack your suitcase this month, as travel opportunities in the name of business beckon you temptingly. Positive financial gains are likely to be the happy outcome. This is definitely a good month to ensure that your passport and other travel documents are valid and in order. Those among you who work in the entertainment industries will also experience an increase in business, with an increased number of clients and customers. If you're married, consider going on a vacation with your spouse as this is an extremely ideal time to foster even closer ties with your loved one.

農曆十月 (November 8th - December 6th) 乙亥

Pay attention to any negative external features outside this sector of both your home and office, as the presence of these can heighten the risk of fire hazards. In any case, ensure your safety by double-checking all the electrical wiring and gas outlets in your home by a professional. This is one thing worth spending time on! People working in the fashion industry, whether in design or retail, might find travelling to be the way to go this month. Doing so will increase your revenues and lead to greater business opportunities.

農曆十一月 (December 7th 2019 - January 5th 2020) 丙子

If you work in public and civil service or are somehow involved in politics, this will be a good month for you. You stand to gain a promotion or career advancement, but you need to ensure that you're willing to double your efforts and step up to the plate. A possible salary increment is also in store for all your efforts, so you will have quite a bit to look forward to! Things are pleasant and even joyful on the home front, which gives you plenty of reason to stay at home and spend time with your loved ones.

農曆十二月 (January 6th - February 3rd 2020) 丁丑

You might well be feeling rather hostile, aggressive or irritable lately. Keep a tight rein on your emotions, as any altercations with the law or confrontation with other parties would only land you in a pickle. That aside, this is a suitable month to widen your network of contacts especially if you're working in the communications industry; you would only stand to gain by doing so. The energies of this room will also work well for you if you work in invention and ideas-building.

| Main Door | Northeast | Bedroom Sector | West |

農曆正月 (February 4th - March 5th) 丙寅

Short-term passionate flings rather than long-term affairs will be the result this month for people using this bedroom. If you have any romantic designs on someone and want them fulfilled, it's best to keep this in mind. It's a month to mind your own business. Because, if you meddle in other people's affairs, you are likely to get into arguments rather than be on the receiving end of a wave of gratitude. Resentment and anger are thus the likely results. Office politics are simmering to boiling point this month, and this will therefore be a period of sharp competition and intense rivalries.

農曆二月 (March 6th - April 4th) 丁卯

Make a name for yourself in your field of industry this month, as you stand to make greater acquaintances and thus establish and cement your position. Try to go after joint-venture deals and partnerships that you began awhile back, as the outcomes are likely to bring strong profits in your favour. This is the month to go for broke, rather than sit back and wait for the opportunities to fall into your lap!

農曆三月 (April 5th - May 5th) 戊辰

This is not the month for you to dabble in shares and equities, as there are plenty of tough challenges ahead for you. It would be best for you to consider working on another aspect of your life, instead of focusing on making financial decisions – or even personal ones. Clarity of mind is lacking for you at this point, and so any major decisions you make may be clouded by uncertainty.

農曆四月 (May 6th - June 5th) 己巳

Those of you involved in the world of academia will find that you receive recognition for your work this month if you use this room. People will finally start to know you for the work you do. Be careful if you are involved in any joint ventures and partnerships this month, because these just may have hidden legal entanglements that will take you by surprise. Romantic relationships will be on the upswing this month for those using this bedroom, but you need to be careful if there are water features outside this sector.

| Main Door | Northeast | Bedroom Sector | West |

農曆五月 (June 6th - July 6th) 庚午

Overseas and offshore business opportunities will enhance the bottom line for your business this month, so grab these opportunities as they crop up. Those in the furniture business will find that financial gains will be made this month. However, a loss of wealth and legal problems are possible this month as a result of betrayals and rumours spread about your business. You may need to watch your back and safeguard your interests as much as possible and employ some form of damage control if the backbiting becomes too rampant.

農曆六月 (July 7th - August 7th) 辛未

If you're married, you should be careful of third-party gossip causing you some amount of tension in your relationship. Guard against unwarranted and unreasonable jealousy, as this will cause a certain amount of problems. There is a chance of miscarriage for pregnant women using this sector this month, so move to another room if it's possible. Those in the real estate business will find that property deals return good profits this month and you are likely to enjoy some good financial gains.

農曆七月 (August 8th - September 7th) 壬申

Use your inner talents of wisdom and knowledge to gain the promotion you deserve. If this requires you having to speak up about your talents and abilities and making it known, so be it! You've been humble and self-effacing for far too long. If you're involved in professional, competitive sports, you will do well in international competitions this month if you use this bedroom. Elderly people should be careful of head injuries especially if there are negative features and structures outside this sector.

農曆八月 (September 8th - October 7th) 癸酉

Those aspiring to achieve literary success should showcase their talents this month. You'll find that people are receptive to what you offer and you have a greater chance of meeting publishers, agents, and editors. If you're in professional or competitive sports, your luck continues well into this month and you should maximise efforts while the going is good. However, do bear in mind that mental instability and emotional stress are significant problems this month for those using this bedroom.

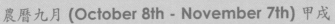

農曆九月 **(October 8th - November 7th)** 甲戌

Water-related industries such as tourism, travel, logistics and the spa industry will have some positive publicity and should return favourable profits as a result. Those of you who work in those fields are likely to see a bigger bonus this year! Spouses may feel a bit neglected this month, as one partner is busy making money while the other is being sidelined. Ensure that you devote enough time and energy to your relationship and don't sacrifice it for the sake of your career. Look into property investments this month, as there are good deals to be had with good financial rewards that could keep you comfortable for some time.

農曆十月 **(November 8th - December 6th)** 乙亥

Bear in mind that those of you who use this room will have to battle poor health this month. While the implications are not serious, it is however strong enough to merit your care and concern. In particular, pay special attention to any problems that crop up with your head and mouth. This is not the month for romance either, so it would be best for you to stay away from all forms of it lest it results in a diminished reputation and markedly lowered spirits.

農曆十一月 **(December 7th 2019 - January 5th 2020)** 丙子

This is a good month to make progress with your personal reputation in your field or industry, or even to gain recognition at work. You need to ensure that people recognise you for what you do, and how you do it. As such, accept the credit given to you and enjoy it with good grace! Complicated relationships or estrangements can be smoothed out and amicably resolved if you are using this room, so use it to your advantage if you need to make amends with someone. Joint venture opportunities are likely and plentiful at this point in time; these should be followed-up, as they should end in good profits in the long-term.

農曆十二月 **(January 6th - February 3rd 2020)** 丁丑

Do not deal in shares and equities this month, as you may face some tough challenges ahead. Avoid making any important personal or financial decisions this month, as you will not be able to see the situation clearly and may end up making wrong choices that you will regret. Pregnant women may face some complications while using this room this month and also while travelling.

農曆正月 (February 4th - March 5th) 丙寅

Prepare for some backstabbing and betrayal from within the company. If you own or manage one, be sure that you keep your employees at the forefront of the company eye this month. Gastrointestinal problems will plague the elderly using this bedroom, so they will need to take extra care where stomach issues and troubles are concerned. There is a possibility of concluding property deals this month. However, as soon as there is any indication of volatile or argumentative bargaining to secure the investment, withdraw from the deal as the outcome will not be worth the effort.

農曆二月 (March 6th - April 4th) 丁卯

Get a qualified electrician or technician to check the wiring of your property because the risk of fire hazards is high. Those among you who are advocates and solicitors, you might find it hard to put your points across this month in presenting your case in court. Don't be unduly frustrated, though. If you keep your wits about you, you should be able to remain calm and patient as you go about executing your duties. Married couples or those of you in committed relationships will also be put to the test this month. But don't allow a bad patch to ruin your entire relationship. Instead, find ways to overcome it.

農曆三月 (April 5th - May 5th) 戊辰

Religious enthusiasm could end up in fanaticism for people using this bedroom this month. If there are people out to incite you to pursue dubious-sounding religious affiliations or groups, it would be best to stay away. Monetary issues and relationship problems may cause added stress this month, casting a shadow on the domestic front. Those in the political arena, and looking for some sense of advancement, will find that friends and acquaintances will be around this month to help them with their political aspirations.

農曆四月 (May 6th - June 5th) 己巳

Good profits can be made from conservative property deals but to benefit from these opportunities, you will need to watch the markets carefully. Carefully avoid taking any untoward financial risks. Younger children in the home may have health problems this month in the form of ligament, muscles and tendon injuries. In general, relationships don't fare well this month. Those using these rooms should be patient with their loved ones. Avoid getting impatient and losing your temper, because it will only make things worse. As much as possible, avoid falling into petty arguments.

Main Door	Northeast	Bedroom Sector	Southwest

農曆五月 (June 6th - July 6th) 庚午

Unless you're prepared to face up to the consequences or repercussions of a casual fling, no thanks to a night of binging, do not overindulge in alcohol or spend too many evenings at the pubs and nightclubs. You might find that you're taking away one type of stress and bringing on another! Also, those suffering from poor health should seriously consider moving out of this bedroom to mitigate the risk of having their health worsened by a skin or liver ailment. This month promises to be a challenging one at work as well, where rivals and competitors will heat up the competition and challenge you considerably.

農曆六月 (July 7th - August 7th) 辛未

Those involved in the legal or arbitration business will be pleased to know that with the proper amount of effort, you will be able to enjoy the fruits of your labour sooner than you expected. However, this month you should refrain from giving personal loans especially to relatives and family members. You can't afford to be impudent and you might not see the money again. Children using this bedroom are likely to be more rebellious and difficult to control or discipline this month.

農曆七月 (August 8th - September 7th) 壬申

Ambitious or optimistic as you may be, this is simply not the right time to embark on a new enterprise or venture as the probability of tasting early success is very low. Instead, it might be more prudent for you to wait for a more suitable time to make your move. The end results could be a lot sweeter! Resist the temptation to gamble and engage in any form of speculative investment, as you may end up poorer than when you first started. Elderly ladies suffer from the risk of appendicitis or oral disease if they use this room this month, consider putting them in another room.

農曆八月 (September 8th - October 7th) 癸酉

Expectant mothers should avoid using this bedroom this month, as the risk of miscarriage is quite high. If you're a business owner or manager involved in the tourism, travel or media business, you should be prepared for your sales targets to fall slightly below the mark this month. Scholars and academics, on the other hand, will find the energies of the month auguring well for their reputations. Go forth and publish that paper you've being toiling away at or present your findings at a conference. This will be a good way for your star to shine brighter.

農曆九月 (October 8th - November 7th) 甲戌

This month, you should steer clear of any high-risk investment deals, as they could well burn a hole in your bank account at the end of the day. Those working in the entertainment industry will find it tough-going this month. It is a particularly lonely month, what with your superiors and co-workers apparently being unable or unwilling to back you up. Remember that you can still make a difference by working smart, instead of just working hard! Health issues to watch out for are eye or heart-related problems.

農曆十月 (November 8th - December 6th) 乙亥

Women who use this room should have a mammogram this month, as there is an increased risk of breast cancer. Avoid all forms of business expansion and growth this month, if possible. This is because you will end up making incorrect decisions that are most likely to end up in financial losses for both yourself and your company. Pregnant women should avoid sleeping in this room for the month, as the risk of miscarriage is possible and the chances of other complications also high.

農曆十一月 (December 7th 2019 - January 5th 2020) 丙子

Those among you involved in any business partnerships should not discuss important issues this month, as communication is at an all-time low. In fact, if it particularly involves negotiations or deal-breaking, it should be kept to another time. Couples may find it hard to conceive if they use this room this month, so if you are keen to start a family you may want to consider using another room. Also, beware of possible health issues may appear in the form of kidney and water retention.

農曆十二月 (January 6th - February 3rd 2020) 丁丑

Monetary issues and relationship problems may cause added stress this month. You will have to be more astute with your budget to prevent any loss of finances or to find yourself lacking it. If you're involved in the political arena, you will find that friends and acquaintances will be around this month to help them with their political aspirations. Bear in mind also that if you use this room, you may be susceptible to emotional turbulence and confused thoughts.

Main Door	Northeast	Bedroom Sector	South

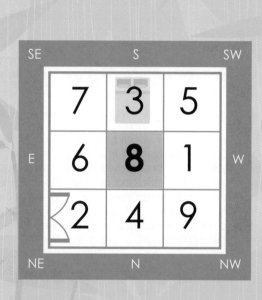

農曆正月 (February 4th - March 5th) 丙寅

Where possible, avoid traveling for business-related purposes, as the outcomes from such trips will not be favourable to you. It would just be an added expense that won't really lead to anything solid. If you've been toiling at your job and sense that a promotion is just waiting for you, you just might be right! If it comes, you will be elevated to a position with more power, status and authority, which as you probably know is more than well-deserved. Male adolescents using this room will be slightly more temperamental and rebellious than usual, so parents will need to be prepared!

農曆二月 (March 6th - April 4th) 丁卯

Resist the temptation to gamble and indulge in any form of speculative investments this month, unless you wish to risk accumulating huge financial losses – which, let's face it – no one does! If you have by chance come into extra money lately, it would be advisable for you to remain discreet and prudent on your financial status. There are people out there keen to stretch out their itchy fingers and take what's not theirs. Be careful also of health problems that will appear in the form of ulcers, gallstones or liver-related ailments; have these treated at the first sign of trouble.

農曆三月 (April 5th - May 5th) 戊辰

Fraud and embezzlement by friends and family members will result in a feeling of betrayal for those who use this bedroom this month. You will have to be discerning with the people whom you choose to confide in with sensitive information. Those working with heavy machinery should be extra careful this month, as there is an increased risk of injury while at work. Exercise more caution than you typically would and never neglect or overlook your own personal safety. Employees will find that petty politics raises its head at this point in time and should not be tempted into arguments and disputes; these could end up in legal problems. The best thing to do would be to play it subtle and take no sides in an argument.

農曆四月 (May 6th - June 5th) 己巳

There's a likelihood of disputes brewing within your family members, so try to prevent it from escalating into something serious. Also, pay attention to personal safety this month as the risk of robberies and muggings is high. Bear in mind this month that by failing to keep abreast of current trends and stay on top of your game in your industry, you only risk losing your share of the market or even niche market. This month, additionally, pay particular attention to communication. Lack of it could potentially undermine your endeavours and set you back.

| Main Door | Northeast | Bedroom Sector | South |

農曆五月 **(June 6th - July 6th)** 庚午

Couples using this room might run into a spot of trouble, so both partners must be patient and tolerant. Avoid listening to other people instead of each other. Refrain from playing the blame game and pointing fingers, as this will only make the situation worse. Additionally, stay away from gambling this month, as the result will be a significant loss of wealth. Those in poor health should avoid using this bedroom this month as all forms of illnesses could take a turn for the worse.

農曆六月 **(July 7th - August 7th)** 辛未

This promises to be a profitable month for most people using this room, especially for those in the construction industry. Seize every opportunity to embark on business trips, as these will yield positive outcomes for you. Couples using this bedroom should be more sensitive to each other's emotions this month. Be more tactful and sensitive in your daily interactions and avoid taking each other for granted. Keep a look out as well for liver-related problems or any feeling of light-headedness, more so if you notice the presence of a negative form outside of this sector. Seek immediate treatment at the first sign of trouble.

農曆七月 **(August 8th - September 7th)** 壬申

You will do well to hold your tongue, rather than offer unsolicited advice to those who are incapable of appreciating your good intentions. Instead, focus on building yourself up. Where business is concerned, review and go over your strategies. This is a good month for strategising and decision-making in general, but not for business expansion and growth. Be prepared for unexpected surprises as well, if using this bedroom. Nothing is quite what it seems.

農曆八月 **(September 8th - October 7th)** 癸酉

Those among you who are involved in the real estate and property market should aggressively market yourselves, as this is a good chance to make money. This is not the month to be overly humble or self-effacing when it comes to your talents and capabilities! Those in the service industry will have opportunities to make money this month, but you will need to pay all taxes earned as the tax officials will be on your tail otherwise! On the domestic side, do note that there is a potential for disharmony between mother and son this month; this will cause arguments that could result in family feuds.

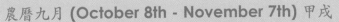

農曆九月 (October 8th - November 7th) 甲戌

If you've been feeling poorly as of late, you need to be extra vigilant this month because the risk of physical injuries is quite high. Seek the advice and treatment of a physician at the first sign of trouble; otherwise the situation could well become serious. The risk of fraud and theft is also high this month. Nothing's absolutely certain, but you can always play your part in averting such risks by ensuring that good security controls are in place. There will be windfall gains for those involved in business ventures with overseas or offshore partners.

農曆十月 (November 8th - December 6th) 乙亥

Hostile and aggressive takeovers are possible for your corporation, so if you sleep in this room then you should be aware of competitors who will take you on as well. In general, this is a favourable bedroom for children, as it will be beneficial for their studies and academic work – particularly if they're sitting for exams. Health problems may come in the form of liver trouble this month and if there are negative structures outside this sector, then the impact of this will be markedly worse.

農曆十一月 (December 7th 2019 - January 5th 2020) 丙子

Children who are using this room will find that leg injuries are cropping more often than usual, especially if they're involved in sports or athletics this month. Those in the cell phone industry will have a very good month, and you'll be able to make good financial gains and profits from a well-performing business. There are plenty of business conflicts this month and as a result concluding deals should be left for a more suitable time when there is less acrimony.

農曆十二月 (January 6th - February 3rd 2020) 丁丑

If you're a salaried employee, you will find that your workplace would be rife with petty politics. Legal problems can be expected as a result of getting into disputes and arguments at work, so it's best to keep your head low for this month. Fraud and embezzlement by friends and family members will result in a feeling of betrayal for those who use this bedroom this month. Those working with heavy machinery should be extra careful this month, as there is an increased risk of injury while working. Exercise more caution than you typically would.

Northeast Sector Main Door

農曆正月 (February 4th - March 5th) 丙寅

This is a good time to watch your health, especially if you've been feeling rather unwell. Otherwise, you risk falling ill and acquiring some form of blood disease or suffering from food poisoning. Males, in particular, have to avoid over-indulging in alcohol for both physical and mental reasons. If you happen to work in the civil service or are a politician, this is the time to keep a low profile and avoid attracting unnecessary attention to yourself as it will likely backfire and set your cause back a few steps.

農曆二月 (March 6th - April 4th) 丁卯

Seek the limelight at work if possible, and let people know what you're doing. Your ascent up the career ladder should thereby proceed in a smoother manner. Students and anyone who's due to sit for important examinations soon will also do well to tap into the positive energies of this room. Stay away from nightclubs and places of unsavoury reputation this month, as otherwise you could attract more trouble than you know what to do with!

農曆三月 (April 5th - May 5th) 戊辰

This month, property investments should yield good returns but you need to make sure that all deals are scrutinised properly before being signed. Otherwise, legal problems could arise and come back to haunt you later. Fire hazards are a problem this month and any old buildings should have the electrical circuits checked by a professional as a safety precaution. There could be an increase in stomach-related problems this month, especially for elderly women using this room. If it gets to be increasingly bad, consider using another room.

農曆四月 (May 6th - June 5th) 己巳

This looks set to be a favorable month for people working in the communications industry, so seize the opportunity to enhance your reputation and expand your clientele. However, avoid making any significant investments this month as wealth luck will not be on your side. You may be greeting losses instead of gains! You might also face some intense business rivalry or competition at work, with the situation being further compounded by the risk of theft or burglary this month. Stay calm and keep your wits about you, it will be more than needed at this point.

| Main Door | Northeast | Bedroom Sector | Southeast |

農曆五月 (June 6th - July 6th) 庚午

Those of you working as salaried employees, stay out of office politics and gossip as you could well find your words being used against you by your rivals or enemies. You might also find your relationships with others plagued by conflicts and disagreements, no thanks to jealousy rearing its ugly head at the wrong time. Seek first to understand others, before you make yourself understood. And needless to say, think before you say or do anything that will cause you regret later on.

農曆六月 (July 7th - August 7th) 辛未

Certain health problems come to the fore this month. So, drink lots of water, get plenty of rest and be on guard for any possible throat ailments. This is also the time of the year when communication is at an all-time low and misunderstandings abound. As such, couples need to be more patient and understanding of each other's emotions and wants. At work, be sure to communicate coherently. Otherwise, you risk having your words being misunderstood or misrepresented thereby leading to stickier problems.

農曆七月 (August 8th - September 7th) 壬申

Expectant mothers need to seriously consider changing bedrooms, at least until the month's over, to negate the risk of pregnancy complications. Married females living in close quarters have to be careful of getting into a tiff with their mothers-in-law, as these could have long-term consequences. However, on the bright side of things, your personal and professional relationships are looking good this month, so take advantage of them to expand your network of contacts.

農曆八月 (September 8th - October 7th) 癸酉

Lawyers, advocates, solicitors and those dabbling in the legal profession will find this month to be a fairly favourable one. This month, it pays to be prudent and discreet with the amount of information you share with the world. The risk of robberies and theft is high, so don't share information with others if you've recently come into some wealth. Those involved in a serious relationship might find things to be a little strained or tense this month. It might be better off giving each other room to breathe instead of trying to immediately 'fix' the situation.

農曆九月 (October 8th - November 7th) 甲戌

Property deals could go sour owing to a breakdown in negotiations, which is a direct result of a miscommunication especially if you are in the mining, minerals and semi-precious stones industries. Avoid new romantic relationships this month, as these could end up in scandals and cause more misery than joy for you. It will be best to focus on another aspect of your life. Do not make any major personal or business decisions this month, as discussions over these matters may have been clouded with miscommunication. You will end up making some bad choices if pressed into it.

農曆十月 (November 8th - December 6th) 乙亥

You should be prepared for a conflict between the women of the house this month. This will primarily be caused by misunderstood words and hurtful comments. If you're female, be careful of your speech this month to avoid stepping on anyone's toes. There is an increased risk of fraud and embezzlement from employees this month. So, if you own or run a company, you may need to keep a watchful eye without resorting to being overly suspicious and hostile. Pregnant women should try to find another room to sleep in this month, as there is a high risk of complications and miscarriage.

農曆十一月 (December 7th 2019 - January 5th 2020) 丙子

Those among you in the fashion, apparel and cosmetics industries will find that the financial side of the business takes off this month. However, companies that are having problems attracting new clients should consider implementing some changes in their approach. Don't just go with the tried-and-tested methods that are stale and outdated. Relationships are generally quite rocky this month; great care should be taken to keep the peace and the relationship will be on track.

農曆十二月 (January 6th - February 3rd 2020) 丁丑

Property investments should yield good returns but you need to make sure that all deals are scrutinized properly before being signed so that legal problems do not arise at a later stage. Fire hazards are a problem this month, any old buildings should have the electrical circuits checked as a safety precaution. In terms of health, there could be an increase in stomach-related ailments this month; especially for elderly women using this room.

Northeast Sector Main Door

農曆正月 (February 4th - March 5th) 丙寅

This is generally not a good month for those in the entertainment industries, as well as the electrical and electronic industries. Demand for your services and products will be somewhat diminished, resulting in a loss of profits. Defer any important decision-making as far as personal and professional relationships are concerned to a more suitable time. This is because it will be hard for you to be rational and logical this month when emotions are running high. Elderly people using this room this month will be more susceptible to heart attacks and strokes. As such, they might want to consider moving to another room.

農曆二月 (March 6th - April 4th) 丁卯

You will receive the accolades, recognition, advancement and financial rewards you've worked so hard to achieve success in your professional life. It's time to kick back, put your legs up and let the accolades pile up! Investment and merchant bankers who specialise in stocks, equities and corporate deals and mergers also stand to make substantial monetary gains on-the-job, so double your efforts if you want to gain more out of it. Couples using this room will enjoy a heightened relationship with closer ties and a better sense of fulfillment.

農曆三月 (April 5th - May 5th) 戊辰

Those of you working as analysts will find this an exciting month as their career takes off as a result of strategic positioning in the equities market. You can expect to gain good profits for your work. Entrepreneurs and those wishing to start new ventures should use the good energies of this sector to go out and make a new start. Noble People in the form of coaches and mentors are present in your life this month, so take their advice and act on these suggestions to achieve success. If you happen to arrive at a stumbling block, they will be able to offer you pertinent advice.

農曆四月 (May 6th - June 5th) 己巳

Couples will have a happier month this month and you will do well in your chosen careers as well. Both your professional and personal lives will complement the other nicely, leading to much contentment. Children using this bedroom this month will be rebellious and difficult to control; parents may have to exercise greater authority than necessary. If your job involves strategic thinking or analysis, you will find that you have the chance to advance your career and make a name for yourself this month. Don't hesitate to grab the opportunities to promote yourself.

| Main Door | Northeast | Bedroom Sector | East |

農曆五月 (June 6th - July 6th) 庚午

Investment and merchant bankers concluding deals in the share and equity markets this month will benefit from good profits in the months to come. Therefore, if something appears promising, do your best and go for it! You will receive the recognition, career advancement and financial reward you deserve this month. Your career would be raised to new heights and bringing a new level of job satisfaction. Newly-married couples will find this a very good month for harmonious relationships and you will enjoy better communication and improved ties.

農曆六月 (July 7th - August 7th) 辛未

For those of you trying to make an honest living from a regular job, don't bother with trivial disputes or arguments at the workplace this month. It could fester into legal complications if blown out of proportion. Ignore your rivals and the proliferation of backstabbers at work and concentrate on your job. The rewards are a lot more fulfilling than being caught up in office politics. Those who are actively involved in the trading of stocks and shares will be pleased to know that there will be gains to be made from their transactions. Garner the input and help from more seasoned investors, if you're unsure how to proceed.

農曆七月 (August 8th - September 7th) 壬申

Engineers, technicians and people generally involved in the technical and engineering professions will find your career prospects looking more promising this month. Keep up your good work, as these can lead to possibilities that never occurred to you before. The sweet taste of success will come to you in time. Investment deals, especially risky ones, are a big no-no this month. If you proceed anyway, you're particularly looking forward to ending up with legal problems on your hands! Athletes and sportspersons should also guard against any sports-inflicted injuries; particularly those affecting their legs and feet.

農曆八月 (September 8th - October 7th) 癸酉

For those of you using this room, this is the month when your efforts and capabilities are recognised by your superiors and things start looking up as far as your job is concerned. You've been doing something right all this while, so keep up the good work. Real estate or property specialists will equally be pleased to welcome repeat-customers, and new ones as well, as they find their clientele base expanding. Additionally, couples looking to conceive and start a family should use this bedroom this month.

Main Door	Northeast	Bedroom Sector	East

農曆九月 (October 8th - November 7th) 甲戌

Those of you involved in consulting businesses, think tanks, strategic decision-making processes, and others whose work requires wisdom and intelligence and critical thinking will attract fame and good fortune this month. In other words, your talents and capabilities will finally get its due reward. In general, for most of you, your wisdom and intelligence at work will be recognised and superiors will entrust important projects and deals to you that could result in advancement and promotion. To put it simply, it may be your month to shine at work, so don't shrink from the limelight! For those wanting to start a family, this will still be a suitable month in which to do so.

農曆十月 (November 8th - December 6th) 乙亥

People working in the engineering field will find sudden advancement in their careers, so enjoy the good stuff that will come your way! Those of you who are working as salaried employees should sit tight this month and avoid looking for new work, as the energies of this room for this month does not support this. New endeavours should preferably be postponed to another month when the outcome will be better. There is an increased risk of car accidents that may result in leg injuries, so be careful while on the road – even as a pedestrian.

農曆十一月 (December 7th 2019 - January 5th 2020) 丙子

Those of you working in the construction industry will find this a good month, with minimal labour disruptions and improved output. You'll be able to work smoothly. People in the real estate industry should take advantage of the good energies in this sector and invest in property deals, as these will return good profits this month. If you're in the metaphysics field, you should venture out and expand on your business as this is a beneficial month for you. You are likely to be able to grow your knowledge and skills.

農曆十二月 (January 6th - February 3rd 2020) 丁丑

Lawyers and professionals dabbling in the legal field will find their services much sought-after this month. In any case, you should also be on the lookout for disputes and office politics in the form of power struggles. At the same time, stay out of them to avoid running into any legal entanglements later on. Don't give your heart away too easily because chances are, any romantic fling will remain what it is. So, don't expect anything solid or long-term to develop out of it.

West Sector
Main Door

This section contains the monthly outlook for all 12 months of the year, for different bedroom sectors in a property with a West Main Door.

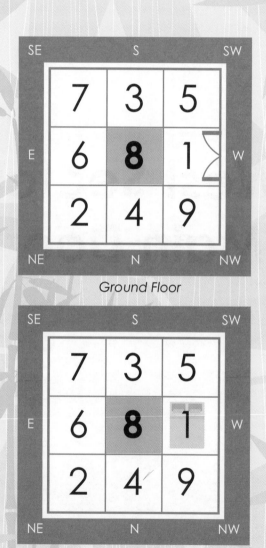

Ground Floor

First Floor

農曆正月 (February 4th - March 5th) 丙寅

Get ready to enjoy warm and cozy ties with your family members this month. Bear in mind, however, that travel will bring about injuries for people using this room. It will be a good idea to invest in some form of travel insurance before embarking on any trip. Academics and those in the research and development fields should market their research this month. At the same time, you should also be mindful of those who will take advantage of your ideas and discoveries. Be circumspect about the people with whom you share your work and don't reveal more than necessary.

農曆二月 (March 6th - April 4th) 丁卯

Those of you involved in politics will find it a very good month, as you do seem to be blessed with Midas touch! It will be a favourable time for you to push forward with your new policies and strategies as you'll be able to garner good, solid support from among the grassroots and your constituents. As your people skills start to pick up, you'll find it a good month in general to form bonds and alliances with other people and forge networking ties.

農曆三月 (April 5th - May 5th) 戊辰

The threat of financial loss looms over this month, robbing all speculative investments, primarily those equity, of its fun. It would be best to avoid all risky investments and to stay away from gambling altogether. You won't be happy, otherwise, staring at an empty bank account balance! Health issues also come to the fore this month for people using this room, especially serious ones like breast and liver cancer. Go for a thorough medical check-up if certain signs are troubling you.

農曆四月 (May 6th - June 5th) 己巳

This is a favourable room for students and scholars facing important examinations this month. It will work well during the preparations for the exams, leading to much favourable results. Any deals involving asset acquisitions concluded this month should do very well, especially if these are overseas investments or if you're dealing with contacts abroad. You'll find yourself being drawn into good relationships with others this month, both your personal and professional ties will enjoy a nice boost.

Main Door	West	Bedroom Sector	West

農曆五月 (June 6th - July 6th) 庚午

People who work in the furniture industry will find this a rather good month, as you will be able to enjoy significant profits that will give your business a boost. However, be on the alert for anyone who might potentially be a backstabber as betrayals will cause a loss of wealth and result in legal problems this month. Don't trust too easily, especially those who are keen to help you sell the moon – but at a cost. Partnerships and new alliances should be avoided this month, as they will result in a financial loss for you that will be hard to overturn.

農曆六月 (July 7th - August 7th) 辛未

Older women who are sick, or feeling frail of health, should avoid using this room this month if possible. It might be better to move them into another room for the meantime, as otherwise the possibilities of their ailment getting worse. Avoid picking fights over small things this month or it could result in serious arguments for couples using this room. Where possible, let the small things blow over or else it could turn into something serious. The energies of this sector are favourable for those in the real estate business, as deals are likely to be quite profitable this month.

農曆七月 (August 8th - September 7th) 壬申

Those of you who are using this room for the month need to be prepared to receive lots of media attention, publicity and recognition. Put on your best face forward as you may have to get used to being in the spotlight! In general, this will prove to be a month to make changes for the better and begin anew on certain matters as there will be substantial rewards awaiting you. This is also a good month to take on an ambitious endeavour, as success is practically certain. There are many mentors who will be around to help and guide you and they will be instrumental in making your ideas a reality.

農曆八月 (September 8th - October 7th) 癸酉

Businesses like health centres, clubs, spas and discos will do well financially this month. If you're in these industries, you need to take advantage of this favourable time to close or negotiate all the good deals that crop up. This is a good month to ask for a promotion as your superiors notice your talent and abilities in the business. Don't be afraid of basking in the limelight and receiving the recognition, because you've certainly earned it. Couples using this bedroom this month will see an improvement in marital relationships, signifying greater harmony and an increased intimacy.

農曆九月 (October 8th - November 7th) 甲戌

Those among you in the oil and gas industries will have a financially favourable month, especially if you're bold enough to grab the bull by the horns and make full use of all the opportunities that crop up. You should be alert and quick enough to capitalise on these chances, as they may not always come twice! Those who wish to be in the literary world should use this bedroom this month, as you might find that doors are beginning to open where they were previously shut. If you're a salaried employee working on special projects, you will have a chance to shine as there are a lot of good outcomes expected with what you're working on. Be prepared the accolades that are bound to come forth!

農曆十月 (November 8th - December 6th) 乙亥

Those among you who earn your bread and butter in the financial industry will find new clients this month. This will occur as a result of fortuitous word of mouth, especially if you travel quite a lot for your work. Travel will increase your chances of profits, so try not to refuse any of these opportunities. This month, you should strive to keep out of office politics as you could come out of it worse than you expect. You may even be saddled with legal issues as a result. Romance heats up this month with possibility of short-term passionate flings. Unfortunately. these may not develop into anything more serious or long-term.

農曆十一月 (December 7th 2019 - January 5th 2020) 丙子

If you're involved in professional and competitive sports, you're going to find this a good month. There is much in the way of advancement coming up for you, leading to much career progress and development. Certain developments may seem new or overwhelming; but as long as you're certain of your abilities, you're likely to do well! Also, get out there and make the most of all the connections you make with all the people you meet, as this is also a good month for exactly those activities.

農曆十二月 (January 6th - February 3rd 2020) 丁丑

This is not a good month for speculative investments, especially equity investments and gambling. There is a likelihood of losses otherwise, and some may have more serious consequences than expected. It will be best to play it safe this month. Couples who use this room may have to battle issues concerning jealousy and suspicion. In terms of health, breast or liver cancer risks could be heightened in this particular area.

| Main Door | West | Bedroom Sector | Southwest |

SE	S	SW
7	3	5

E		W
6	**8**	1

2	4	9
NE	N	NW

農曆正月 (February 4th - March 5th) 丙寅

Mothers and older women who use this bedroom for the month will find an increased risk of kidney problems and related ailments. If possible, you might want to move them to another room to lessen the impact. In general, bad external formations outside this sector can lead to an increase in accidents and illnesses for the occupants. As such, ensure that there are no negative structures outside this sector. Do not try to make property acquisitions this month, as this will likely end in failure.

農曆二月 (March 6th - April 4th) 丁卯

Those among you who are entangled in sticky lawsuits should just cut to the chase and avoid getting involved a long, messy drama. Try to settle the case out of court because if you don't, it's likely to cost more time, money, and energy for everyone involved. Bladder and kidney problems are key health concerns that come up for the occupants of this room this month.

農曆三月 (April 5th - May 5th) 戊辰

It will be a dry month for new business contacts and associates, as your mentors and superiors will not be around to help you get your act together. Don't be too reliant on them, as that won't be able to help you very much. You've got to be able to put together the skills you've learn in order to be able to handle matters yourself, especially if the situation demands it. Risk of health complications are still present this month, so don't ignore any of the warning signs.

農曆四月 (May 6th - June 5th) 己巳

Business owners should avoid any expansion this month and instead focus on consolidating their current position. It will be best in the long run to pay extra attention and care to customers and clients. Bear in mind as disloyalty amongst employees is rife, they will seek to undermine you through your most sensitive point – your clientele. Conservative property related deals will bring good financial gains this month, but those of you who own a business will lack the leverage to benefit from positive investment outcomes.

農曆五月 (June 6th - July 6th) 庚午

Competition and rivalry will affect the people using this room for the month. If you're not careful, this could digress into a very emotional issue that could result in acute psychological warfare. You will need to be on guard, at the same time however, don't overreact and resort to petty responses. Lawyers will have a tough time putting their case across this month and may need to use every ounce of strength to fight. In general, people using this room should be careful as accidents could be caused by mishaps with other people, resulting in muscle and tendon injuries.

農曆六月 (July 7th - August 7th) 辛未

Those among you who play sports for a living and compete professionally will find the competitions an uphill battle this month. You should instead use the time for some physical improvement that can bring future benefits. Stress and depression may end in mental instability or neurosis this month, especially if there are negative external forms located outside this sector. Health issues may also arise in the form of migraines or headaches this month, so try to relax more and not let worries and anxieties get to you. Sometimes, it's just not worth it to sweat the small things!

農曆七月 (August 8th - September 7th) 壬申

Stay away from the fashion and apparel industries, as the outcomes for those industries are likely to be quite disastrous this month. If you're working in those lines, it will be best to lay low and postpone any plans for expansion. For business owners this month, everything that can go wrong will go wrong. This includes the things that usually run smoothly as they will cause trouble and obstruction. You will need to be prepared and have a backup plan. Pregnant women should be careful when using this bedroom this month, as there is a risk of complications and troubles. If possible, switch to another room for the duration.

農曆八月 (September 8th - October 7th) 癸酉

Speculative investments and gambling should be resisted this month, as it is likely to bring financial losses. You'll do well to curb all your instincts to gamble and take a risk! Problems arising this month will be difficult to solve as the cause is not easily evident and your rivals will take quick advantage of this factor. It is imperative that you keep your guard up. Stay away from casual relationships this month, as it is likely to result in sexually-transmitted diseases and will be more trouble than it's worth.

農曆九月 (October 8th - November 7th) 甲戌

Those involved in labour negotiations or in the legal field will find this a good month, as the outcomes are generally promising and you are likely to gain a victory. This month, you'll need to pay close attention to your behaviour as unwise remarks and a lack of common sense will give rise to problems that will be hard to shrug off in the future. You'll be a magnet for bad investment advice this month, so you will need to double check all tips that you receive as deals signed this month may well turn sour.

農曆十月 (November 8th - December 6th) 乙亥

Disputes and negligence will result in property investments turning sour this month. If you're not careful, you'll ruin your good relationship with your contacts as well. There will be many unforeseeable problems this month, so contingency plans will need to be in place to avoid major setbacks. If you already have a good Plan A, be sure to work out a secure Plan B as well! Those of you involved in competitive sports should be careful of accidents resulting in bone, ligament and tendon injuries.

農曆十一月 (December 7th 2019 - January 5th 2020) 丙子

This will be a trying month for business partners, as there is a possible fallout from accumulated tension and stress that have built up over the months. If you're not careful, you will find it leading to further complications that could deplete your wealth and income. People using this room for the month should also guard against possible health problems, as otherwise serious complications will be the result.

農曆十二月 (January 6th - February 3rd 2020) 丁丑

You may find your business networks somewhat dwindling this month due to a lessening of mentors and superiors. It will be best for you to adapt to learning some of the necessary skills yourself so that you can cope with it should the need arise. Those of you in romantic relationships or marriages might feel pressured and stressed due to constant arguments. Take extra care of your health this month as well and watch out for any ear problems or kidney diseases.

Main Door	**West**	Bedroom Sector	**South**

	SE	S	SW	
	7	3	5	
E	6	**8**	1	W
	2	4	9	
	NE	N	NW	

農曆正月 (February 4th - March 5th) 丙寅

The situation on the domestic front starts to get a little harried this month as parents whose children use this room will find them a little hard to tame! Getting angry or impatient won't help matters any, so try to be more guile and tact in trying to impose some form of order. Avoid getting yourself involved in other people's affairs this month, because people are unlikely to be grateful – just the opposite, in fact! People who do business dealings should not expand at this point in time – they should instead consolidate their position for future, long-term gain.

農曆二月 (March 6th - April 4th) 丁卯

Those in the fashion business or retail will find this a month of excellent gains. Make full use of the opportunities that come up to widen or expand your business. In general, it's also a favourable month to make a fair amount of money from property and real estate – using your past experiences and in-depth knowledge to great advantage!

農曆三月 (April 5th - May 5th) 戊辰

This month requires you to be alert and cautious, as theft and fraud are potential problems. These are likely to take you by surprise, as it is likely to be committed by close friends and family members. Therefore, it would be advisable for you to put more financial controls in place and be more vigilant over where your money goes. Those among you pursuing deals with overseas partners and contacts will be able to make some windfall gains this month.

農曆四月 (May 6th - June 5th) 己巳

People using this room should prepare for a new position that affords them more power and authority, especially if you've been long due for career advancement. Do bear in mind however that with more authority (and a higher pay!) comes greater responsibilities. As such, ensure that your expectations are moderate to avoid disappointment. There will be strange power disputes between friends this month. So, if there is tension imminent, try to diffuse it before it gets out of hand. Parents with teenage sons using this room will find them to be more hardheaded and rebellious this month.

Main Door	West	Bedroom Sector	South

農曆五月 (June 6th - July 6th) 庚午

This is not the month to dabble in speculative financial investments, as losses are possible – and in worst-case scenarios, lawsuits and legal entanglements. Avoid spending all your hard-earned money on gambling, because the losses may be greater than your calculated risks. Be careful of potential health problems that come in the form of ulcers, gallstones, and liver troubles. Get a professional medical opinion if it's needed.

農曆六月 (July 7th - August 7th) 辛未

Romance issues come to the forefront this month and those of you who are in relationships should put in more effort. There is competition looming on the horizon and if you take your partner for granted, you are likely to be left licking your wounds! People using this room will have to battle some emotional and psychological problems this month. Those among you who work in research and development are likely to get noticed for your abilities this month. This is especially true if you are dealing with companies and associates abroad.

農曆七月 (August 8th - September 7th) 壬申

Be wary of road travel this month as those of you using this room are prone to getting into car accidents. If you drive, be especially watchful and careful with how you conduct yourself on the road. People who are involved in politics and those who rely heavily on their oratory skills will find it a very good month to perform well and get favourable results. Those among you who work in the analytic or scientific fields will find this to be a good month as well, you are likely to achieve a breakthrough in your line of work.

農曆八月 (September 8th - October 7th) 癸酉

Marriages are likely to come under fire this month, as both partners will be especially tense and stressed out. Instead of taking out their frustration on each other, they should address the situation promptly with tolerance before the outcome ends in a divorce. Those among you working in advertising and events management will have a particularly profitable month. It would be especially so if you consider making timely changes to your business plan. Where your professional life is concerned, you need to address the arguments, quarrels, and gossip that crop up in a diplomatic and thoughtful manner. Otherwise, it could result in legal issues.

農曆九月 (October 8th - November 7th) 甲戌

People involved in the legal field will find this a good month for increased business because there is a demand for your expertise and skills. You will have your hands full, but this will be a good thing! If you're senior personnel at work, be prepared for possible theft and fraud as there are unscrupulous third parties just waiting for the opportunity to extort large sums of money from you. Those among you working as mentors or counsellors will also be inundated with new clients this month.

農曆十月 (November 8th - December 6th) 乙亥

In general, people who use this bedroom will be able to enjoy some good gains. You will also have the wisdom and foresight to protect what you get, but you will need all your wits about you in order to outsmart the fraudsters who are out to pull the wool over your eyes. Bear in mind, however, that competitors could get nasty this month and attack you out of the blue – which may end up in hostile takeovers. It will be hard to make any deals this month, and even those that seem available will have to be concluded carefully.

農曆十一月 (December 7th 2019 - January 5th 2020) 丙子

Generally, this month brings about potential financial success for you. However, don't have too much of a good time enjoying your accomplishments that you ignore the attention from people around you looking with envious eyes. The green-eyed monster may be disguised as a charming, solicitous colleague or acquaintance; so be on guard. If you're not careful, their jealousy could be strong enough to prompt them to resort to malicious, ill-intention actions. Additionally, it's a good month to dabble in some property or real estate investments.

農曆十二月 (January 6th - February 3rd 2020) 丁丑

People who are having health problems should be on extra guard this month, especially if using this bedroom. There is the risk of injuries and if one does take place, then don't ignore the symptoms or resulting consequences. You'll find it easy to make a good financial profit from deals made with overseas partners or contacts abroad. But, bear in mind that you should put extra financial controls in place this month. This should be adhered to because theft and fraud are likely to take place, especially among people you thought you could trust.

West Sector Main Door

農曆正月 (February 4th - March 5th) 丙寅

Things are not so smooth on the domestic front, or at work, where women are concerned. There could be some tense relations or full-blown disagreements that could cause stress for the people around them. Health-wise, those of you with respiratory problems should be extra careful this month, as it may worsen and exacerbate other health issues. Leisure travel bodes well for you this month. However, be sure that you are alert to times of departure as otherwise you could find yourself in a last-minute fix!

農曆二月 (March 6th - April 4th) 丁卯

Those who work in dangerous and hazardous jobs should be extra careful as there is a risk of occupational injury this month. This will most likely be to the limbs, so don't be negligent when working with heavy machinery or sharp implements. There is little prospect of making financial profits this month and if you own or manage a company, you must be careful of employees defrauding the company. Keep an eagle eye on your staff, but don't succumb to mindless suspicion as you could alienate the trustworthy ones.

農曆三月 (April 5th - May 5th) 戊辰

Expectant mothers should steer clear of using this room for the month. It would be best for them to try to find another room or shift to another place as otherwise complications could set in. Doctors and medical professionals in general will find this a good month, as more people flock to you for your services through very favourable word of mouth!

農曆四月 (May 6th - June 5th) 己巳

People who work in the entertainment business including those who run bars, pubs, and nightclubs will find that there is no such thing as bad publicity this month! Even if it seems like the only thing that comes about is notoriety, you should ride out the publicity wave and try to gain some good business gains! However, for politicians or those of you in public service, you should try to keep a low profile and avoid attracting attention this month. In your case, there is such thing as bad publicity and your reputation will suffer as an outcome.

| Main Door | West | Bedroom Sector | Southeast |

農曆五月 (June 6th - July 6th) 庚午

Publicity and heightened fame comes about for most of you in the professional field this month, so don't hide from the limelight! It'll be exactly what you need to give your career a good boost and wait for the accolades to come pouring in. There will be problems in the office involving female colleagues as they largely try to show off their abilities and compete with one another. Your public image and status also stands to improve from increased travelling this month. Take heed, however, that your stress levels will also increase as a result of unstable emotions.

農曆六月 (July 7th - August 7th) 辛未

Word of mouth deals within the property industry can result in financial gains for you, so you need to keep your ears to the ground and cultivate your network of contacts. In general, most of you will be able to take on your competitors this month and with renewed zeal and energy. Go full steam ahead, as you're likely to attract new customers by doing so as well. Teenagers using this room will be subject to a whirlwind of emotions and feelings. They should be careful not to be swept away by the current of their feelings, as otherwise it could result in haphazard decisions and actions.

農曆七月 (August 8th - September 7th) 壬申

Guys should be on guard this month, because there will be gals with the gift of gab who will prove to be extremely tempting – but in all the wrong ways! Proceed carefully, or you could find yourself in an embarrassing situation. Be on guard where your personal safety is concerned, as robbery and theft are serious threats. Those of you involved in businesses like reflexology or massage should avoid going into new ventures, as these are unlikely to turn out well.

農曆八月 (September 8th - October 7th) 癸酉

Elderly women who use this bedroom should be careful of their health, especially where stomach ailments are concerned. This is especially true if there are negative structures located outside this sector. In general, professional rivalry and competition starts to heat up this month – resulting in possible physical violence if the arguments become explosive! Try not to add to the problem, but instead seek to calm the situation. Those in the legal and judicial fields will do well this month as the demand for their services increases.

農曆九月 (October 8th - November 7th) 甲戌

All business deals that are undertaken this month should preferably be concluded in writing, as otherwise miscommunication is rife and there will be plenty of trouble to follow. In general, avoid making any decisions in both professional and personal capacities because the outcome is unlikely to be good. Couples will find misunderstandings to be commonplace this month, so both partners should make an effort to communicate openly. Work a little bit harder to stabilise your relationship and things are likely to progress well.

農曆十月 (November 8th - December 6th) 乙亥

People who are professionally involved in the academic and media fields and using this room are likely to see an increase in fame and recognition for their work this month. Acclaim is in the bag for all your hard work thus far. Those of you who are required to sign documents should try to put it off for a future time, as otherwise trouble could be the result due to the increased likelihood of misunderstandings affecting you this month. This is not a good room for use by pregnant women, as complications are likely to set in. It might be better to switch to another room.

農曆十一月 (December 7th 2019 - January 5th 2020) 丙子

Those of you who are involved in business will find this a favourable month. Good word of mouth is likely to generate more customers and referrals for you, increasing your profits! Make an effort to cultivate your network of contacts and grab these opportunities to expand your circle of acquaintances – because everyone is a potential customer!

農曆十二月 (January 6th - February 3rd 2020) 丁丑

If you're a doctor, you will find that you have greater opportunities to perform your services this month. Those who are employed should look for opportunities to make some side income this month as there are good profits to be made from sound opportunities. Pregnant women should avoid sleeping in this room, as there is a chance of miscarriage. Where possible, a transfer to another room will be better.

Main Door	West	Bedroom Sector	East

農曆正月 (February 4th - March 5th) 丙寅

Professional sportspeople should be careful of leg injuries or accidentally hurting themselves if they use this room this month. Don't neglect these injuries if they occur, get medical treatment as soon as you can. There is an increased risk of car accidents and injuries this month, so be especially cautious if you're on the road. There will be increased tension between father and son this month, particularly if there are negative structures located outside this sector.

農曆二月 (March 6th - April 4th) 丁卯

Salaried employees may find that you face obstructions in career prospects this month, but you need to be patient and wait it out as this is only temporary. Continue to put in good effort and don't skimp on the quality of your work. Women may experience gynecological problems this month if they use this bedroom, so any complications or troubles should be checked out immediately by a medical professional.

農曆三月 (April 5th - May 5th) 戊辰

Those among you involved in the tourism and spa businesses will do well this month, especially if you travel to seek out new business prospects and contacts. Don't be afraid to go all out in pursuing these leads as it will lead to greater gains that could have you laughing all the way to the bank. This will be a good room for entrepreneurs and business people, as new ventures are likely to bode well for them. There is much to experience and plenty to learn.

農曆四月 (May 6th - June 5th) 己巳

Parents should avoid putting children in this bedroom this month if it can be helped, as they will be rebellious and difficult to control. Otherwise, a potentially tiring month is in store for you! There may be internal bickering this month so you will need to keep a low profile at work and make sure that you keep out of the office politics. Avoid taking sides and playing the blame game. Older males using this room should take care of their health, especially with regards to high blood pressure or lung disease.

Main Door	West	Bedroom Sector	East

農曆五月 (June 6th - July 6th) 庚午

A change in career, a pay raise or some form of career advancement is likely this month. This could result in financial rewards that would make you very happy! This is not a month to be afraid of new things. Investment and merchant bankers who engage in stock and corporate deals will make good financial profits this month. Most of you in general will find that there are coaches and mentors around to offer good advice, so take heed of their suggestions. You are able to achieve financial success if you consider their suggestions wisely.

農曆六月 (July 7th - August 7th) 辛未

Senior personnel in communications industry will be able to see an increase in profits this month. It might be a month of physical aggression for males, as jealousy and rivalry amongst them could result in fights. These could likely end up in the law courts. Therefore, it might be good to put the bravado aside and consider the situation using brains instead of brawn and ugly legal wrangles can be avoided. This is a month for short-term flings rather than long term relationships. If you're comfortable with that, then you should be able to enjoy it. Just don't set your expectations too high and you should be fine!

農曆七月 (August 8th - September 7th) 壬申

Employees may become rebellious this month and superiors will find them difficult to handle. General tact and diplomacy will be needed to ensure that situation does not explode out of control. Good profits can be realised this month, but a more hands-on approach is required to maximise profits. As such, you should not be hesitant to get your hands dirty! This bedroom will benefit you if you're into professional sports and are participating in any competitive events this month, as you're likely to see more victories than losses.

農曆八月 (September 8th - October 7th) 癸酉

Family relations are strained and tense this month. It is better however just to keep the peace, as this is not a good time to thrash it out with the family. It's best to save the emotional probing to a more conducive time in the future. There are opportunities to make money from property investments this month, but you will need to have a good knowledge of the market to be successful in this venture. In other words, study the property market inside out before attempting anything in it! Alternatively, at the very least, consult an expert.

農曆九月 (October 8th - November 7th) 甲戌

Those in the academic and literary fields will benefit from new ideas and inspiration that are likely to bring favourable financial gains this month. Don't ignore an idea even if seems crazy, as that just might be the ticket! If you are in metal trading or share and equity trading, this is a month where good deals will be concluded and financial gains are made. Scholars and students who are facing important examinations should make use of this room for their study preparations, as academic results are likely to be favourable.

農曆十月 (November 8th - December 6th) 乙亥

Travel-related problems could result in leg injuries this month, so be especially careful on any of your travel trips. Consider investing in a good form of insurance just to be safe! Minor health issues could be a problem as well, but don't neglect any of the troubling signs that crop up. It could lead to more serious problems further down the road. Employees in the engineering field will gain a lot of support and encouragement from superiors this month and financial reward and recognition are likely to follow.

農曆十一月 (December 7th 2019 - January 5th 2020) 丙子

Those among you who are deeply involved in the spiritual, religious, or even metaphysical fields will find plenty to look forward to this month. Growth and expansion of knowledge will likely set you off in new and exciting directions. You'll find this a good time to also meet with like-minded individuals who share your interests. Those of you who work full-time for an employer will not have an easy month of it, but don't lose heart because things will get better.

農曆十二月 (January 6th - February 3rd 2020) 丁丑

Those of you who are experiencing a rocky relationship or a floundering business partnership will most likely have to face the end of the tie or connection if you use this bedroom this month. However, don't think of it as a bad thing, because it paves the way for auspicious new beginnings. But, if you'd like to maintain what you have, be sure to take extra care of your manner of speech and behavior with your partner. Those of you in the spa and tourism business will do well to do some travelling because it will help lead you to new business prospects and contacts.

West Sector Main Door

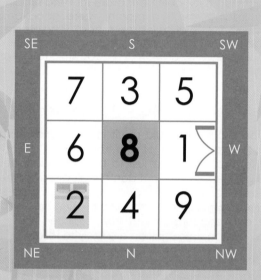

SE	S	SW
7	3	5
6	**8**	1
2	4	9
NE	N	NW

E (left side)   W (right side)

農曆正月 (February 4th - March 5th) 丙寅

Couples using this room will be distracted at work as a result of your romantic involvement, so don't allow your relationship to affect your professional life. It is just a rough patch that will soon return to normal, so in the meantime concentrate on your career instead of blowing it off. Investment in gold mines this month will return good profits for you. So, if you've always wanted to invest in gold mines, this is the time to do so! Ill health is also a problem this month, with head and brain problems coming to the fore. Take note of any sudden headaches and it will be best to go for an early medical check-up if it troubles you.

農曆二月 (March 6th - April 4th) 丁卯

Those of you who have property portfolios to divest should do so this month, as you are likely to gain some very pretty profits from it! The name of the game this month is work, work and more work – and this is especially true for salaried employees. Don't be disheartened if the benefits of hard work are not immediately apparent at this point in time, because it will come soon enough.

農曆三月 (April 5th - May 5th) 戊辰

If there is a need to sign legal documents, be particularly careful this month. You will need to exercise extreme caution in all your legal dealings. If you need to enlist professional legal advice, so be it. There are greater gains to be earned doing so than going it alone and suffering greater losses. Be careful of potential financial losses caused by negligence, though. This is the month to step up on your vigilance.

農曆四月 (May 6th - June 5th) 己巳

Mothers and daughters-in-law will be having tense relations this month. So, if you're either one of the above, it will be best to exercise tact and diplomacy in your dealings with the other! Women in the literary field will have a time to shine this month, as they will receive awards and achievements for all their creative labours thus far. This is a time for self-cultivation and if the opportunity arises, you should take a self-development course. It is a good month to work on improving yourself, and you're likely to feel a lot better about your life in general.

| Main Door | West | Bedroom Sector | Northeast |

農曆五月 (June 6th - July 6th) 庚午

Make sure that all taxes and fines are up-to-date this month as you may find yourself in trouble with the law otherwise! Getting yourself extricated out of that mess might require all of your creativity and ingenuity. Couples should make sure that they spend as little time together as possible, because they will end up with tense and stressful situations if they share this room this month. It will be better instead to give each other some much needed space. This is a good sector for those who wish to become involved in religious or spiritual endeavours.

農曆六月 (July 7th - August 7th) 辛未

If you're in the medical field, you will find that your skills are in great demand this month and you can expect to enjoy an increase in profits. Those of you wishing to invest in property will find that this a good month to get involved in the venture, as the returns will be quick and profitable. Get the advice of the experts for guidance if you need it. Women who are pregnant should avoid this sector for the time being. Chances are, miscarriage or some other form of complication is possible.

農曆七月 (August 8th - September 7th) 壬申

While your financial luck is somewhat good, you will need to exercise some caution and not get too carried away. Don't spend too much of your money too soon as you'll be left with nothing if you're too gung-ho with your wallet. Maintain good ties with your friends and family and don't let any arguments escalate out of control this month, as you'll have a hard time putting the pieces back together otherwise. Don't be too gullible this month, people may tend to take advantage of you if you're not careful.

農曆八月 (September 8th - October 7th) 癸酉

Put your guard up in your business dealings this month, as things are not what they seem and rivals are out to deceive you. Foster a healthy sense of skepticism and don't be easily misled. Remain doubtful of the person or circumstance that seems to be too good to be true! Academic luck is not good this month and as such, if you're a student you may find that your thought processes lack clarity. This in turn translates to your work being muddled as a result. There is a possibility of discord, arguments and family disharmony for people who use this bedroom this month. It would be advisable to pay more attention to your communication and ties with each other.

農曆九月 (October 8th - November 7th) 甲戌

Paranoia and superstition may set in this month, resulting in emotional setbacks for those you who succumb to the worries and excessive agitation. The key thing is to maintain some form of emotional strength despite the negative feelings and possibly share your worries with a trusted friend. Gastric and intestinal problems will plague those using this bedroom this month. If you are prone to these issues, you should take care of yourself. If you are involved in politics and consider yourself to be senior, you will find that you make good headway in the political field and you will receive recognition for your work in the community.

農曆十月 (November 8th - December 6th) 乙亥

There is a possibility for you to make money this month from side investments that will return good profits. If you make smart decisions, you can expect to enjoy a well-padded wallet! However, be careful not to work too hard and skimp on rest! If you're a doctor, you will find that you have increased business this month. Couples in this house may find that they are unable to have children and using this bedroom this month will complicate things further. If possible, you should try shifting to another room in order to improve the situation.

農曆十一月 (December 7th 2019 - January 5th 2020) 丙子

As an employee, you will find that you are working harder this month, but income and deal closure do not seem to be concluded. In other words, the benefits of your hard work are not clearly visible – but don't give up faith just yet! This is a good month however to make financial gains from the sale of property assets, so you might want to divest off your portfolios. Those involved in religious pursuits or those gaining spiritual knowledge should use this bedroom this month, as it is conducive for exactly those types of activities.

農曆十二月 (January 6th - February 3rd 2020) 丁丑

Health issues come into the fore this month. Typically for elderly women using this room, this will come in the form of abdominal illness. Don't put off a medical consultation for too long. It will be best to consult your doctor at the first signs of discomfort. Be careful when signing legal documents this month because all legal dealings are fraught with potential risks at this point in time. This is especially true for those of you working or involved in finance and trading.

| Main Door | West | Bedroom Sector | North |

農曆正月 (February 4th - March 5th) 丙寅

There will be harmonious relations for those who use this bedroom this month, but they have to be careful if there are no water features outside this sector. Those of you working in the arts and culture industry will be able to generate good exposure from the media this month, leading to increased recognition for your work. You can expect to prepare for your moment in the spotlight! This is a good month to build alliance partners abroad or embark on business expansion, so consider focusing your endeavours on the international arena at this point in time.

農曆二月 (March 6th - April 4th) 丁卯

Relationships are generally on the upswing this month and those using this bedroom should take full advantage of them. Make an effort to reconnect with old friends, spend more time with family and further strengthen your marriage and love relationships. All your endeavours in this particular area of your life are likely to go down well, giving you favourable results. However, this is not a good time to travel as your rivals will make inroads into your client base whilst you are away. It will be best to stay closer to home and keep an eye on your business proceedings.

農曆三月 (April 5th - May 5th) 戊辰

There is much good news to look forward to on the professional front for people using this room. You stand a very good chance of getting that promotion or career advancement you've longed for, or at least receive some significant form of recognition for all your hard work thus far. This is especially true for those of you work in the real estate and property fields. In addition, there are profits aplenty to be gained from investments in the property market.

農曆四月 (May 6th - June 5th) 己巳

Words need to be used with care this month, as there is a tendency for misunderstandings arising out of words misconstrued. Therefore, think carefully before saying anything this month, as you might find yourself having to eat quite a lot of your words otherwise! Those of you in the business of furniture retail will have a good month, but you will need to be careful when signing any legal documents. Double-check everything at least once. If your work involves being at construction and work sites, then be careful while using sharp metal objects.

| Main Door | West | Bedroom Sector | North |

農曆五月 (June 6th - July 6th) 庚午

It's a good month for both personal and professional relationships. So, if you want to cultivate closer ties, this would be the ideal time to do it. This is especially the case in communication0 as the more you work on making it better, the greater the results will be! As much as possible, though, avoid dabbling in speculative investments – especially in equities, shares, and futures. Losses can be quite huge, so it would be best to avoid it altogether. Your stature, reputation and name will improve if you travel to conduct business this month, so strive to make as many business opportunities abroad!

農曆六月 (July 7th - August 7th) 辛未

This is not a month for gambling, because financial losses are the only thing looming on the horizon. In that vein, those among you who have dabbled in speculative investments – particularly involving property or real estate – should withdraw from these deals or divest their investments before they endure any significant losses. Ladies using this room are likely to run into some serious health problems this month, so to be safe it would be best to schedule a mammogram to rule out possibilities of breast cancer.

農曆七月 (August 8th - September 7th) 壬申

Health problems is ever present this month, with asthma and bronchitis being some of the major ones plaguing people using this room. If you show symptoms of these illnesses, get medical treatment so as not to worsen your situation. Gambling activities should continue to be avoided this month Women who own businesses will find that travels abroad to conclude deals lead to very good financial gains. Make the most of the work travel opportunities that crop up this month!

農曆八月 (September 8th - October 7th) 癸酉

Those of you who are artistically creative should make an effort to approach the international market as the demand for quality work is high. You are likely to receive creative support for your work in addition to acclaim. Those travelling this month should expect some sudden changes or last-minute problems. It would be best for you to invest in some good travel insurance. Children using this sector could be encouraged by peer pressure to get involved in rebellious activities. If you're a parent, it pays to be more aware of your children's friends and their leisure habits.

農曆九月 (October 8th - November 7th) 甲戌

Female employees will have an excellent month, especially those of you who work in the real estate industry. Profits will be pouring in for you! However, as competition amongst women employees intensify, little progress may be made on the actual work projects for those of you in the other industries. Try not to get caught in the middle of professional rivalries. This is a good month to invest in self-cultivation; this is achievable either by attending new courses or learning a new trade. Consider taking a class in something that you've always wanted to try.

農曆十月 (November 8th - December 6th) 乙亥

It's a good month for relationships this month, and those of you who have long wanted to take yours to the next level should do so at this point in time! If you've wanted to propose marriage for some time, then the outcome is favourable for you to do it now. Those among you who work as authors and journalists should make a vested effort this month to look for publishers and give your written work its proper platform! If you're sitting for examinations, it'll also be beneficial for you to use this room.

農曆十一月 (December 7th 2019 - January 5th 2020) 丙子

This is a good month to conclude all the deals you've had juggling in the air for a while now. There are plenty of profitable and lucrative investment opportunities available for grabs this month, but you'll need to be eagle-eyed and alert to spot them as they come up. Therefore, make it your mission this month to make an outstanding closing. Those of you using this room will also find it a continuing good month for relationships.

農曆十二月 (January 6th - February 3rd 2020) 丁丑

Joint ventures will benefit you greatly this month, especially if you're already using this room. If possible, try to dabble or try your hand in gilt bonds and shares to see how you will do. The likelihood is that you'll be able to rake up the profits! In general, those using this room will enjoy a good month especially if involved in the real estate and property industry. There is a good chance that you'll see a marked increase in stature as a promotion or likely recognition comes your way. In general, profits come from the property market.

West Sector Main Door

農曆正月 (February 4th - March 5th) 丙寅

Health concerns come to the fore this month, leading up to some troubling matters if you're not careful. In particular, food poisoning is very likely and this is especially so if there are negative structures located outside this sector. If you are not careful, it's likely to lead to stomach and digestive problems that cause you much discomfort even if it's not serious. Stick to low-profile, conservative investments this month, as financial loss rather than gain is likely to be the norm.

農曆二月 (March 6th - April 4th) 丁卯

You'll face quite a bit of difficulty at work this month, as very little support is received for your ideas and projects. Without the encouragement and help from others, the obstacles in place are likely to be harder to overcome. If possible, avoid starting any major or important projects this month. It will be better to just lay low and do your planning at this stage, conserving your energy and productivity for a more fruitful time in the future.

農曆三月 (April 5th - May 5th) 戊辰

Things at work start to get a little demanding and you might have to juggle multiple projects to please your superiors. If it becomes overwhelming, you need to speak up and ask for help. There is no shame in doing that, because you only succeed in providing half-hearted work if you don't have the time or the energy to give it your best!

農曆四月 (May 6th - June 5th) 己巳

Those of you using this room will find it a very good month for romance. If you're already in committed relationships, you'll find that your relationship can progress comfortably to the next level with very little effort on your part. If you're single and looking, this is the month to step up the pace or make a move if someone has already caught your eye! Those of you working in the engineering or travel industry should go forth and ask for a promotion this month as results are likely to be good.

| Main Door | West | Bedroom Sector | Northwest |

農曆五月 (June 6th - July 6th) 庚午

This will prove to be a very good month, professionally, for people using this room. There are strong chances for a promotion for salaried employees, while those among you who are self-employed or own businesses will be able to enjoy an enhanced reputation. Fame and increased business are likely to be the results of that. Personal relationships will also do well this month, so make an effort to forge closer ties with your loved ones.

農曆六月 (July 7th - August 7th) 辛未

Make this your month of self-improvement as any attempts at self-cultivation will be fruitful and leave you feeling satisfied. Consider embarking on a new program for living or take up meditation and other soul-replenishing activities. Clarity of thought is at its unvarnished prime this month, so it will be a good time to make an important decision you've been holding off. Health will generally be good but do ensure that there are no negative features located outside this sector.

農曆七月 (August 8th - September 7th) 壬申

People using this bedroom will be able to celebrate with some good news this month. Married couples may be able to welcome a new crying, squirming bundle of joy into their arms! The rest of you in committed relationships should be able to go forth and pop the question – and receive the desired answer. In terms of finances, it's all looking quite rosy as well – as property investments are likely to bring in positive results.

農曆八月 (September 8th - October 7th) 癸酉

Your bad temper will be a prominent feature this month, as your mood will be lot sourer than usual due to the effects of sleeping in this room. This might lead you to be very anti-social and you'll find it difficult to get along with others and simply enjoy a good time. Don't worry too much or push things along, because it will blow over soon. Partners in relationships should avoid being too clingy this month, as both of you need more space.

農曆九月 (October 8th - November 7th) 甲戌

Trouble comes this month in the form of openly defiant and rebellious subordinates and employees. Try to find out the reasons behind this, as they are most likely disgruntled over some issue that proves to be quite significant. This is not the time for heavy-handed authority, as they are more likely to respond positively when you show some compassion and diplomacy. This way, the problem can be easily solved and everyone can benefit from the resolution.

農曆十月 (November 8th - December 6th) 乙亥

This month starts off with a very small bang, so it would be highly advisable for you to keep a low profile! This means playing it cool and keeping your cards close to you both in the personal and professional areas of your life. There is a tendency for a significant loss of wealth this month if you're not careful, so keep your investments conservative. If something seems too risky at this point in time, avoid it. There will be better opportunities cropping up in the future.

農曆十一月 (December 7th 2019 - January 5th 2020) 丙子

People using this room will find that it does not bode well for their academic or learning pursuits this month. As such, students and scholars who are sitting for their examinations will be better off using another room if they wish their results to be better. Otherwise, don't be surprised if what you get is below your expectations.

農曆十二月 (January 6th - February 3rd 2020) 丁丑

Those of you who are salaried employees will find that your employers' expectations start to increase substantially this month! Dealing with their demands will be somewhat difficult, yet all you can do is to try to fulfill them to the best of your ability. If you find that the workload is too much to cope with however, try to discuss this with your superiors and find a middle ground that works for everyone.

Southwest Sector
Main Door

Southwest Sector Main Door

This section contains the monthly outlook for all 12 months of the year, for different bedroom sectors in a property with a Southwest Main Door.

SE	S	SW
7	3	5
6 (E)	**8**	1 (W)
2	4	9
NE	N	NW

Ground Floor

SE	S	SW
7	3	5
6 (E)	**8**	1 (W)
2	4	9
NE	N	NW

First Floor

農曆正月 (February 4th - March 5th) 丙寅

It's a good month for you to stick your toes in property dealings, but maybe one toe is just about best for now! It's better to be conservative with your finances than to splurge all-out this month. Any problems that come up in your relationships and marriages at this point in time should be handled with maturity, diplomacy and tact. Young children and toddlers are at risk for muscle, tendon and ligament problems and injuries this month. As such, pay extra attention to their movements this month.

農曆二月 (March 6th - April 4th) 丁卯

Any disagreements or conflicts that crop up with your family members and loved ones at home must be addressed with diplomacy and goodwill this month, or else they risk escalating into something more serious. Be patient and listen to what others have to say before drawing your own conclusions. Those in the legal profession, such as lawyers and advocates, will have some trouble putting their cases across this month. Your chances of winning your cases this month are quite slim, so it might be best to push forward your litigation to another time where possible.

農曆三月 (April 5th - May 5th) 戊辰

At the workplace this month, things are liable to get somewhat nasty. Put all sharp implements away as backstabbing is rife! What you need to do is duck when you have to, and run when you need to. There is no sense in getting involved in office politics because it will only bring you pain and stress. Work pressure starts to mount, in general, so be aware of the effects this will have on you and your relationships.

農曆四月 (May 6th - June 5th) 己巳

This is not a good month for both professional and personal relationships, so avoid rocking the boat whenever possible. This is not the month to make a stand or put your foot down! Instead, focus on your own thing and stay out of the line of fire until things start to improve. Don't get involved in property deals that are particularly risky as you stand the chance to lose in a big way. Be cautious when it comes to your finances, this will help you go further in the long run. Health-wise, be careful of nerve and tendon injuries.

| Main Door | Southwest | Bedroom Sector | Southwest |

農曆五月 (June 6th - July 6th) 庚午

Vocal abilities are under strain this month for people using this room, so be especially careful if you need to deliver speeches and presentations. Bear this in mind as well if you are scheduled for any speaking engagements. It will be a challenging month for lawyers in general, and not just because of the vocal trouble, as you'll find yourself facing some obstacles in putting your case across. People using this room will also find the competition heating up from professional and personal rivals, resulting in emotional situations heavy in manipulation and confrontations.

農曆六月 (July 7th - August 7th) 辛未

Your Wealth Luck is somewhat weak for this month, so all investment deals should be steadfastly avoided in the best interests of your bank account! This is also not the month to be particularly tender-hearted when people come by asking you for loans, as you're unlikely to see your money back if you lend it out. Health-wise, be careful of any physical injuries that could result in head or bone injuries. If any minor health ailments crop up, it would be best for you to get yourself bundled off to the doctor at the first chance possible to avoid serious complications in the future.

農曆七月 (August 8th - September 7th) 壬申

Where your professional life and work are concerned, this is a month for you to lay low and keep a low profile. Getting involved in anything too ambitious this month will only backfire. Likewise for all new projects and endeavours – best to begin it at a more favourable time in the future. In terms of your health, get all minor illnesses that may present itself checked out – otherwise, you might have a more serious problem on your hands. If possible, avoid long-distance travel by car or automobile this month because accidents are very likely. Avoid breaking traffic laws as well.

農曆八月 (September 8th - October 7th) 癸酉

Pregnant ladies should be careful this month, because complications with your pregnancy are likely if you're using this room. If possible, you should switch to using another room. Other health problems that are likely to affect people using this room include liver infections and skin disease. As much as possible, get adequate rest and give yourself plenty of respite so as to not overstrain your body. Be prepared for a fierce fight put up by your rivals and competitors this month. So, get geared up for a battle that is likely to leave you feeling quite drained.

農曆九月 (October 8th - November 7th) 甲戌

The risk of fire hazards is quite strong this month. As such, be careful of your stove and kitchen gas outlets. Check all your electrical wiring as well. Where your work schedule is concerned, you need to take some time to plan and organise your projects carefully. If you find that your plate is overflowing or even filled to the brim, then make your opinion known and demand for a more reasonable timeline.

農曆十月 (November 8th - December 6th) 乙亥

This is not a good month to indulge in gambling and speculative investments as you may find yourself counting your losses more than anything else otherwise! It will be best for you to be conservative instead and avoid all forms of risky financial endeavours. Romance luck is not too favourable for this month. Boring as this may sound, you will be better off focusing on your career at this point! Elderly ladies using this room should be careful of any stomach problems that crop up.

農曆十一月 (December 7th 2019 - January 5th 2020) 丙子

For people relying on communication skills this month, whether it's your bread and butter or you're simply using masses of it to get things done, this month will give you some problems. You'll have trouble trying to articulate exactly what you want to say or you may end up misfiring and sticking your foot into your mouth. As much as you can, think before you speak! Also, any pending legal matters in your life should ideally be put to rest – forever – this month. Otherwise, it could end up draining your finances, which is something you definitely do not need.

農曆十二月 (January 6th - February 3rd 2020) 丁丑

This is a month that can be overwhelming for some, as stress and work pressure will cause relationships to be tense and difficult. Schedule some time for heart-to-heart communication with your loved ones so that they understand your situation. Betrayal by employees making a play for power will bring you stress, so you will need to maintain courage under fire. Stay out of nasty office politics as much as possible in order to remain unaffected.

農曆正月 (February 4th - March 5th) 丙寅

Things on the career horizon are looking bright for you and all the hard work and effort you put into your job will not go unnoticed! You might be looking at a possible promotion and/or raise that are bound to keep you happy. Where your physical health is concerned, it's a good month for you to get moving and head to the gym! If you've ever wanted to lose some weight, there's no better time to start than now. However, the possibility of car accidents is very strong; be carefully when you're behind the wheel and limit long-distance travel.

農曆二月 (March 6th - April 4th) 丁卯

Those of you who have been feeling under the weather and somewhat physically weak should avoid using this sector as much as possible. If any of your illnesses become worse, it would be best to consult a doctor as soon as possible. Decisions involving your business deals should be postponed to a later time. Otherwise, the risk of disputes or slander is high. This is the kind of trouble you don't need at this point. You'll need to be a little more eagle-eyed with your staff than normal, as there are a few of them defecting to the other side... or just attempting to get away with some fraud.

農曆三月 (April 5th - May 5th) 戊辰

Those of you who have business deals or connections with partners abroad are likely to have some unexpected financial gains this month. Health-wise, people who are already battling infections and illnesses should be extra careful this month as internal injuries are likely. Be especially vigilant and don't take your physical wellbeing for granted. There is also the unfortunate chance for robberies and thefts to occur this month. With that in mind, be cautious with your belongings, cash, and assets. Conceal the existence all valuables as much as you possibly can.

農曆四月 (May 6th - June 5th) 己巳

Elderly males who are using this room will have to be careful with their health this month, as potential lung problems can develop into something serious. Take all proper precautions and visit the doctor as soon as something seems slightly amiss. Male teenagers who are using this room, meanwhile, will be a lot more rebellious and insolent than normal. It would be a wise idea to consider using a different month to cool that defiant spirit. Those of you who are due for some form of progress in your career are likely to see a possible new position that brings with it greater power and authority for you.

| Main Door | Southwest | Bedroom Sector | South |

農曆五月 (June 6th - July 6th) 庚午

If you're working in the service industry, you'll be enjoying relatively good business this month. But, remember that you must keep on top of your taxes or otherwise all that good effect will be negated! People in the real estate or property industries will have to push a little harder this month to see any form of revenue. Don't be afraid to try new things instead of sticking to the tried and tested. Things on the home front will be less than rosy, especially in families where mothers and sons are living together. Arguments and conflicts are likely between these two members of the family, so the best way to overcome it is to let each other enjoy more space.

農曆六月 (July 7th - August 7th) 辛未

If you use a bedroom in this sector as a bedroom, emotional and psychological problems are likely to plague you and cause some discontent. Feeling edgy and anxious will be the hallmarks of the effects generated. People in the marketing and media fields will find the month tough going in many respects; it will seem that despite all your pushing and prodding, not much results or gains are likely. In terms of striking business deals, this is the month to play it safe. Go with your gut instinct to trust people you've dealt with before instead of going down a whole new path.

農曆七月 (August 8th - September 7th) 壬申

Watch your words this month, as any words spoken out of rash anger or emotion are likely to get you into some trouble. This is trouble you don't need, so you're much better off remaining silent when you can't think of anything nice to say. In terms of romance, any new encounters this month should be kept casual and light as the chances of those becoming serious and long-term are slim to none. Fraudsters and conmen are out to make a killing, so go into any deals or professional negotiations with your eyes wide open and your guard up.

農曆八月 (September 8th - October 7th) 癸酉

If you're in real estate and property investment, this is a good month for you to give your portfolios a nice boost. Strong results are likely. Those of you who are married will find this month bringing about its fair share of tension and stress, putting some pressure on your relationship and causing more discord between the two of you. As serious fights could lead to separation or even divorce, don't let anything fester for too long. As much as possible, avoid fighting over anything as well as these are likely to end badly.

農曆九月 (October 8th - November 7th) 甲戌

Where health is concerned, liver-related trouble and illnesses are what you need to watch out for this month. If you work in the travel industry, you can expect some abrupt changes and developments that could actually turn out very well for you. It could also lead to some nice increased profits! Those in the midst of negotiations will find that things are going well, only to have rug abruptly pulled out from under you. Try to keep your expectations low and don't put all your eggs into one basket.

農曆十月 (November 8th - December 6th) 乙亥

This month, it will be good to have your wall of scepticism back up. There will be plenty of fraudsters around ready to offer you too-good-to-be-true investment deals once again. Avoid getting into any of this or you'll risk a serious financial loss. But, rest assured that your mind is in top form at this point and your thoughts have a clear-cut purpose and clarity to them – so it's the ideal time to put your strategic plans into action. You're likely to get the results you want.

農曆十一月 (December 7th 2019 - January 5th 2020) 丙子

If you've long been in love and have been ready to take your relationship to the next level, then this is the month where you should pull out all the stops. It's a favourable month for you to pop the big question or at the very least, bring the topic up! The results are likely to be what you want. You might be doing well in your life and enjoying a few successes, but resentment and envy are ripe all around you. Don't feed the flames of others' jealousy by boasting about your achievements; instead, play it cool and keep a low profile instead. Better to share your happiness with those nearest and dearest.

農曆十二月 (January 6th - February 3rd 2020) 丁丑

There is a likelihood of a loss of wealth as a result of fraud or theft. Be careful of all your personal belongings and your material assets. Do not leave valuable jewellery lying about the house in easy-to-reach areas and do also pay close attention to your personal documents – especially those relating to your financial accounts and statements. Confidential business documents should also be kept in a safe place and guarded closely.

農曆正月 **(February 4th - March 5th)** 丙寅

People in the mobile industry can expect a challenging month as they will have to battle annoying technical problems and glitches. It will take up all of your time and energy trying to put these things to right. If you're an actor or a doctor, you'll incite the interest of the media this month – and this will be a good thing! Your reputation will enjoy a nice boost that will bring in further accolades and benefits. This month, err on the side of caution and try to be conservative. Otherwise, you'll find yourself trapped in some sticky legal complications that will require the intervention of lawyers.

農曆二月 **(March 6th - April 4th)** 丁卯

You might be overwhelmed by the demands of your relationship this month. But, at the same time, it's not an excuse to run away. In fact, don't try to dance or party your sorrows away in clubs and bars since you'll be mired deeper in unwanted problems. This is a good month to look on the bright side of things, and failing that, do some soul searching. You just might be able to find the solutions to your problems if you look hard enough. Career-wise, you are ripe for some recognition. However, you need to be wise enough to find the avenues to carve out a good name for yourself.

農曆三月 **(April 5th - May 5th)** 戊辰

Expectant ladies who use this room could suffer a possible miscarriage, so it might be better to consider using another one. In general, people who use this room will be prone to stomach-related illnesses and trouble, especially elderly women. Take proper precautions and don't neglect your health. Fire-related accidents and hazards are very likely this month, especially if there are negative landforms or structures outside this sector.

農曆四月 **(May 6th - June 5th)** 己巳

If you've been harbouring thoughts about starting new ventures in the communications industry this month, think again – because there are many impediments along the way that will slow you down and cause unnecessary delays and losses. It will be best to attempt this at a more favourable time in the future. Those seeking some short-term romantic pleasure will find that flings will bring their fair share of mud being slung at you! You don't need more trouble at this point, so don't go looking for any. Ladies who invest in business deals and ventures in another country are likely to enjoy good profits.

農曆五月 (June 6th - July 6th) 庚午

Fire hazards crop up again this month, so do be careful with your electrical appliances and double check all electrical wiring and gas valves and openings thoroughly. Don't be negligent and careless, as the risk is high. Avoid getting into any joint ventures at this point, because they could bring you financial losses instead of success. If you're an entrepreneur or a businessperson, let your wildest, most innovative idea take root – it will bode well in terms of promoting you and your career and you will gain admiration and acclaim.

農曆六月 (July 7th - August 7th) 辛未

There are plenty of opportunities for you to smile this month, as you are likely to enjoy good Wealth Luck – with opportunities to make a small killing in the property and real estate industries! Additionally, your personal relationships are enjoying some good vibes. As such, make an effort to spend more time with the people you care about as this emotional investment will bring about its own rewards. If you own a business, this is the right time to attract new customers and clients that could lead to solid financial returns. It would be advisable for you to make a concentrated effort to pull them in. Try out new ideas and techniques that could give you a different response.

農曆七月 (August 8th - September 7th) 壬申

Be careful with your personal belongings, money and valuables as there is an increased risk of robbery and theft this month. At the same time, professional rivalry really starts to heat up. You'll need to protect your material and intellectual properties equally, so it'll be a balancing act for sure! Married men should steer clear of temptation and avoid doing anything that will compromise the sanctity of your marriage vows. Otherwise, you might risk causing some serious damage to your relationship. In general, people using this room should be careful of potential injuries to the limbs.

農曆八月 (September 8th - October 7th) 癸酉

Lawyers and solicitors are likely to have a good month of it, as business prospects come your way and you reaping the benefits of all that! Enjoy the results of your hard work. Elderly women who use this room should be prepared for possible limb-related injuries or health problems, so don't take any warning signs lightly. People in the mobile and telecommunications device industries will enjoy a good month as financial profits come rolling in.

農曆九月 (October 8th - November 7th) 甲戌

Those of you who are just starting out professionally in the sports arena will find this a good month to focus on the specific sport you're interested and develop your talent. The results are likely to be very good. Women involved in business ventures, especially those in the medical field, will do well to make some wise and clever business deals that could rake in some huge profits. At work, keep an eye on your competition as otherwise you could find yourself mired in a messy argument or lawsuit.

農曆十月 (November 8th - December 6th) 乙亥

Pregnant ladies using this room should be careful, as possible complications can arise as a result of using this room; especially in relation to the confinement period. Try to use another room for the month if possible. In general, for everyone using this room, health problems to watch out for include possible kidney ailments. People in the media and publishing fields will find that any investments that are made this month are likely to bring in profits, so go all out in pursuing the leads that seem particularly good.

農曆十一月 (December 7th 2019 - January 5th 2020) 丙子

Economists among us will find this a good month, as their skills and expertise are more in demand than ever – giving a nice boost to their income while cementing their professional reputation. People who work in the sports equipment and fitness apparel industry can look forward to good results, but only after overcoming quite a few obstacles. While the initial hard work can be demotivating, persevere on because the end results will be more than worth the effort. In general, the risk of theft and burglary is high. So, take extra precautions and enforce a home security system.

農曆十二月 (January 6th - February 3rd 2020) 丁丑

There's no better time than the end of the year to forge closer ties with your colleagues and business partners and affiliates, along with your family and friends. Thriving, well-nurtured relationships are the bedrock to a happy existence and you'll have plenty of chances to water yours with love and care this month! Your Wealth Luck is also good this month and there will be plenty of chances for you to make some good profits from the entertainment and property industries. While this is a good month for you in all aspects, be careful of international business deals and contracts. You might miss something in the legal fine print that could cause some problems. Have a lawyer look over your documents to be safe!

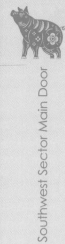

Southwest Sector Main Door

Main Door | **Southwest** | Bedroom Sector | **East**

農曆正月 (February 4th - March 5th) 丙寅

Fathers and sons will run into problems with each other this month if they use this room, so it might be best to keep them out of this sector where possible. Some minor health issues could also be quite bothersome; take the time to treat it properly as otherwise it could grow into more serious complications. Steadfastly avoid all forms of speculative investments this month, unless you're in the engineering industry – in which case you should expand and actively seek out new clients and customers.

農曆二月 (March 6th - April 4th) 丁卯

You will enjoy a positive and harmonious relationship with your partner this month, so take advantage of this time to cultivate the relationship and foster closer and more intimate tie. In terms of wealth, you'll be able to gain some money from investments previously made in the real estate and property industries. In general, this month brings about some happy tidings for you – so don't be afraid to indulge in a few celebrations!

農曆三月 (April 5th - May 5th) 戊辰

While your health troubles are not prominent this month, you still need to be careful of potential headaches and migraines. Ensure that you get enough rest as too much stress will only make things worse. If your job role involves strategic thinking and analysis, this will be a good month for you! You'll see chances to advance your career and strike a reputation for yourself. Use your talents and skills to your best advantage and plan carefully on how you can let others see the best of your true abilities.

農曆四月 (May 6th - June 5th) 己巳

Long-term investments bring about great dividends for you this month, but steer clear of getting overconfident by trying to continue your winning streak the wrong way. Don't get into any short-term investments at this point hoping to make a quick buck, because the opposite is likely to occur. Sons who use this room may be particularly defiant towards their fathers and some discord could be likely on the home front. Otherwise, health and relationships are both good for most people using this room and you'll definitely feel a sense of rest and relaxation seeping into your life.

| Main Door | Southwest | Bedroom Sector | East |

農曆五月 (June 6th - July 6th) 庚午

If you find yourself in need of help this month, don't be afraid to ask for it. There is no shame in being sincere and upfront about your needs. This may be particularly relevant where your business projects are concerned. Consider asking the opinion of an older or wiser mentor and you just might see the negative transforming into the positive faster than you expected! Stress and mental pressure affect you quite strongly this month and that in turn will play havoc with your ability to think clearly and reason things out. Ensure you have some time-out for relaxation; don't overstrain yourself.

農曆六月 (July 7th - August 7th) 辛未

People who work in the legal and advertising industries will find an increased demand for your skills, which will have good repercussions in terms of bolstering your finances. However, for most people, jealousy and competition will start to heat up at the workplace. As a result, some messy legal issues are in store if left to escalate out of control. If possible, try to play the role of peacemaker and smooth over ruffled feathers lest the situation explodes into something that no one can handle. Those of you in the throes of new love would do well to bear in mind that these are likely to be short-term rather than long-term, so keep your expectations in proportion.

農曆七月 (August 8th - September 7th) 壬申

This is not the best time for you to consider thoughts of business expansion, as it will not work out in your favour. Spend your time concentrating on your core products or services instead and wait for a better time in the future to consider further development. High-risk investments should be avoided this month at all costs, because it could bring about some potentially severe legal problems. People who work in the engineering industries will be well-supported by their bosses and superiors, leading to some nice financial remunerations!

農曆八月 (September 8th - October 7th) 癸酉

That's the sound of Cupid's arrow hurtling through the air that you're hearing this month! Romance in all its flowery and sweet guises is likely to sweep you off your feet, so if you're single and ready to mingle – go out and do it! Health-wise, however, possible eye ailments or infections are likely so do take care of them. You'll need to be in top shape if you were to scope out your potential romantic partners. If your line of work falls under state security and defense, this month requires you to do your homework before you invest in any new technology. Knowing exactly what you're doing will help you increase your profits.

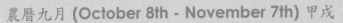

農曆九月 (October 8th - November 7th) 甲戌

If you work in the printing, courier, or logistics industries, you will need to travel out of the country to seek new markets for your products and services this month. However, look upon these travels with a bright eye. These travels are likely to help you rake in the profits. People using this room will suffer from mental stress and emotional instability, so be prepared for some topsy-turvy thoughts and feelings. However, it's a good month to reach out and forge a new alliance with another party or person; it will likely lead to a profitable future.

農曆十月 (November 8th - December 6th) 乙亥

Adolescents using this room will be hard to handle this month, being more rebellious and insolent than usual. Parents might find it hard to make them see reason. If you think it's worth the effort, it might be better moving them into another room and out of this sector. If you're into professional sports, be careful this month as leg and tendon injuries are very likely. Those of you in the engineering and paper industries will find it a good month in terms of increased business and profits.

農曆十一月 (December 7th 2019 - January 5th 2020) 丙子

Put your health as your first priority this month, because you're likely to be facing some health issues that could be further exacerbated if you're negligent. In particular, kidney and stomach issues could crop especially if there are negative forms or structures located outside this sector. People with real estate investments should consider selling off some of their property this month, as the value would have appreciated and the chance to make some profits is high.

農曆十二月 (January 6th - February 3rd 2020) 丁丑

Those in the logistics, courier and tourism businesses should benefit from increased profits this month. If your job involves strategic thinking or analysis you will find that you have the chance to advance your career and gain a name for yourself this month – so don't be hesitant in putting your best foot forward and making strategic attempts to improve your reputation.

| Main Door | **Southwest** | Bedroom Sector | **Northeast** |

農曆正月 (February 4th - March 5th) 丙寅

All of you professionals in the legal field will enjoy a boost in reputation this month! Your contribution to your field of work will earn you the respect and esteem of others, cementing your reputation as one of the top ones in your line of work. Health-wise, the presence of any negative landforms outside this sector could cause some serious health implications which can include diseases as severe as cancer. There are substantial financial gains to be made from all your business dealings, but make sure you know exactly what to do in order to actually see these profits.

農曆二月 (March 6th - April 4th) 丁卯

There is much money to be gained from property investments this month, so use all your knowledge in this field to make it work for you! Your personal life is not going as smoothly as you'd like, because those of you who are married will be facing some problems with your in-laws. Smooth over these problems as best as you can, as there is no point in fanning the flames with more anger. Where your physical health is concerned, be careful of any illnesses that could affect your spleen or internal organs. You're likely to be seeing the interior of a hospital more often than you'd like if you were to let your symptoms be.

農曆三月 (April 5th - May 5th) 戊辰

This sector will be well-suited for activities related to spiritual or religious knowledge and pursuits. Using it as a bedroom may cause some emotional turbulence or instability, and in some extreme cases, depression. Be on guard against this and sleep in another room for the time being if possible. At work, you'll find yourself putting your nose to the grindstone but the likelihood of seeing any rewards for that is slim.

農曆四月 (May 6th - June 5th) 己巳

If you're in the medical industry, or work as a medical professional, you're likely to do well this month. Pregnant ladies on the other hand are advised not to use this room, because the risk of complications and miscarriage is high. If you're in doubt, it would be best to seek the advice of your doctor at the first sign of trouble. The same applies to elderly ladies using this room – if something seems amiss, seek professional medical advice to avoid worsening complications. For those of you sitting for examinations, this sector should be avoided as well this month, as otherwise your results may not be good.

| Main Door | Southwest | Bedroom Sector | Northeast |

農曆五月 (June 6th - July 6th) 庚午

You'll be facing quite a bit of stress at the workplace and if you're not careful, this could lead to health problems – such as gastrointestinal issues and ulcers. If you can't avoid the stress, you will do well to learn how to manage it. There is no point in sacrificing your health for work! There is a strong likelihood that you'll be able to make money from investment in the property industries, but ensure that you take the time and effort to do your homework and analyse the deal from every angle. The worst thing you can do for yourself is to rush into something blindly just because the opportunity presents itself.

農曆六月 (July 7th - August 7th) 辛未

Those of you in marriages or committed relationships will find this a particularly difficult month, so you will both do well to be more tolerant and forgiving. There's no point in uttering the first hurtful word that comes to your mouth; you'll only do your relationship a disservice and bring about needless pain. Those of you who are writers – or wishing to be one – should stop dreaming about doing it and actually do it, as the energies are conducive for your literary pursuits. With that in mind, get those journals and notebooks out and start scribbling!

農曆七月 (August 8th - September 7th) 壬申

If you already gravitate towards spiritual and religious pursuits, the energies prevalent in this sector could precipitate the inclinations further this month. Where health is concerned, however, you might want to get a professional medical opinion if some particular situation is troubling you. Otherwise, it could become a persistent illness or symptom. It's a favourable month for those of you dealing in real estate and property and it'll be a good time for you to acquire new portfolios, even if these are small ones.

農曆八月 (September 8th - October 7th) 癸酉

This month, you'll do well to steer clear of signing important documents and contracts. This is because things are not what they seem, you'll have to ensure that you're paying attention to the fine print and understanding all that each and every word implies. If you're sitting for a major exam this month, avoid using this room if possible. In general, arguments could plague domestic harmony this month. This would cause family members to exchange heated words with each other. If you can't exactly prevent every argument, then keep your cool throughout each and every one to avoid saying anything you will regret later.

| Main Door | Southwest | Bedroom Sector | Northeast |

農曆九月 (October 8th - November 7th) 甲戌

Depression and stress-related mental anxiety will plague the people using this room this month. You need to manage your lifestyle carefully, or otherwise risk paying the heavy price of emotional disturbance. The plus point is that it will generally be a problem-free month for people using this room. If you're committed to finding peace of mind, you're likely to find it! Make an effort to streamline your life according to your desires, and you're likely to feel rested, peaceful, and well-adjusted.

農曆十月 (November 8th - December 6th) 乙亥

Deals and negotiations made under the table could cost you more money in the long run. besides exploding in your face. So, you should ensure that everything is on the straight and proper. Rivals in the workplace, or even some of your subordinates, are looking for ways to step over you and pull out the rug from under your authority. Be wary and just a little bit guarded or you'll risk being caught by surprise. There is money to be made from property deals, but the legal details must be all sorted out first.

農曆十一月 (December 7th 2019 - January 5th 2020) 丙子

If you're looking to conceive or start a family, then avoid using this room for the month as the energies will not be conducive. Watch out as well for potential fire hazards and risks, so take all proper precaution and don't be negligent in any way. Also, be more careful when you're around hot water as the chances of burns and scalding are high. On the whole, be careful of the tiny mishaps involving water, electricity, and fire.

農曆十二月 (January 6th - February 3rd 2020) 丁丑

Mental and emotional stress may cause depression and even hallucinations for those using this bedroom. It will be important for you to talk to people close to you or seek help if you find yourself becoming increasingly confused and disoriented. This also applies if you are unable to deal with regular, day-to-day problems that you had no problem with before. This sector is best suited for those in religious pursuits or for gaining spiritual knowledge.

Southwest Sector Main Door

| Main Door | Southwest | Bedroom Sector | North |

SE | S | SW

7 | 3 | 5

E | | W

6 | **8** | 1

2 | 4 | 9

NE | N | NW

農曆正月 (February 4th - March 5th) 丙寅

Singles who are looking for love will find this sector to be favourable this month, but this is only if there are no natural water formations located in this sector. In general, it's a good month to consider expanding your business or building alliances with international partners. At the same time, do consider revisiting business connections made in the past as these will bode well for you. People in the mining and engineering industries will find that their business would do well this month and profits come trickling in.

農曆二月 (March 6th - April 4th) 丁卯

This will not be the ideal month to engage in speculative or high-risk investments, so it's best to just lay low and keep your money safe. Otherwise, you'd end up with less than what you first started out with! However, it is a good month to focus on building relations with your colleagues, business affiliates, partner, and loved ones. Generally, all relationships will be infused with an air of contentment and intimacy; it will bode well in sustaining long-term ties. If there is work-related travel in the cards for you this month, grab the opportunity as it will bring about an enhanced stature and reputation.

農曆三月 (April 5th - May 5th) 戊辰

People in the forestry and dairy farming industries will find business demands increasing this month, which is good news for you because revenues and profits see a happy upward spike too! In general, it's a good month for you to make a property-related investment or enter into property deals. Elderly women using this room might have migraines, or in worst-case scenarios, a stroke. Pay attention to all and any signs that indicates something's amiss.

農曆四月 (May 6th - June 5th) 己巳

If you're a lawyer, legal advisor, or someone working in the legal field, your expertise is very much in demand this month! It's best that you gear up for a productive but busy time ahead. However, it's best that those of you using this room steer clear of conflicts, arguments, and quarrels this month. They might take a turn for violence and this is not something you want to be caught up in. Be particularly careful when working with sharp tools and implements this month, like knives and scissors.

農曆五月 (June 6th - July 6th) 庚午

For professional sportspeople and individuals involved in competitive sports, this is the month to make a name for yourself and cement your reputation as one of the best. However, bear in mind that it won't necessarily come with financial rewards! Romantic relationships will start to take on a whole new level of intensity and commitment this month. It will be a good time to make important decisions together or to have that talk you've both been putting off for awhile now.

農曆六月 (July 7th - August 7th) 辛未

For people using this room, it would be best to avoid business deals, ventures, and investments this month as the outcome will not be favourable. There will be more chances of losses than gains. Married couples will have to endure strained, tense relations this month. Instead of pushing the matter, simply give each other more space and things will return to normal. This is not a good month to play in the stock market, as only financial losses could result.

農曆七月 (August 8th - September 7th) 壬申

Females in the professional arena with female superiors and bosses will find this a month of recognition. You'll finally be duly recognised for your diligence and hard work. It's also a good month to satiate that wanderlust in you, so get your bags packing and get on that plane to that far-flung island you've been dreaming about! For those of you in management and consulting, there are good financial benefits to be gained and profits to be enjoyed. You will see a substantial increase in your wealth standing.

農曆八月 (September 8th - October 7th) 癸酉

If you're travelling this month, you should be prepared for last minute changes and problems that could hamper an otherwise smooth trip. It might also require you buying some health insurance. Those in the fashion and cosmetic industries will find this a good month in terms of increased exposure and revenue. Where your professional life is concerned, things seem to be on an upswing; recognition is coming your way and a promotion and advancement are to be expected. But, you have to remember that these come with its own set of responsibilities and issues.

農曆九月 (October 8th - November 7th) 甲戌

You might run into some problems with female subordinates at work, so be particularly cautious this month. Ensure that all your communication is clear and direct. You'll have good opportunities to make a profit from property dealings abroad; this will work out even better if you're required to travel to sign the documents! If you're interested in meditation and reading, this room will be conducive for those activities.

農曆十月 (November 8th - December 6th) 乙亥

Students and scholars set to write important examinations should probably spend more time in this room or use it for their studies and revision. People who are involved in research and development should probably also grab the opportunities presented this month and go forward and publish their thesis or papers. Newly-weds and those of you starting on the first rosy steps of new relationships will find this month rewarding in all things romance! Minor conflicts are easily smoothed over and a general sense of harmony and contentment pervades.

農曆十一月 (December 7th 2019 - January 5th 2020) 丙子

Business deals that take place this month will be golden. So, any opportunities that come up this month should be grasped without hesitation! Females who work in the entertainment industry will benefit tremendously this month as you'll be subject to accolades and acclaim. You will be deservingly rewarded for months of hard work and effort. Couples who have long pondered the issue of matrimony can officially set the date for wedding bells to ring.

農曆十二月 (January 6th - February 3rd 2020) 丁丑

This is a good month to enter into property deals, so you need to be ready to make the right move when the opportunity strikes. Strokes and migraines may be a problem for older women who use this bedroom; it will be wise to pay close attention to any of the warning signs. As early as possible, if something seems amiss, it will become necessary to seek professional medical advice. Don't put it off or ignore the symptoms.

Southwest Sector Main Door

農曆正月 (February 4th - March 5th) 丙寅

Those of you involved in the fields of counseling and psychology will see an increase or surge in people's recognition and need for your skills. More than ever before, people will be flocking to you for your expertise and you'll be more than able to help. Students and scholars sitting for examinations will be happy to see some good results coming in this month.

農曆二月 (March 6th - April 4th) 丁卯

This month you should be a little more patient and diplomatic when dealing with unpleasant or plain weird situations. Becoming rash and hasty as a result of your temper or impatience will only serve to set you back further. So, exercise a little willpower and you'll be all the better for it. Romance luck in general improves for people using this room. Use this time to grow a current relationship of yours or start a new one that bears promise.

農曆三月 (April 5th - May 5th) 戊辰

If you're working in the academic, mining, or engineering fields, this is a particularly favourable time for you. Make great opportunities of what comes your way and be especially crafty with using your vast network of contacts. People can be your ticket towards gaining more revenue and opening up new vistas. As your professional and personal relationships start to improve, you can make more of an effort to cultivate your ties with the various people in your lives to keep the important ones permanent.

農曆四月 (May 6th - June 5th) 己巳

Things are good if you are interested to pursuit matters of the spiritual or religious nature. If you've been doing a little meditation and mind-development exercises of late, this is the beneficial sector to use. If you work in the cosmetic and fashion industries, you need to remember that one day you're in, and the next day you're out... so make the most of your opportunities this month to promote and market yourself aggressively! There is gold to be struck but only if you're willing to put in the effort and the legwork.

農曆五月 (June 6th - July 6th) 庚午

Cupid will smile upon couples using this bedroom for the month. If you've long been in a relationship that's heading towards matrimony, don't be too afraid to propose to your loved one if you feel like it's time! If you're married and have always wanted to start a family, this is also a good month to try. Professionally, people dabbling in the real estate and property industries will be able to make quite a few profits from their worthy investments made earlier.

農曆六月 (July 7th - August 7th) 辛未

If you own a business, conduct regular audits to ensure that nothing amiss is taking place as fraud will prove to be quite a costly burden to bear this month! There is never such a thing as being too safe when it comes to these matter, rather than being regrettably sorry. Make the most of your connections this month, because you'll have a chance to take some of your contacts and make them work for you – in terms of gaining profits. It's a good time to begin some mass exposure for your business or your work by engaging the mass media, so go all out on a well-planned and well-thought out publicity blitz.

農曆七月 (August 8th - September 7th) 壬申

Be disciplined and be cautious, especially if you're involved in metal, futures, equities, or stock trading. For those of you working for others, this is the month to toe the line and smile sweetly. Challenging or questioning authority can lead to embarrassment for you. Also, a possible defeat is likely. Don't think too much about them and concentrate instead on your work. Parents who find their kids disobedient or rebellious should consider moving them into another room. Otherwise, you can expect plenty of conflicts and high-pressure negotiations!

農曆八月 (September 8th - October 7th) 癸酉

This will be a month to give your mind a break, so avoid having to make big decisions. You're under quite a bit of pressure from your work and you're not in top form where mental reasoning is required. You'll be somewhat short-tempered too as a result, so it's best to keep to yourself. This is at least until the month ends. Otherwise, you'll find yourself embroiled in a nasty fight that does nothing to assuage your stress! Watch out for possible illnesses like heart or eye disease. Get a thorough check-up if it's overdue.

農曆九月 (October 8th - November 7th) 甲戌

This will not be the ideal room to use this month if you're a student or scholar sitting for an important examination. It might be better for you to do your revision and studies in another sector. If you're female, you will be facing some trouble at the workplace as you'll find it hard to be suitably supported by your superiors in all that you do. Be careful that you don't step on any toes. If you need something clarified in black and white, then that is what you should ask for. The rest of you, especially those who own your own business or company, will find it a good month to increase your reputation as long as you keep an eye on potentially-disloyal employees. They could besmirch your good name through acts of fraud.

農曆十月 (November 8th - December 6th) 乙亥

A pat on the back for you for your diligent perseverance thus far! This is the month when you can sit back and say, "I did it!" The rewards and recognition come fast and furious. With it, there is a chance for a career advancement in store for you. Forget about being humble and modest for once, because this time you deserve it... so enjoy it! Those of you who are sitting for exams this month will enjoy the energies present it this sector, because it will be conduit for you to do well.

農曆十一月 (December 7th 2019 - January 5th 2020) 丙子

Good luck with possible romantic partners follows you around this month if you use this room. If you've long been single and antsy to get into the dating scene, this is a good time to begin! Those of you working in the engineering and travel industries should take this month as a chance to make the most of every opportunity that comes your way. The ability to gain some wealth increases, so make the most of it and be on a lookout for all the opportunities that are up for grabs.

農曆十二月 (January 6th - February 3rd 2020) 丁丑

It's a very good month for both your professional and personal relationships, so now's the time to foster even closer ties with your those important to you in one way or another. Cultivate more business partnerships and get to know more people in general as it will greatly benefit you. It's also a good month to tap into the energies of this bedroom for education, learning, and scholarly activities – students in particular are likely to benefit.

| Main Door | Southwest | Bedroom Sector | West |

農曆正月 (February 4th - March 5th) 丙寅

Your health continues to be somewhat weak this month, so make an effort to put your physical health first and foremost. Ulcers could cause some problems if you're not careful. This is not a month to stick your nose into other people's problems and affairs, as you could get dragged into some sticky messes. Adding insult to your injury, this will also result in having to bear the brunt of other people's resentments as your reward. Relationships will be distracting you from more important matters at hand, so keep your concentration focused on what is of higher priority.

農曆二月 (March 6th - April 4th) 丁卯

Your personal reputation takes centre stage this month, and not in a way you might have imagined! In fact, it could be that your name and character are called into question. Appropriately, don't provide fuel to the fire in any way by making missteps. Pay close attention to your words and actions, particularly by being careful not to do or say anything in a fit of anger or carelessness. If you're a professional sportsperson, you will do well this month. However, it will be best to be wary of competitors.

農曆三月 (April 5th - May 5th) 戊辰

Those of you in the property and real estate industries will find this a particularly tough and challenging month. This is mainly due to the fact that you have trouble organising your thoughts and achieving some form of clarity in your analytical processes. This might cause you unnecessary problems when it comes to making decisions, so it might be better off for you in the long run to delay those decisions to a better time in the future if possible.

農曆四月 (May 6th - June 5th) 己巳

Where health is concerned, kidney problems might plague the people using this room this month. As such, watch out for signs of those and seek medical opinion early if necessary. Children or students who need to sit for important examinations should be careful about using this room for revision and study, as any negative structures or landforms outside this sector could cause some problems. If you have any offshore deals in the making, best wait for a more favourable time in the future before finalising them.

| Main Door | Southwest | Bedroom Sector | West |

農曆五月 (June 6th - July 6th) 庚午

This room could cause fights and arguments that would result in couples to be at odds with each other if they were to use this room. This is a month to be especially careful with the things you say. Weigh each word carefully before uttering them. Legal problems might happen this month and possible betrayals are likely. People might turn against you, poisoning the reputation of your business. This is will no doubt bring about its fair share of stress and anxiety, and the rumours are likely to affect your business relationships – but keep your head low and endure it, as it will blow over very soon.

農曆六月 (July 7th - August 7th) 辛未

Elderly males using this room will do well to get their health problems checked out early this month. In the real estate business, there are plenty of good deals to be made and struck. However, you will need to exercise your analytical powers to choose the right ones and make a home run! It will be worth your time to be completely thorough in checking out credentials. In fact, it is particularly important that you sift through all the information you come across this month, because people are out to pull the wool over your eyes.

農曆七月 (August 8th - September 7th) 壬申

Temptation does its devilish dance in front of most people using this room this month and it's a particularly testing time for newly-recovering alcoholics. The best way to cope? Put yourself out of the equation and avoid all forms of temptation. In general, romance fares quite poorly for this month. Possible affairs are likely, or the temptation is there for one, causing strain to fall on the relationship. Be careful with how you proceed, as the consequences are serious and break-ups and separation are likely.

農曆八月 (September 8th - October 7th) 癸酉

Relationships that begin this month or were begun in the recent past are not likely to have long-term potential. It would be wiser for you not to invest your all into it. It will be a better long-term investment, instead, for you to focus on your career and work on building up your professional life. Medical problems that start off as minor and unimportant could become more serious in the future, so get medical treatment even if it seems like a trifling issue at this point. If you work in the entertainment industry, exercise extreme care and deliberation when signing contracts; don't put pen to paper if even the smallest thing seems amiss.

農曆九月 (October 8th - November 7th) 甲戌

If you're married, pay more attention to your spouse if you feel you've been spending too much time on your career. If you're the neglected one, then make your feelings known instead of letting it fester inside. Those of you in real estate, or with property deals and investments, will find that profits find their merry way to you this month – but you'll need to be quick enough to make the most of opportunities as they crop up. Health problems involving the lungs might crop up this month, so take extra care.

農曆十月 (November 8th - December 6th) 乙亥

A month of jealous tensions could cause some marital discord or relationship trouble for people using this room. Don't let pent-up resentment dictate the flow of your actions or words, as some of that will be hard to undo in the future. If you're signing documents this month, don't! It might be better to put it off to a better time, as legal issues might cause some problems this month. On the home front, you will need to check all electrical wiring and be careful of any fire-related hazards.

農曆十一月 (December 7th 2019 - January 5th 2020) 丙子

Joint ventures or partnerships are very fruitful this month, so it will do you well to take advantage of the opportunities that appear! Don't delay in taking action when it is needed; this month requires courage and swiftness on your part, before any form of rewards or benefits could come your way. If you're involved in competitive sports, this could be a stellar month for you. However, you need to be aware that there are plenty of people around wishing to bring you down. Be vigilant.

農曆十二月 (January 6th - February 3rd 2020) 丁丑

Elderly males using this bedroom should be careful of potential head injuries or head-related symptoms and illnesses. This is an especially difficult month for those in the property business, because you will find it hard to zero in on the root of the problem and achieve some mental clarity. You will find it difficult to make decisions. Where possible, defer your decisions to another time when you're feeling mentally stronger.

South Sector
Main Door

This section contains the monthly outlook for all 12 months of the year, for different bedroom sectors, in a property with a South Main Door.

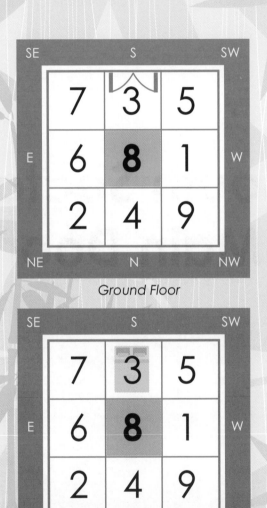

Ground Floor

First Floor

農曆正月 (February 4th - March 5th) 丙寅

Elderly males who use this room or sector will be susceptible to certain health problems and conditions, so it will be best to seek medical treatment immediately instead of pushing it forward to another time. Couples who use this room will need to pay extra attention to your other half this month, or you'll be in for a rough time. Jealous tantrums could rear its ugly head if your partner suspects you of having a wandering eye or behaving dishonestly. If possible, avoid going on any business trips this month!

農曆二月 (March 6th - April 4th) 丁卯

You are prone to injuries this month, particularly those brought on by driving accidents. Drive safely, don't speed; also practice safety habits like wearing your safety belt. Your health isn't looking too rosy this month either. You'll have to battle ulcers, gallstones, and possible liver diseases. This is also a bad month to indulge in your gambling instincts, as any risks you take with your finances will only end in severe losses. All speculative, high-risk investments should also be avoided – as it might result in lawsuits in addition to losses.

農曆三月 (April 5th - May 5th) 戊辰

Monitor your employees closely this month, because they may be involved in illegal dealings such as theft and fraud. Ensure that stringent auditing procedures are in place. Business deals that are negotiated abroad, or done with partners overseas, should be concluded this month. However, before you put pen to paper and sign any legal documents, be sure to read the fine print carefully. If you've recently undergone any medical procedures, it would be best to avoid using this room.

農曆四月 (May 6th - June 5th) 己巳

At the workplace, you will need to keep an eye out on your competitors, because they will be going all out to keep you down. If you let them get away with it, they could keep a possible promotion out of your path. Be cautious around heavy machinery and dangerous tools this month. Untoward accidents could happen due to your carelessness or negligence. In general, you're also at risk for car accidents and travel-related mishaps.

Main Door	South	Bedroom Sector	South

農曆五月 (June 6th - July 6th) 庚午

Curb any impulse to gamble this month because you are likely to suffer from heavy losses. What's more, you will be incapable of making good judgement calls and will be somewhat reckless this month. Even speculative investments are a no-no at this point, as financial losses are not the worst that can happen – legal troubles are! Employees and subordinates are likely to be defiant and rebellious at this point, and a confrontation might take you aback, so be ready to act to prevent things from getting out of hand.

農曆六月 (July 7th - August 7th) 辛未

People in the media and marketing industries will enjoy the fruits of this month, as it brings great achievements and high honour. Maximise the good fortune that comes your way without worrying too much about the future. However, if you're one of those who suffer from depression and mood-related issues, it might be better to vacate this room for the month. Bear in mind that covert, underhanded schemes by your competitors will only lead to financial loss, and possible legal problems through fraud or embezzlement.

農曆七月 (August 8th - September 7th) 壬申

Those of you who work in analytical or scientific fields will enjoy the positive energies of this sector, and may find this affecting your work in good ways. You'll have clear breakthroughs in projects or tasks that you were working on. Those of you in politics should go all out on a campaign this month, as your personal charisma will be irresistible, bringing you much success! If you're in the communications or construction industries, you will be able to make good headway into your competitors' markets this month.

農曆八月 (September 8th - October 7th) 癸酉

This will not be the ideal month for you to ponder upon your relationship, or spend endless hours musing about 'where it's going' and 'what it all means.' You do not have luxury of time to get lost in your head. At this point in time, you will need to be more action-oriented. It's a good time to conclude any of your property deals, but be specific on the details – or otherwise, messy legal issues will rear their ugly head! If you fall ill this month, don't ignore the signs – what may seem trivial could lead to something a lot more serious if you don't nip it in the bud.

農曆九月 (October 8th - November 7th) 甲戌

Rumours and gossip will be swirling around you this month, causing conflicts. It might be best for you to switch to another room if this is affecting your peace of mind. Those of you working in the publishing or printing industries will find this a good month in terms of financial profits, especially when it comes from sales abroad. If you're involved in any arbitration work, you are likely to see good results as your skills are very much needed.

農曆十月 (November 8th - December 6th) 乙亥

It would be advantageous for bright young kids to use this room for exam preparation and studies. They would likely pass their examination with stellar results because the room is conducive for mental alertness and stimulation. Watch the words that come out of your mouth this month, because any words said in haste or tactlessness could come back to bite you – bringing along some legal problems with it! Beware of competitors stinging you when you least expect it; to recover you need to be quick on your feet and agile in the mind, and be ready to flexibly import new changes if the need arises.

農曆十一月 (December 7th 2019 - January 5th 2020) 丙子

Be prepared to put in some long hours in the office this month if you want to keep your business flourishing and see the profits continue to tumble in! Put in some extra labour now and you'll taste the sweet results of it for long after. Use expert knowledge, whether gleaned from your own research or through word of mouth, to accumulate profits from the real estate and property markets. Intense arguments could put your personal relationships under too much strain; make a concerted effort to keep things civil and diplomatic if you want to preserve your relationships and come out with minimal damage.

農曆十二月 (January 6th - February 3rd 2020) 丁丑

Seek sound financial advice from the experts this month – you will gain useful tips which you can use to make your business more profitable. Accumulating wealth takes careful planning - so if money is on your mind, you know what to do! This is also a good sector to use in terms of academic endeavours and studies. Business people, however, should be wary of fraud or embezzlement – scrutinize all business transactions and legal documents meticulously to check for anything odd that arouses your suspicions.

South Sector Main Door

SE	S	SW
7	3	5
E 6	**8**	1 W
2	4	9
NE	N	NW

農曆正月 (February 4th - March 5th) 丙寅

It's a good month for female entrepreneurs to venture into markets abroad, because there will be substantial profits to be gained from deals and agreements concluded in another country. But in general, people using this room should refrain from beginning new commercial ventures this month. You're likely to face some serious obstacles from the start, which will delay your progress and waste your time. It will be best for you to wait for another time. Romance will be rocky this month; you could find that the romantic liaisons of yours will turn out to be short-term flings, which may cause some heartbreak.

農曆二月 (March 6th - April 4th) 丁卯

For those of you who've been bitten by the travel bug, this is a good month to satisfy your wanderlust. Get your bags packed, book your flight, and get ready to expand your horizons! It's also a good month for prospective business people, because if you've long wanted to begin an enterprise or start a business, this will be the right time to pursue your dreams. However, beware of potential unstable emotions that may plague you, and lead to a tarnished public image. Keep a tight lid on those explosive emotions, as otherwise it will get the better of you and ruin your reputation to some extent.

農曆三月 (April 5th - May 5th) 戊辰

Doctors and medical practitioners using this sector will find a demand for their skills increasing, as more people become aware of your expertise and want your services over that of others! Where romance is concerned, this might be a good month for you attempt a new relationship. This might be best among your own circle of friends and acquaintances, as you'll be able to skip that awkward 'getting-to-know-you' phase. Make sure your electrical equipment and wiring are in good condition to prevent any potential fires caused by faulty wiring or short circuits.

農曆四月 (May 6th - June 5th) 己巳

If you own or run a business, proceed with caution when you launch or undertake any new ventures and projects this month. You'll also need to be a little more eagle-eyed with your employees than normal, as some disgruntled ones are capable of committing fraud or embezzling your company. Avoid walking in dark alleys and be aware of your surroundings at all times as a safety precaution against robberies and thefts. Males using this room need to be careful of flirtatious, sweet-talking females… especially if your will is weak. Otherwise, you're likely to get yourself entangled in a sticky situation.

| Main Door | South | Bedroom Sector | Southeast |

農曆五月 (June 6th - July 6th) 庚午

This will be an auspicious month for females to conduct business deals abroad and travel for investments overseas. For most of you, good publicity will come your way this month, putting you in the limelight and catapulting your career forward in a good way. In general, people using this sector will do well to avoid disreputable nightclubs and entertainment outlets – because visiting these places will bring about more problems than fun!

農曆六月 (July 7th - August 7th) 辛未

Those working in the cell-phone and communication industries could be beleaguered with problems this month, so you'll need to be prepared and adaptable to changes, in order to fix what could potentially go wrong. This month, in general, people need to be careful about what they say to others. Your casual or flippant remarks may go down the wrong way, which could result in problems. In personal relationships, too, watch out for potential jealousy issues that could cast a shadow over your happiness. Avoid responding with jokes or humour – this is a situation that requires maturity and tact.

農曆七月 (August 8th - September 7th) 壬申

It will be prudent for pregnant ladies to use another room this month, to avoid any possible complications with your pregnancy. The will be some friction among ladies living together in close proximity this month. Avoid all domestic problems by being neutral, and avoid fanning the flames with thoughtless remarks and insinuations. If you work in the travel and communication industries, it is likely to be a favourable month for you if you need attention and publicity to further your work.

農曆八月 (September 8th - October 7th) 癸酉

If you're single, available, and looking to start a relationship, then this will be a good month to scope for potential prospects among your friends! Short-term investments also bode well for you at this point, but you need to keep an eye out on the possibility of robbery or theft that will make any wealth you have a short-lived experience. Business people will enjoy a significant boost to your reputation, particularly among your social network and business partners. Maintain your high standards of service.

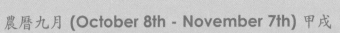

農曆九月 (October 8th - November 7th) 甲戌

Fire hazards are very likely this month, so check the electrical circuits and wiring in your home, as well as all your gas outlets. Don't be negligent or careless with your safety. Those who are preparing to sit for important examinations should avoid using this room. Expectant mothers should also refrain from using this bedroom to avoid possible complications.

農曆十月 (November 8th - December 6th) 乙亥

For mothers and daughters using this sector for the month, there will be some tension and stress to battle through – resulting in frayed relations. It would be best for both parties concerned to steer clear of each other and give each other some space until things start to improve soon. Negative publicity, and misunderstandings that arise out of that, will cost you your job if you're not careful. Play your cards well and be very careful. Nevertheless, it is a good month for those of you in the travel industry; you can even consider expanding your business as you will see good returns.

農曆十一月 (December 7th 2019 - January 5th 2020) 丙子

Put priority on your personal safety this month; watch where you go and what you do. Do not take unnecessary risks and implement all necessary precautions to avoid any untoward incidents. People working in the fashion and beauty industries will see their profits increase this month, which will generally lead to lighter spirits and moods among the employees. For those of you in the courier, logistics, and transportation industries, be on guard against deals that appear too good to be true – remember that all that glitters isn't really gold!

農曆十二月 (January 6th - February 3rd 2020) 丁丑

Those of you in real estate or property development, or have invested in those industries, will stand to gain a good amount of financial profits this month. Generally, this is an ideal time for you to bring down all your competitors in the same field. You can look forward to significantly expanding your customer base. Students and scholars who use this room to prepare for examinations will find the results positive.

| Main Door | South | Bedroom Sector | East |

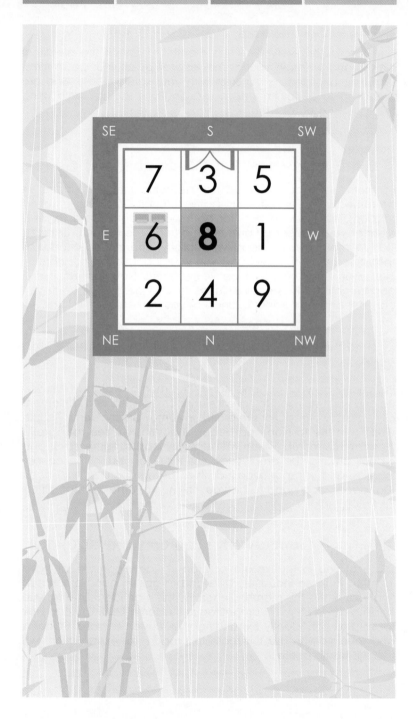

SE	S	SW
7	3	5
6	**8**	1
2	4	9
NE	N	NW

農曆正月 (February 4th - March 5th) 丙寅

Fathers and sons using this room will find themselves at loggerheads, and this tension will be further exacerbated if there are negative structures and forms outside this sector. For the elderly members of the household using this room, do not neglect to address any signs of minor ailments. Delaying medical treatment could result in further complications down the road. Professionals in the engineering industry will glean unexpected recognition, and possible financial rewards, if they use this particular room.

農曆二月 (March 6th - April 4th) 丁卯

In general, for most people using this bedroom, there is plenty to smile about as there is quite a bit of good news awaiting. If you have been working diligently at your projects and activities, you will find your efforts paying off handsomely this month. It's also an ideal time of the year to take up some property or gilt investments, but it requires you to occasionally enter unchartered territories and take some risks. There are several ill-intentioned souls out to put a dent in your plans, so be on the alert for that.

農曆三月 (April 5th - May 5th) 戊辰

For those of you in jobs or career positions that require strategic thinking and detailed analysis, this will be a good month for you to advance your career and push forward. You'll be able to gain a name for yourself within your current company, or the industry that you're in. In general, most people should seek the advice of life coaches and mentors, as they can share with you their insights and useful nuggets of wisdom. Rocky, struggling business relationships and partnerships will enjoy the benefits of the good energies of this room, as potential break-ups can be averted and harmony restored.

農曆四月 (May 6th - June 5th) 己巳

Those of you in the entertainment and electrical industries should take caution, as you could suffer from serious financial losses due to a few bad business decisions. You might have to make more of an effort than usual in order to keep things going at an even keel. People holding positions of power and authority should be aware that there may be rumblings of dissent below you, creating various forms of challenges. At the home, this can be seen through disputes between sons and fathers, or sons defiantly challenging their father figures. Employers should be careful with labour relations and arbitration, because employees are likely to be rebellious and difficult to manage.

| Main Door | South | Bedroom Sector | East |

農曆五月 (June 6th - July 6th) 庚午

Good financial gains can be made by taking some risks and really making an effort to put yourself out on a limb; but focus on property or gilt investments because these are likely to give you high profits. It will be a profitable time for investment and merchant bankers engaging in stock and corporate deals. Elderly people using this bedroom for the month should try to use a different room, as there is a possibility of the risk of heart ailments.

農曆六月 (July 7th - August 7th) 辛未

At the workplace, you should be prepared for competition starting to heat up. Because of the intense rivalry among colleagues, jealousy and backstabbing could come into the mix, causing a toxic environment at work if the situation escalates into hostility. There could even be legal issues as one of the ramifications. The best thing to do at this point would be to keep your head down and concentrate solely on your work. Those of you who are sticking your toes into the waters of love this month will find these new relationships to be fleeting, short-term affairs. Avoid investing too much of your time or emotions into it.

農曆七月 (August 8th - September 7th) 壬申

People in the engineering industry will find this quite a good month to realise their career aspirations and fulfill their dreams. It will bode well for you at this point in time, especially if you have worked hard to gain these financial rewards and acquire some recognition. Fathers or sons using this room are likely to experience tense and strained relations. To ease the situation and make the relationship smoother, both should preferably be using rooms in other sectors. Negative formations located outside this sector could result in headaches or leg injuries for the occupants.

農曆八月 (September 8th - October 7th) 癸酉

In general, the situation at work will be less than ideal. Employees and subordinates are feeling disgruntled and defiant, and they are liable to betray their employers and their companies. At the very least, they may fall into behaviour and actions that could cost their company a significant amount of money. Be wary of hostile takeovers this month – it would be wise to take pre-emptive actions and be prepared to remedy the situation, rather than allow yourself to be taken by surprise by the consequences. People using this room might also suffer from headaches and migraines, largely brought upon by stress.

農曆九月 (October 8th - November 7th) 甲戌

People in academia and those in the civil service will receive due recognition for their work and research, and will also enjoy a heightened status within their industry. Besides that, this is a generally good month to invest your money, as you are likely to see good returns. However, be prudent so that you don't put your money into bad deals which will result in a loss. Spend a considerable amount of time improving both your personal and professional relationships, as these will bear fruit in the later months. This is a good month to focus on intensifying your connections.

農曆十月 (November 8th - December 6th) 乙亥

Avoid all forms of speculative investments this month, as the profits are likely to be anything but good. However, if you're in the engineering industry, this will be an ideal time to expand and seek new clients and business. Avoid unnecessary travel this month, as there are possible travel-related injuries, especially to the limbs. If you're involved in competitive sports, you will need to be careful of potential sprains and tendon injuries that could end up being more serious. This is especially true if there are negative formations outside this sector.

農曆十一月 (December 7th 2019 - January 5th 2020) 丙子

Those who are dabbling in property and real-estate related investments will enjoy a good windfall this month. This will be especially true if you've long been negotiating some serious discussions to conclude it. People using this room will tend to be overcome by some mental pressures, resulting in emotional volatility. If you already suffer from depression, you might want to consider using another room to avoid exacerbating the situation. If you're involved in the metaphysics field, or have strong interest in it, this is a good month to take advantage of the good energies of this sector.

農曆十二月 (January 6th - February 3rd 2020) 丁丑

Those of you in a rocky relationship or business partnership on the verge of breakup will be able to salvage your relationship, if you are using this bedroom. Coaches and mentors are present, so take their advice and act on these suggestions to achieve success. If your job involves strategic thinking or analysis, you will find that you have the chance to advance your career and gain a name for yourself within the company or the industry you're in.

| Main Door | South | Bedroom Sector | Northeast |

	SE	S	SW
	7	3	5
E	6	**8**	1	W
	2	4	9
	NE	N	NW

農曆正月 (February 4th - March 5th) 丙寅

Unfortunately, a month of unforeseen and unexpected problems is in store for you. You will need to be quick on the uptake to be able to respond in a timely manner to these problems. To avoid yourself from being caught unaware like a deer in headlights, you should prepare yourself with a Plan B, and a Plan C too... for good measure! Your relationships will be plagued by misunderstandings, largely caused by tumultuous thoughts and emotions. It will be better for you to lay low and avoid pressing the issue or engaging too closely with others. What you and everyone else needs right now are more breathing space and time to let things simmer down.

農曆二月 (March 6th - April 4th) 丁卯

Health problems and troubles are likely to crop up this month, resulting in colonic or gastrointestinal illnesses. Seek medical treatment as soon as something is amiss, as neglecting the symptoms will only make you feel worse in the long run. Writers and poets, or those with talents in the literary field, will find due recognition and rewards this month. Married women who are using this room and living in the same home as your in-laws will find that relations are testy and strained this month – so keep a low profile and try not to engage too closely with them.

農曆三月 (April 5th - May 5th) 戊辰

If you're involved in spiritual pursuits, or interested in developing your spiritual or religious knowledge, this would be the ideal room to use. The energies present here are very conducive for those types of activities. Good financial gains could arise out of smart real estate ventures. However, bear in mind that this could bring with it its fair share of stress and tension, so try not to sacrifice your own peace of mind simply to gain more money. For those who are earning a monthly wage, you will find yourselves having to work much harder this month, yet your income or benefits do not seem commensurate with your efforts.

農曆四月 (May 6th - June 5th) 己巳

Sudden business opportunities and deals that come up this month should be carefully considered and dealt with. You may want to enlist the help of experienced, skillful lawyers to help you weed out any irregularities before you get entangled in something messy. Haphazard thoughts and emotions could send relationships spiraling out of control this month, so most of you will do well to maintain a low profile and give each other more breathing space. It's not a good time to force any issue. This month, legal professionals -particularly judges and lawyers - will receive recognition and appreciation for your efforts.

| Main Door | South | Bedroom Sector | Northeast |

農曆五月 (June 6th - July 6th) 庚午

If you are working in public relations, media and communications or journalism, you will have an abundant of opportunities to accumulate your wealth this month! Make the most of it, as you will have worked hard for these rewards. People involved in real estate will have ample opportunities to dabble in property-related speculative investments at this point in time. Most of you using this sector will find it a good time to immerse yourself in self-improvement and self-cultivation, so grab any chances that arise that enables you to take a course or program to improve your knowledge or skills.

農曆六月 (July 7th - August 7th) 辛未

Relationships come under fire this month for people using this room or sector, and constant arguments and quarrels are very likely. Try your very best not to contribute to the tension. Instead, aim to alleviate the situation by approaching it calmly, and without reacting to everything in an emotional manner. If you work with other people, avoid taking sides or getting drawn into workplace politics and gossip. Otherwise, these could erupt into large-scale problems that no one will be interested to clean up in the end.

農曆七月 (August 8th - September 7th) 壬申

The situation at work is a little tense for you this month, because there are plenty of jealous subordinates and co-workers who will be ever-ready to undermine your efforts and hard work. Do not engage with them but concentrate on your work instead, and you will remain unaffected! Avoid getting into any deals that promise short-cuts, or even underhanded methods of obtaining swift results. In the long run, it could turn out very sour and cost you quite a bit of fortune. However, your personal relationships are likely to do quite well this month.

農曆八月 (September 8th - October 7th) 癸酉

Married couples should watch out for discords in marriage, resulting in arguments and general family disharmony. Make an effort not to let your emotions get the best of you. Endeavour to deal with the arguments and quarrels with a sense of proportion, and be patient and tolerant because it will go a long way! For those who are property developers or involved in real estate, there are opportunities to make good, sound investments in property. However, you need to first ensure that you read the fine print carefully, or hire a skillful lawyer to vet the documents before you sign, to catch any irregularities.

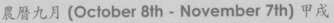

農曆九月 (October 8th - November 7th) 甲戌

Love is likely to bloom for singles who are available and on the lookout! You will find this a good month to meet a person who will capture your interest and send your pulse racing, so don't waste the opportunities that present themselves! Those of you involved in business ventures that require plenty of logic and deduction applied in order to produce your income may run into difficulties. To improve your business opportunities, most of you should consider focusing on networking, as meeting new people could be the ticket to more profits.

農曆十月 (November 8th - December 6th) 乙亥

It will be a good month for property investments, whether it may be in existing property or those in the development stages. You are likely to see some good financial benefits from these deals. Those of you who are interested in making a big career move or looking to gain a promotion – this will be the month to fulfill your dreams. Moving up to the upper echelons of society is also possible, for those who desire such an ascent. This will be the ideal month to make significant changes to your home, or to put your house on the market if you've been waiting for the right time to do that.

農曆十一月 (December 7th 2019 - January 5th 2020) 丙子

Those among you who are doctors will find business prospects increasing this month. This is not so much that people are falling ill at a more alarming rate, but more because they flock to you for your superior skills and expertise! There is a very strong chance for most of you to make a decent amount of money from side investments this month. These investments are likely to bring you increased profits.

農曆十二月 (January 6th - February 3rd 2020) 丁丑

Employees will find that they seem to work harder this month but your income does not seem to be proportionate to your efforts. If you feel that you are plugging away at the same old opportunity without any signs of interest or profit forthcoming, it might be time to give it a rest and focus your energies elsewhere. Those involved in spiritual pursuits or in gaining spiritual knowledge should use this bedroom this month.

Main Door	South	Bedroom Sector	North

農曆正月 (February 4th - March 5th) 丙寅

Be extremely careful when handling any sharp instruments this month, as chances are very high that you might incur an injury from a knife or metal tool. Apply the same caution even when signing legal documents and important papers this month – double-check every thing on the page thoroughly, and pay attention to the fine print. You will also be prone to having serious arguments and conflicts that could turn ugly, so try to be less argumentative and reactive, and more invested in maintaining your peace of mind. Keep a tight lid over your more explosive emotions and you will do a world of good in making yourself feel better.

農曆二月 (March 6th - April 4th) 丁卯

Pregnant ladies will have to be extra careful this month, especially if you are embarking on long distance travel which could result in accidents, or even pregnancy complications. Those of you who have to regularly deal with difficult clients or customers, or even business partners, will find it a good month to exercise diplomacy and patience. There are many rewards to be reaped from equities or share deals. If you're required to travel for work or business, consider it a lucky break – you'll be able to enhance your reputation and status.

農曆三月 (April 5th - May 5th) 戊辰

Entrepreneurs and businesspeople will find their employees putting in the extra legwork required to produce good results. This will be a result of their loyalty to you and the company, so if you value their work be sure to register your gratitude. If you're in the real estate business, you will need to exercise some ingenuity and creativity, because you will need to adapt your methods to different needs before you're able to make the most of your investments and capitalise on it. Tensions and friction between married couples could escalate this month. Be patient and kind towards each other to maintain harmony.

農曆四月 (May 6th - June 5th) 己巳

If you've been bitten by the travelling bug, then this is the month to let it take full control! It is the ideal time for you to take a vacation or consider travelling to distant shores. In addition to boosting your spirits, you just might encounter some romance while you're travelling! However, keep your expectations in proportion and don't assume it will lead to anything long-lasting. There will be no lack of ideas and inspiration for those of you working in the artistic and creative fields. Inspiration is bound to come to you wherever you go, so make the most of this time to generate original new work.

| Main Door | South | Bedroom Sector | North |

農曆五月 (June 6th - July 6th) 庚午

Married couples are likely to hit another rocky patch this month. It is important to rein in your temper and learn to accept each other's shortcomings. This is not the time to give your partner the cold shoulder or to be overly condescending in your remarks! Domestic disagreements could cause some serious disruptions in your home, and it will affect you in particular if you're female. Cultivate your inner sense of calm so you're less likely to be blown about by every wind, and hence react emotionally. If you have children, especially those who are of the school-going age – keep a closer eye on them. Don't neglect paying attention to their needs, or they may be adversely influenced by peer pressure and trouble.

農曆六月 (July 7th - August 7th) 辛未

Those among you who own a business should ensure that all your deals are on the straight and narrow. If not, the chances of you encountering losses as result of legally dodgy deals are very high, and it's too steep a price for you to pay simply to cut a few corners. To make successful speculative investments in the property field, you'll need to have some valuable knowledge on the subject. In other words, doing your homework will pay off handsomely. On the romantic front, both partners will need to give each the requisite amount of space and an innate sense of trust for the relationship to work.

農曆七月 (August 8th - September 7th) 壬申

Where health is concerned, you'll have to watch out for potential bronchitis. Those of you who are asthmatic will find your symptoms flaring up, and it's possible that some of you might develop it at this point in time if using this room. If you're an artist, pluck up the courage to put up your works for exhibit, because this will greatly enhance your reputation and put your name on the artistic map. The media is an ideal vehicle for those of you in the mining or agriculture industries to promote yourself and advertise your services – the media exposure will bring more customers to you, which will lead to greater profits.

農曆八月 (September 8th - October 7th) 癸酉

You can expect see some positive changes at your workplace that directly involves you, if you're using this room. It's bound to come in the form of promotions and advancements, or some form of major recognition. For people in the fashion and beauty industries, this is a month of increased business connections. This translates into increased profits and bonuses! By all means, go out and cultivate more of these connections. Where matters of the heart are concerned, single people in search of love will have good opportunity to find it!

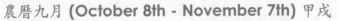

South Sector Main Door

農曆九月 (October 8th - November 7th) 甲戌

Literary types, or even those who work in the literary and media industries, will be happy to know that this month bodes well for you! Financial gains and profits are very much possible, so if there was ever a time to double your efforts – this would be it. For those who wish to purchase new properties, you have to be willing to travel in search of good properties worth investing in. Senior citizens using this room, however, need to be careful where their health are concerned. Watch out for arterial blockages, blood circulation problems, or even a possible stroke. If you're able to move to another room, so much the better.

農曆十月 (November 8th - December 6th) 乙亥

There will be positive news this month for those of you who work in the research and development fields. Any changes in your company or place of work should not deter you in any way. In fact, welcome these changes with open arms because these will bring positive financial gains! Those of you using this room will be able to enjoy good, solid relationships this month – except if there are negative external structures outside this room. This room is particularly beneficial for students and scholars to use for exam preparations; your results are likely to show the positive effects.

農曆十一月 (December 7th 2019 - January 5th 2020) 丙子

If you are a part of the entertainment industry, you will be in the spotlight and gain a considerable of fame and publicity this month – courtesy of the ever-curious media. You'll need to make the most of this lucky break in order to propel your professional life forward, but just be careful that this does not affect your private life. In general, those of you who are involved in the arts, culture, and entertainment will see an increase in media attention and publicity if you use this room. It's also a good month to begin some joint ventures with others, because financial gains are likely to be forthcoming.

農曆十二月 (January 6th - February 3rd 2020) 丁丑

Those of you in the real estate business will need to adapt and review your methods when speculating on property, in order to maximize the profitability of these investments. Sticking to the same old strategies and tired methods will only create negative and adverse scenarios, so attempt to brainstorm on how to improve and shake things up to your benefit.

Main Door	South	Bedroom Sector	Northwest

SE	S	SW
7	3	5
6	**8**	1
2	4	9
NE	N	NW

農曆正月 (February 4th - March 5th) 丙寅

Any problems or issues that come up this month should not be left to fester, because it could bleed over into long-term trouble and resentment. Even if the issue seems trivial, you should be ready to solve every problem swiftly. If doing so is beyond your own capabilities, don't be hesitant to seek counsel from someone older and wiser, or simply a person with more experience. For those of you who want to engage in investment deals, seeking help from a financial advisor will also be beneficial.

農曆二月 (March 6th - April 4th) 丁卯

Those of you with a strong curiosity and interest in esoteric and metaphysical subjects and disciplines, are well-advised to cultivate your interests. What might start out as a minor enthusiasm or hobby could well develop into something more specialised and professional – which in itself could lead to greater opportunities beyond your imagination! This is also a good month for people who have made significant investments in real estate and properties, because they are likely to gain sizeable profits that may have them laughing all the way to the bank.

農曆三月 (April 5th - May 5th) 戊辰

All of you using this room can expect to see your careers progressing by leaps and bounds. You can expect to hear news of a promotion, and with it an elevation of your status and authority at the workplace. In terms of relationships and matters of the heart, you'll be able to enjoy an increasingly harmonious relationship with your partner. Bear in mind, however, that this is only true insofar that there are no negative external forms outside this sector.

農曆四月 (May 6th - June 5th) 己巳

This will generally be quite an auspicious month for you, so make the most of this period to push forward your plans. In particular, those of you who work in the fashion and beauty industries will be able to reap the rewards and profits if you have put in your fair share of effort. Health-wise, most of you will enjoy a good forecast this month. It's also a good time for people using this room to take a break or go on a retreat to clear your mind, relax and rejuvenate the self.

Main Door	South	Bedroom Sector	Northwest

農曆五月 (June 6th - July 6th) 庚午

If you're looking to cash in on any potential real estate or property investments that you've made in the past, this is the time to do it. The financial rewards that you reap from these investments will be splendid, and you'll be able capitalize on your profits. Politicians and civil servants will also reap the benefits of this month, because there are lots of possibilities that enable them to enhance their reputation at work and get ahead. For couples who wish to start a family, this will be the right time to do so, using the positive energies of this room.

農曆六月 (July 7th - August 7th) 辛未

In matters of the heart, couples who use this room may run into some problems and issues. Your relationship ties will not be at their highest point this month, so you will need to put in more effort to communicate with each other, and ensure that ties are strong. Those of you own a business will be wise to utilise the power of the media at this point in time. The extra publicity will bring you more potential customers. People in public relations, event management or advertising and promotion industries will also stand out this month – but you will need to be vigilant of potential fraud or embezzlement that could cost you dearly.

農曆七月 (August 8th - September 7th) 壬申

You'll be happy to know that your relationships enjoy a good boost during this month, and for people using this room, it is likely to be harmonious and fulfilling - not only in terms of your personal relationships, but also in your professional relationships. You are able to make more of an impact in your career, as well, if you use this room. New opportunities and avenues will open up for you – it is high time that you got that promotion, salary raise and recognition from your superiors. However, this only applies if you've been pulling your own weight thus far! You may also make some fast money through speculative investments.

農曆八月 (September 8th - October 7th) 癸酉

For those using this room, there will be a strong need for you to control your temper and keep a cool head in this month! This is because you could lose your head while dealing with others, leading to some friction and tension in your relationships that could lead to long-term repercussions. Furthermore, you'll also have some problems maintaining clarity of thought and will have to battle some amount of stress and emotional volatility. Negative structures or features located outside this sector will exacerbate the issue, leading to health issues like food poisoning and liver trouble.

農曆九月 (October 8th - November 7th) 甲戌

Where romance is concerned, people using this room will enjoy a heightened sense of intimacy and closer ties with their other halves. It's also a beneficial room and sector for people in the academic and educational fields, because you'll be able to make some visible progress in your work. However, be wary of your competitors who are out to throw a wrench in your plans. Students sitting for examinations will also derive much benefit from using this room, so it will be wise to use it in the midst of their study preparations.

農曆十月 (November 8th - December 6th) 乙亥

At the workplace, you will need to seek the advice of your seniors, or of experienced professionals, before you engage in any form of investment deals this month. Going into it with half-baked knowledge will not help you in any way, and the reverse is entirely possible. Remember that you have nothing to lose by gathering more information and using professional expertise. You'll be surprised to note that people are more than willing to help you out, and the help that you receive is likely to go a long way.

農曆十一月 (December 7th 2019 - January 5th 2020) 丙子

Pregnant ladies who are using this room or this sector are under risk for complications. It might be best for you to consider moving to another room, just as a precaution, to prevent a possible miscarriage. In general, it's a good month for you to make long-term investments in real estate and properties. You can expect to see some substantial profits and financial returns. If you've long thought about dabbling in investments in these two industries, this will be the right month for you to make your move.

農曆十二月 (January 6th - February 3rd 2020) 丁丑

It's a favourable month for personal relationships for those of you using this room this month. Couples should try to spend more time together. However, it will be best to ensure that there are no naturally-occurring water formations outside the room. Those intending to embark on a major research project, where substantial research and development expenditure is required, will find this a suitable month to look for sponsors.

Main Door	South	Bedroom Sector	West

農曆正月 (February 4th - March 5th) 丙寅

There's a time to be nosey, and there's a time to keep your nose strictly out of other people's affairs – and this is one of those times to do the latter! If you become enmeshed in the lives of others, you're likely to see resentment and brickbats being flung your way, as opposed to gratitude and bouquets. Those who are travel-bound or going out of town this month should get your travel and health insurance updated.

農曆二月 (March 6th - April 4th) 丁卯

For most of us, networking forms a big part of our day-to-day jobs. This month will prove especially beneficial for networking attempts, especially if you're out to corral in new clients and customers. So grab the bull by the horns to get things rolling! For those who have important examinations to sit for this month, it would be favourable for you to use this room to get your preparations and studying done. If you're in politics and looking to move ahead, it's a good month for you to solicit support from within your party or constituency.

農曆三月 (April 5th - May 5th) 戊辰

Your romantic relationships this month could be perturbed by jealousy, so you will need to make an effort to keep everything at an even keel. Don't let the green-eyed monster take control of you, because when jealousy and suspicion takes over the relationship, it will lead to a break-up. Those of you in travel, logistics, and courier industries will find that this is the month to be vigilant and careful, as the turnover will be adversely affected.

農曆四月 (May 6th - June 5th) 己巳

Any form of speculative investments, especially in asset acquisitions, will bring about a surfeit of profits. This is particularly true if these investment deals are made or finalized abroad. If you have any important examinations taking place this month, you will do well to use this room – because it bodes well for scholarly pursuits. In general, you'll be able to enjoy favourable relationship conditions, but watch out for the presence of water in this sector. It could result in possible relationship scandals that will cause a significant amount of stress and anxiety.

Main Door	South	Bedroom Sector	West

農曆五月 (June 6th - July 6th) 庚午

Where your business relationships or partnerships are concerned, you will have to be careful of possible tensions and problems that could cause a strain. It will be best to avoid forming new alliances at this point in time, because it's not likely to work in your favour. You should also be prepared for possible rumours dogging you and your business endeavours this month. While the rumours may seem trivial, they could cause a loss in wealth, a smeared reputation and potential messy legal issues. Relationships could also come under pressure this month, so you'll have more tolerant and less apt to losing your cool.

農曆六月 (July 7th - August 7th) 辛未

Gossip arising out of third-party interference will cause tensions in your marriage and relationships this month, so be careful to what you listen to, and to whom you put your trust. Otherwise, it might cause your relationship painful lingering problems, which could deteriorate into long-term repercussions and consequences. If you choose to make investments in property this month, you are likely to enjoy some profitable results.

農曆七月 (August 8th - September 7th) 壬申

It's a month to take on significant and ambitious projects, as there are plenty of mentors and advisors around who will help you do what you need to do. Don't be afraid to ask for help when you need it, as you will find the right people who are willing to assist you. For people involved in creative industries, you'll need to be ready to step into the limelight because you're likely impress everyone and make a name for yourself. If you find that your career has been stagnant thus far, now is the time to make hay while the sun shines.

農曆八月 (September 8th - October 7th) 癸酉

For people who are in the food and beverage or entertainment industries, this will be a relatively profitable month. Go all out to make the most of the deals that will be headed your way! If there are any romantic interludes to look forward to this month, they are likely to be short-lived. It will be better for you not to put too much of yourself into it, and to focus on other aspects of your life instead, such as your health. Watch out for heart and eye ailments, as these are likely to develop into something more serious.

農曆九月 (October 8th - November 7th) 甲戌

Those of you involved in the property field will be astounded by the many spectacular deals that are within your grasp. Keep an eagle eye out on possible good ones and make a quick move to seal your deals this month. This is an opportune month for all business deals in general. Where matters of the heart are concerned, your spouse might feel neglected this month, as your focus on your career could sideline intimacy and bonding time.

農曆十月 (November 8th - December 6th) 乙亥

If you work in finance, you will need to travel quite a bit to solicit potential business prospects. See this as a good thing, because moving about to seek new clients and customers can bring very good results for you. Where work is concerned, in general, there will be quite a bit of competition and rivalry to deal with. Office politics will be at its height, requiring your adeptness at circumventing the stuff. Prospects are not looking rosy on the romantic front. Tread carefully, as your reputation might be the casualty of careless flings. It might be best to focus your energies elsewhere.

農曆十一月 (December 7th 2019 - January 5th 2020) 丙子

For those of you preparing to sit for examinations this month, it will be advantageous for you to use this room in this particular sector. You will find the energies present here rather conducive for studies and revision. As such, you will be able to make the most of any form of scholarly or learning activities that you do here, to ace your exams. If you are in politics, you will find this a good month, especially if you need to ascend the political ladder, and gain the support of the grassroots. It's a good time for you to do networking, as it will bring about good results and stronger connections with your clients and customers.

農曆十二月 (January 6th - February 3rd 2020) 丁丑

You might feel as though you have hit an invincible wall this month, so it will be fruitless to continue to push forward ambitiously. The smarter alternative will be to pull back, review your situation and recoup your losses. Then plan for a new strategy in the months ahead. Ask for help from mentors or trusted friends on how best to implement your new strategy. On matters of the heart, romantic relationships will be plagued by jealousy this month, so you should refrain from mingling too closely with others if it bothers your partner.

| Main Door | **South** | **Bedroom Sector** | **Southwest** |

農曆正月 (February 4th - March 5th) 丙寅

It's not a good month for your finances, and this is largely in due part to disloyal subordinates undermining your moves. Also, be wary of potential accidents caused by careless people around you, leading you to suffer from possible muscles or tendon injuries. In general, using this room will aggravate any existing health problems, and create potential new ones. This is especially the case with eye diseases, or head injuries.

農曆二月 (March 6th - April 4th) 丁卯

Where your health is concerned this month, try to avoid eating out. You might have to battle some indigestion and stomach troubles. It will be best to prepare your food at home, for the sake of your physical wellbeing. Lawyers will find their number of clients increasing this month, so you should make the most of your extra business! Be conservative about making any significant financial investments this month, especially if you're in the communications industry – as the risk of losses is very high.

農曆三月 (April 5th - May 5th) 戊辰

Older males using this room will find themselves being promoted to a position of greater authority, but it could end with disastrous results if you're not careful. If you own or run a corporation, be on the lookout for rumbles of discontent rising from among your employees. Disloyal ones are likely to pull the wool over your eyes to undermine the company and its superiors. Most people using this room will need to be wary of stress and depression this month. You might be feeling less emotionally and mentally anchored than usual.

農曆四月 (May 6th - June 5th) 己巳

Pay closer attention to your health this month. If you have any persistent minor ailments or symptoms, get them checked out thoroughly, so that you do not develop anything more serious. In general, where work is concerned, it is best to lay low and avoid the ambitious projects this month. Things are not likely to progress smoothly, so it will be to your benefit to keep a low profile. Even in real estate and property transactions, you will do best to steer clear of major deals until a better time in the future.

| Main Door | South | Bedroom Sector | Southwest |

農曆五月 (June 6th - July 6th) 庚午

Females using this room should be careful of potential cancer risks, especially breast cancer. Avoid succumbing to the temptation to engage in speculative or high-risk investments, including gambling. The chances of losses are higher than the potential gains. Problems come to the fore this month, both professional and personal. You will find no easy solutions or compromises, as the source of most of your troubles are also quite obscured. Be careful of potential enemies and rivals looking to take advantage of your situation, as well.

農曆六月 (July 7th - August 7th) 辛未

There is trouble brewing in your work place, and you will need to resolve the issue on your own without relying on your employees. You might find that they will create more trouble for you. It will be best to postpone any projects that require sustained teamwork and the collective support of all your staff. Males might have to deal with some lawsuits this month, especially those that arise out of car or vehicle accidents. People in serious relationships will find this a trying month filled with many arguments, disrupting the general peace.

農曆七月 (August 8th - September 7th) 壬申

It would be prudent for pregnant women to avoid sleeping in this sector for the month, or else complications could arise that could lead to serious problems. In general, people using this room should focus more on their careers than on their romantic lives, as Cupid's arrow is not headed in your direction at this point in time. Hold off on making important decisions if you're trying to expand your business – otherwise, you risk making some hasty or reckless decisions that could cost you a considerable financial loss.

農曆八月 (September 8th - October 7th) 癸酉

Good news for those of you who are in the publishing industry – you will find success and a career breakthrough at long last, but only after slogging through some serious hard work! Also, be wary of certain people who will go all out to undermine your position and point of view. You're likely to experience minor fallouts in your professional and personal relationships this month, so be prepared. It will also be a generally difficult month for lawyers, as you will face problems putting your case across in an effective manner.

農曆九月 (October 8th - November 7th) 甲戌

Romantic relationships continue to be put under stress and extreme pressure, resulting in tense relations and frazzled nerves. If you want to avoid a break-up, it will be imperative for both parties to be more understanding and considerate towards each other. People working in the IT industry will have a superb month, primarily due to new business opportunities springing up from connections and recommendations.

農曆十月 (November 8th - December 6th) 乙亥

If you're looking to renovate or expand any buildings, like your home or your office space, you should postpone all expansion works until a later date. At this point in time, it would be best for you to focus on consolidation. For those hoping to gain some financial profits, it might be favourable to invest in conservative, long-term property deals. Just bear in mind that your investments will take time to bear fruit. People in the insurance industry will have to be extra diligent and work longer hours in order to prevent any potential financial losses.

農曆十一月 (December 7th 2019 - January 5th 2020) 丙子

Ruffled feathers and irritable tempers are more than likely to cast its long shadows over relationships this month. With frequent heated arguments and tensions running high, serious repercussions - such as divorce - are a real possibility, if you don't keep your own grievances and emotions in check. If speeches and presentations are likely to feature in your near future, be careful, because you could suffer from potential problems with your voice.

農曆十二月 (January 6th - February 3rd 2020) 丁丑

Stress and depression may trigger some form of mental instability or neurosis this month among those who are prone to these issues, especially if negative Sha is located in the sector of this bedroom. This may be especially true among elderly people using this room. Older males may find that their promotion to a position of authority ends up in a disastrous situation.

Southeast Sector
Main Door

| Main Door | Southeast | Bedroom Sector | Southeast |

This section contains the monthly outlook for all 12 months of the year for different bedroom sectors, in a property with a Southeast Main Door.

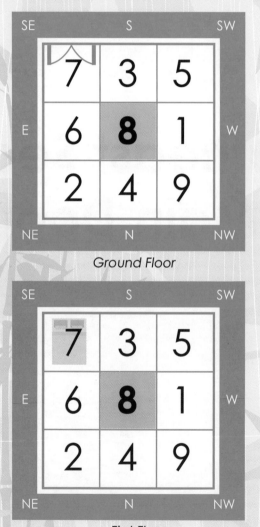

Ground Floor

First Floor

農曆正月 (February 4th - March 5th) 丙寅

If you've been battling strong opposition or intense competition at work, you may finally succumb to fatigue and exhaustion this month. No job is worth sacrificing your personal health and contentment for, so give yourself time to rest and recuperate to get back your energy. Avoid embarking on any new ventures or enterprises this month, because you're likely to come across a few serious stumbling blocks that will put your plans on hold and invite needless legal complications.

農曆二月 (March 6th - April 4th) 丁卯

Engage the services of a qualified electrician to check on all the wiring and electrical appliances in your property, because there is a strong risk of a fire hazard. Here's a tip for entrepreneurs and business owners this month: make full use of the mass media to promote your business's products or services, as it will lead to more revenue! In general, most of you will stand to gain from a greatly enhanced status, reputation and public image, but especially so if your core business revolves around real estate or properties.

農曆三月 (April 5th - May 5th) 戊辰

Doctors among you will likely see a more profitable month, due to your skills and expertise being recognised by a wider group of people. As such, they will choose to flock to you for your superior treatment rather than to go elsewhere! Females in the medical profession and finance industries will find this a bumper month in terms of financial profits. Most employed people will find ample opportunities to make a lucrative side income, so here's your chance to further increase your income and pad out your savings stash!

農曆四月 (May 6th - June 5th) 己巳

No publicity is bad publicity, they say, and this proves to be true for those of you involved in the jewellery or cell phone industries. You will find that a certain amount notoriety will actually help you improve your business! Women will continue to do well this month, although most people in general can expect promotions and recognition to come your way. However, along with this comes an increase in the amount of travelling you will need to do for work. If your health is weak, you should be careful of food poisoning or blood-related diseases.

Southeast Sector Main Door

農曆五月 (June 6th - July 6th) 庚午

This is a good month for travel, so those of you who enjoy it should take advantage of the good energies of this sector and start packing your bags and booking your plane tickets! Take care when using electrical appliances which are in poor condition, as they are fire hazards. Also, examine all your electrical and gas outlets. In general this month, you should be especially careful and refrain from attempting any reckless moves. Those among you who have created new inventions should use this month to launch it into the public domain.

農曆六月 (July 7th - August 7th) 辛未

It will be highly likely that your relationships – both personal and professional – may hit the rocks this month. Usually, the underlying reason behind this unpleasant scenario is plain and simple miscommunication. So learn to listen better and speak to others clearly, not behind their backs, and you'll weather the storm quite nicely. Expect to encounter some disputes or arguments at the workplace, although it's always wise to stay out of any issues that may lead to misunderstandings. Most importantly, scrutinise all legal documents and contracts before concluding any business deals this month, to avoid the possibility of running into any legal complications later on.

農曆七月 (August 8th - September 7th) 壬申

This month, you must make a concentrated effort to mind the words that you say. It's only a myth to suggest that words will never hurt anyone, so pay attention to yours. This is especially true of the words expressed in anger or hurt. Female members of the household should refrain from starting any conflicts with each other, particularly if you share the house with your in-laws. Those of you sitting for exams in near future will do well not to use this bedroom. Professionals in the media and publishing fields can consider expanding their business this month, but ensure that you seek legal advice before you do so.

農曆八月 (September 8th - October 7th) 癸酉

Love comes to those who go out and seek it with an open heart; so if you're single and available, then this is the month for you to enter the game of love! You never know when you might meet the love of your life, but even if you don't, chalk it all up to experience – which is invaluable. There is a heightened risk of theft and burglary this month, so it would be in your best interests to install an alarm and security system in both your home and workplace. Lawyers and legal professionals will find that their services are much sought-after at this point in time, leading to profitable financial gains.

農曆九月 (October 8th - November 7th) 甲戌

If there are negative features outside this sector it would be very unwise to embark on any business dealings at all this month, as these may lead to financial losses – especially for people in the engineering and construction industries. Do not become involved in any property deals because these will end up in legal problems. At worst, you might even wrangle with conmen who are out to cheat you of your money. There will be turbulence in personal relationships this month. Do not resort to drinking too much as a means to escape your sorrows, as this could result in a serious addiction.

農曆十月 (November 8th - December 6th) 乙亥

Those who work in the travel industry should consider expanding their business this month, as it is likely to be successful from the start. The energies are conducive for growth, so start implementing those well-thought out strategies! Actors and doctors will find themselves suddenly attracting positive media attention, which they can use to benefit their careers and enhance their reputation. In general, however, the signing of documents should be kept to a minimum or preferably left for a more suitable time, as there will tend to be complications as a result of misunderstandings or misheard information.

農曆十一月 (December 7th 2019 - January 5th 2020) 丙子

If you've come into some extra money or material acquisitions lately, don't advertise this to others this month as there is an increased risk of robbery and burglary. There is also an increased risk of occupational injury, especially for people involved in hazardous jobs. Be extra careful when handling heavy and dangerous machinery. Negligence never pays, so value your own personal safety. Where relationships are concerned, this is a good month to find your new partner – who could be right in front of you the whole time, from amongst your circle of friends.

農曆十二月 (January 6th - February 3rd 2020) 丁丑

This month, couples who use this room to foster closer ties and promote intimacy will find yourselves feeling very contented with the state of your relationship. In the professional arena, don't just ignore your competitors – engage them in a strategic manner. You'll be rewarded handsomely for your strategic planning, from increased profit margins to gaining a wider customer base. Professionals involved in the property and real estate markets will find plenty of revenue-generating opportunities, but be prepared to deal with a little conflict and misunderstanding that will arise before you're finally able to seal the deal.

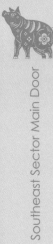

SE	S	SW
7	3	5
6	**8**	1
2	4	9
NE	N	NW

E. ... W

農曆正月 (February 4th - March 5th) 丙寅

You will need to be aware of travel-related problems this month that could result in injury to the limbs. Be careful when you're out on one of your travel adventures, and invest in a good form of insurance. Injuries are also especially prevalent for those of you involved in extreme sports. Those among you who are working as salaried employees should watch out for competition at work and keep out of any arguments, as these could escalate and end up in legal entanglements. On the other hand, this is a good month for those in the engineering industry; you can look forward to getting unexpected recognition and financial rewards coming your way if you use this bedroom.

農曆二月 (March 6th - April 4th) 丁卯

Traders deeply immersed in the precious metals or metal futures market will derive beneficial spin-offs from their investments in these industries this month. Therefore, pursue any new leads with vigour and don't be afraid to take some bold risks. Newlyweds looking for a good start to your new life together should also use this bedroom to build intimacy. Those of you attempting to invest in the stock market will do well to heed the advice of your mentors and financial advisors, and act on their suggestions accordingly. There is no reason for you to stumble about if you're unsure – ask for advice from the right people, and you're bound to receive it.

農曆三月 (April 5th - May 5th) 戊辰

Many of you will receive acknowledgment and rewards for the good work you've put into your job this month. Additionally, your superiors will be inclined to reward you with substantial financial benefits. In general, relationships will run smoothly at this point in time, so if you wish to finalise the partnership, this is the month to take that big step! If you're an analyst, you will find this an exciting month as your career is liable to take off due to strategic positioning in the equities market.

農曆四月 (May 6th - June 5th) 己巳

Those of you aiming for the #1 spot in a professional sports tournament or competition should use this room, as it will be greatly beneficial in your endeavours. Similarly, employees and workers in the courier, logistics and printing industries should double their efforts this month, as you are likely to be rewarded with that promotion and salary increment you've been seeking all along! Married couples, however, are in a spot of trouble. Try to watch what you say and how you say it, so that you don't come off as being insensitive to your partner's feelings and needs in the relationship.

| Main Door | Southeast | Bedroom Sector | East |

農曆五月 (June 6th - July 6th) 庚午

This is not a very favourable month for most – if not all – endeavours, to say the least. Elderly males using this bedroom may find themselves especially susceptible to lung problems this month, so extra care and attention must be paid to their health. Employers might find it necessary to keep a tighter rein on their company's finances, as employees will tend to be disloyal and even dishonest at work. Keep an eagle eye out for all fraudulent activities. Those of you who are salaried workers may find your efforts always going unnoticed by your superiors. Don't lose heart – be patient and continue to work diligently.

農曆六月 (July 7th - August 7th) 辛未

Couples using this bedroom will find their relationship harmonious and thriving this month. Communicating your needs to each other will lead to an increased sense of contentment and happiness! Use this room if you will be sitting for an important examination soon, or if you happen to be involved in the academic and scholarly fields. Meanwhile, those of you in the marketing, consultancy and strategic-planning businesses will find your services and expertise much sought-after this month – so go ahead and show them what you're made of!

農曆七月 (August 8th - September 7th) 壬申

Stay away from any form of speculative investments this month, although you may most certainly use this time of the year to expand your business and widen your clientele base. This will be especially pertinent if you're involved in the engineering business. Health-wise, do not brush aside minor ailments, or they might develop into more serious conditions. Do seek the advice of your doctor at the first signs of any irregularity. If you're going to be travelling this month, be extra cautious and ensure that you have the necessary insurance policies in place. This is to avert the risks of meeting with an accident while travelling.

農曆八月 (September 8th - October 7th) 癸酉

Couples hoping to conceive should try to use this bedroom this month, if you don't already. That is because this room is very favourable in getting your endeavours to bear fruit, so to speak! Meanwhile, metaphysics professionals should also venture forth and expand their businesses, as this is a good time to do so. If you happen to have a portfolio of several properties under your wings, it will be the right time to divest some of these off, and pocket the profits from your investments. You might find yourself laughing all the way to the bank.

農曆九月 (October 8th - November 7th) 甲戌

If you've been considering making long-term investments, this is the month to do your research and get cracking! Those of you who are analysts will also find your career taking off quite nicely as a result of positive developments in the equities and financial markets. Ensure that you strike while the iron is hot. Similarly, academics, scholars and those involved in the literary, creative or artistic fields will find their skills and efforts recognised and possibly even celebrated, thereby bringing them a good measure of fame and brighter career prospects.

農曆十月 (November 8th - December 6th) 乙亥

Fathers and sons will endure increasingly tense and strained relations this month, particularly if either one of them is using this bedroom. Try to move them out to another room if the situation becomes particularly bad. Where investments are concerned, stay away from them – unforeseen legal problems could come up to further derail your plans. Be careful about getting injured from participating in competitive sports this month, particularly sprains and tendon injuries. This risk will be heightened if there are negative formations outside this sector.

農曆十一月 (December 7th 2019 - January 5th 2020) 丙子

This is a good month to re-evaluate your investment portfolio. Consider selling off those stocks that have made good profits while investing in others that appear to have lucrative future potential. People who suffer from mental instability or depression should find alternate accommodation this month, as this room will tend to exacerbate the problem and create further emotional volatility. Those of you involved in family businesses will find opportunities to accumulate wealth. However, you'll need to be extra prudent when signing documents and concluding deals, as other people may be out to con you with shady deals.

農曆十二月 (January 6th - February 3rd 2020) 丁丑

What may seem to you at first to be a promising new relationship will fail to develop into something deeper or more solid, so it's better to keep things casual and save yourself from heartache. Avoid investing too much time and too many emotions into it. Jealousy and intense rivalry threaten to disturb your peace of mind this month, so you will need to manage yourself carefully to prevent this scenario from escalating into something worse – such as a legal issue. On the other hand, this month looks set to be a positive one for legal professionals, as you will find your services and skills to be very much sought-after.

Main Door	Southeast	Bedroom Sector	Northeast

農曆正月 (February 4th - March 5th) 丙寅

Students or candidates bound to sit for examinations soon should refrain from using this bedroom for revision and learning purposes, as it is not very conducive for studies this month. Any unexpected business issues that arise this month should be dealt with carefully and swiftly, with the help of legal professionals if necessary – to prevent these problems from intensifying, with long-term implications. Those of you in the chemical and mechanical industries, however, will find this to be a smooth-sailing, hassle-free month.

農曆二月 (March 6th - April 4th) 丁卯

On the domestic front, try to minimise contact with your in-laws this month, or otherwise you risk inciting some domestic discord that will sour relations with you and your spouse. You need to make a concentrated effort to manage your stress levels properly, or you could otherwise end up with gastrointestinal problems or ulcers as a result of immense work pressure. For those dabbling in the real estate business, there will be opportunities to gain wealth, but ensure you do due diligence before following through all your potential deals.

農曆三月 (April 5th - May 5th) 戊辰

People who are susceptible to spiritual activities and disturbances will find that they are especially adversely affected this month and should consider using a different room. If you are a salaried employee, you may feel that you've been slogging at your job and making sacrifices without gaining much in return. Someone will always be undercutting you and causing unexpected trouble. Be patient, however, because this is only a temporary setback. If there are negative features outside this sector, then there is a chance for you to lose money in the stock market – so avoid dabbling in it at this point in time to be safe.

農曆四月 (May 6th - June 5th) 己巳

Medical practitioners will find plenty of opportunities to serve the sick and needy this month, and enhance their reputation in the process – so continue to do your good work, as all your efforts are recognised by the people who need it most. Be wary any negative external formations outside this sector, as it could spell trouble in the form of stomach ailments, which the elder females in the household are particularly susceptible to.

Southeast Sector Main Door

農曆五月 (June 6th - July 6th) 庚午

Expectant mothers are advised to avoid using this room for the time being, in order to minimise the risk of a miscarriage or possible complications. Couples using this room should be mindful of each other's feelings and sensitivities this month, to maintain harmony within the homefront, and for the sake of your loved ones. Otherwise, you risk being at odds with each other. All in all, the energies of this sector do not augur well for most – if not all – endeavors this month. In particular, students using this room to study in will find their thoughts clouded and distracted, and their academic efforts thwarted.

農曆六月 (July 7th - August 7th) 辛未

Elderly males using this room are advised to go for a full medical check-up at the first sign of trouble, to prevent minor ailments from developing into something more serious and complicated. In general, people should avoid running afoul of the law this month, and conduct their behaviour well in public. If you work in the field of research and development, it is probably best to put off making important decisions this month, as your mind will not be at its sharpest, and you will struggle to think rationally and logically as you normally do.

農曆七月 (August 8th - September 7th) 壬申

This is a good month to invest in viable real estate or property developments, so act shrewdly and prudently, but be prepared to strike while the iron is hot. Those of you looking to sell your home may want to make a concentrated effort to do so this month, as you stand to reap substantial profits from your sale. Additionally, pay special attention to your health to avoid falling ill. If you push yourself too hard and develop any serious illness later, it would cause a lot of money to get yourself treated.

農曆八月 (September 8th - October 7th) 癸酉

Where possible, avoid engaging your female co-workers in unhealthy competition this month, to sidestep the possibility of ending up with a dispute or even legal issue in your hands. It will be best to simply hunker down and focus on your own work instead. Get a qualified expert to check for any fire hazards in your home and office this month, especially if you notice any negative external features located outside this sector. Some of you who are seasoned lawyers will be pleasantly surprised by an unexpected promotion to a position of status and authority this month.

農曆九月 (October 8th - November 7th) 甲戌

This is not the month to bite off more than you can chew, especially when it comes to property investments. Things could easily take a turn for the worse, no matter how promising they may look initially. Try not to spread yourself too thin where your finances are concerned. And while this room is a good one to use to gain spiritual knowledge, watch out for any negative structures outside this sector, as you could end up feeling quite disturbed by the negative energy instead. In general, those of you who have a tendency of emotional or mental instability should avoid using this room this month, to prevent further intensifying your symptoms.

農曆十月 (November 8th - December 6th) 乙亥

In general, do not attempt to make any underhanded deals this month, as it could cost you dearly in the long run. Get good legal experts to help you vet all your documents and ensure that everything agreed is above board. It is not worth it to take a few shortcuts at the expense of potential legal trouble. This is the month to invest in real estate but do your homework thoroughly before investing in anything. If you are secretly hoping to be promoted to a position of influence and higher social status in general, you could find your ambitions being fulfilled this month.

農曆十一月 (December 7th 2019 - January 5th 2020) 丙子

Educators, trainers and speakers will find this a difficult month as you will have significant problems trying to put your point across. This could lead to you feeling intellectually and creatively stymied for a temporary duration. On the other hand, judges and doctors will find this a time when their expertise are most needed. People who specialise in the metal futures markets will do well this month and should stay focused on that specific market and not try to spread themselves too thin, as this will not work. In other words, avoid being the Jack or Jill of all trades or you'll only suffer from a burnout!

農曆十二月 (January 6th - February 3rd 2020) 丁丑

Disputes, legal issues and power struggles may cause business partners to split up this month – so seek to resolve your differences amicably and swiftly. Don't let any conflicts drag and turn into long-term repercussions. Meanwhile, elderly ladies need to guard against injuries caused by sharp or metal objects when using this room for the month. For the sake of your relationship, it might be best not to use this room this month – more so if you find your relationship with your other half to be strained and tense lately. It will be a shame to risk having your relationship end in a separation or divorce, just because of a temporary bad patch which could have been prevented.

| Main Door | **Southeast** | Bedroom Sector | **North** |

	SE	S	SW	
E	7	3	5	W
	6	**8**	1	
	2	4	9	
	NE	N	NW	

農曆正月 (February 4th - March 5th) 丙寅

Sticks and stones may break your bones, and words will find a way to hurt you! So be mindful of the words that come out of your mouth this month, as if you utter something flippantly in haste or anger, it will likely cause trouble to rear its ugly head for some time after. Quarrels will begin at the drop of a hat this month, so bear this in mind and avoid getting enmeshed in one for trivial reasons. Try to resolve all conflicts as swiftly as possible. People working in the media, marketing or publicity will have to vet through all legal documents with care before putting pen to paper.

農曆二月 (March 6th - April 4th) 丁卯

If you're pregnant, this will not be a good month for you to travel or move around too much. As the probability of accidents happening is heightened this month, it will be wise for you to put off any travel until after your delivery. It's a good month in general for improving interpersonal ties, whether it be with your colleagues or loved ones, or even your business partners and affiliates! All dealings in shares and equities are likely to bring in the profits at this point in time, but you will need to do it with thought and deliberation, as opposed to simply rushing through. If you do the latter, the results could be entirely the opposite from good!

農曆三月 (April 5th - May 5th) 戊辰

Those among you in the field of real estate should stop being humble and go all out in promoting yourself and your skills! Your confidence and charisma will draw in new clients, and reap in dividends in the form of professional recognition and a possible promotion. In general, it's a good month to consider buying some property – and it will be even better if you need to travel abroad to conclude your negotiations. Similarly, joint ventures in the property industry will go well, but it will be particularly good if these are consolidated abroad.

農曆四月 (May 6th - June 5th) 己巳

If you are a salaried employee who happens to have a female boss, you're highly likely to be rewarded for your outstanding performance and dedication. It will likely come in the form of a promotion and salary increment, so be prepared to celebrate. For ladies living in the same house as your husband's family, it will not be a month to celebrate, however. The best thing to do would be to keep a low profile and avoid getting in anyone's way, as this could go a long way toward dispelling any tension. Pregnant mothers should avoid using this room for the month to avoid any possible dangerous complications.

| Main Door | Southeast | Bedroom Sector | North |

農曆五月 (June 6th - July 6th) 庚午

It will be a very good month for those of you involved in professional and competitive sports, but in terms of recognition and reputation-building rather than wealth. However, even if the financial gains don't come now, your heightened stature will only lead to greater wealth in the future. On the other hand, those who work in the mining industries or in financial trading will enjoy good profits this month from all your efforts. Relationships are likely to flourish this month, both in the professional and personal sense. In the latter case, you might even want to use this month to consider popping the big question regarding marriage.

農曆六月 (July 7th - August 7th) 辛未

Females come under fire from using this room this month, as you'll be susceptible to stress and increasing pressure and tension. As a result, your emotions might be a lot more topsy-turvy than you'd like! This emotional stress will then manifest itself in the form of ulcers and gastrointestinal issues. For those of you who are married and living with your in-laws, you'll do well to minimise your contact with them to avoid creating any undue strains. Consider taking a vacation to get away and refresh both your spirit and body. However, do ensure that you invest in a good form of travel insurance before you embark on your jet-setting adventures!

農曆七月 (August 8th - September 7th) 壬申

It is a good month to be with other people, as both your personal and professional relationships are blossoming and you enjoy good, harmonious ties. This will be a month to formalise any ties, if these thoughts have lain dormant in your mind for some time. Scholars, academics, and researchers will do well using this room, as the energies here will help them in their work and allow the results to come along beautifully. The same effects are true for writers and journalists – if you are scouting around for a peaceful place to write and let your create juices flow, you will do well to use this room.

農曆八月 (September 8th - October 7th) 癸酉

Be on the lookout for backstabbing and underhanded dealings at the workplace this month. There are a resentful few around you who are unhappy as their career paths seems to be stalled. As a result, they're likely to cause trouble for those around them. In general, the sense of unfriendly competition coupled with deception will also dog professionals in the entertainment industry. Those of you working in the food and beverage industry should be careful of possible health laws. You will do well, with the exception of a few run-ins with the law for this reason which could lead to financial losses.

農曆九月 (October 8th - November 7th) 甲戌

This will be a very good month to make some financial profits, in particular, on property deals abroad. Don't be afraid to travel quite a bit to sign a few documents, as the rewards will certainly outweigh a little bit of trouble. For most of you, consider this a month of self-improvement, as all endeavours begun along these lines will have extensive benefits. Consider taking up that class or new hobby that you've always dreamed about. Married females, however, will have some troubles with their mothers-in-law this month, so be sure to bite your tongue whenever you are angry. Don't be too emotionally reactive or the situation will only get worse for you.

農曆十月 (November 8th - December 6th) 乙亥

This month, couples can use this room to enhance their romantic ties, but it will depend on there not being excessive amounts of water located outside this sector. If there is, the unfortunate result could be extra-marital affairs and dalliances. Scholars and students who will be sitting for important examinations soon will benefit from the good energies of this sector for their revision and studies. Generally, it will be a good month for most to consider business expansion and growth, or to further build alliances with overseas partners and negotiators – particularly for those involved in the mining sector.

農曆十一月 (December 7th 2019 - January 5th 2020) 丙子

If you have made investments in the internet technology industries, you will find that your investments are not just doing well – they are performing far beyond your expectations! Negotiations will be in your favour, and the profits could be quite substantial. Avoid travelling this month however, because you might lose out to some of your competitors while you are away. It will be better for you to remain at home and keep a close eye on what your competitors are cooking up, while staying closely observant of your own management procedures. There will be plenty of joint investment opportunities cropping up this month, so people who are interested should consider pursuing it at this point in time.

農曆十二月 (January 6th - February 3rd 2020) 丁丑

Females using this room should go for a thorough medical examination this month to check for any possible diseases, especially serious ones like breast cancer. If at all possible, avoid using this room for the time-being for the betterment of your health. Avoid all temptations that lead you to gamble or indulge in speculative investments, if not, you could soon be emptying your bank account this month to pay off your debts! On the relationship front, there will be some pressures for budding new couples – the best thing you can do for your relationship this month is to give it some time to grow, and you will find it 'growing' a lot healthier as well.

| Main Door | Southeast | Bedroom Sector | Northwest |

SE	S	SW
7	3	5
6	**8**	1
2	4	9

(E — left, W — right, NE, N, NW)

農曆正月 (February 4th - March 5th) 丙寅

There might be some disruptions to your well-laid plans because of some family issues – but these are likely to blow over quickly, as long as you address those issues swiftly as they come up. Don't allow anything to fester for too long. Be bold at work this month, and you're likely to reap the rewards. It's the right time to strike forward with courage, using all your knowledge and shrewdness to your advantage. You'll be amazed at the financial rewards that await you should you choose to do so.

農曆二月 (March 6th - April 4th) 丁卯

This room will be ideal to foster closer romantic relationships between couples this month. You will want to make the most of this happy time by making an effort to spend more time with each other. You'll be surprised at how it feels like you're getting to know each other all over again – but with the comfort of an established trust between you. Professionals in the engineering and travel industries will be smiling all the way this month, as they are finally given the recognition they deserve for the hard work put in thus far. A promotion, or some form of career advancement, is in order as well.

農曆三月 (April 5th - May 5th) 戊辰

For married couples, the good romantic vibes continue into this month, lending an air of magic to your relationship. However, be careful of the presence of excess water outside this sector, as this could lead to extramarital temptations and affairs. Those of you who've been putting in the necessary long hours and effort at work (and you know who you are!) will be able to enjoy the sweet taste of the fruits of your hard labour! This is your time to shine under the limelight, with an improved stature at work plus more opportunities ahead.

農曆四月 (May 6th - June 5th) 己巳

For those who have to travel abroad this month to close some business deals, do it with a smile because these are likely to bring you immense profits! Grasp all the opportunities that crop up. Personal relationships continue to be a source of joy and contentment this month, bringing you much domestic bliss. Home is indeed where the heart is, and as a result, you'll be happy spending time at your abode with your loved ones. It's also an ideal month to indulge in some personal transformation, or self-cultivation and development.

農曆五月 (June 6th - July 6th) 庚午

For those who are looking to engage in joint ventures or partnerships in order to expand your business, this will be the right time to do so. Profits will increase and you'll be able to make your business more well-known. Travelling in order to conclude deals in property development and real estate will be a boon this month as well. Those of you who are in politics or civil service will be able to push forward and advance your cause, and might even get a promotion and salary increment out of it! However, there are no short-cuts to success, so make sure that you've done the groundwork in preparation.

農曆六月 (July 7th - August 7th) 辛未

There are fire hazards lurking around your home this month, so ensure that you get all your electrical wiring and gas outlets thoroughly checked. Don't be careless and negligent with these things, or a serious problem could occur. People working in the marketing and consultancy businesses will have favourable wealth luck this month, and as a result you'll be seeing higher profit margins! This is likely to be due to your expanded network of contacts, so nurture these professional relationships to the best of your ability. Where personal relationships are concerned, there is a potential for betrayal if a third party enters the picture.

農曆七月 (August 8th - September 7th) 壬申

There will be slight shake-ups and changes at the workplace, but it will likely work in your favour if you're using this room. Whatever surprises that come up, you can bet that they will be good surprises for you! Those of you trading in the metal, futures, stock and equities markets must grab the bull by the horns and be bold this month – without sacrificing shrewdness and wits, of course! Frequent travel this month may cause couples using this room to grow distant from each other – so make the effort to spend quality time together.

農曆八月 (September 8th - October 7th) 癸酉

There is trouble in paradise this month; you and your partner could find yourselves at loggerheads with each other. This is likely to be due to the lack of quality time between the two of you, so now might be the appropriate time to consider taking that long-needed vacation together. It will also keep malicious third-party intruders at bay. For those of you running your own businesses, keep an eagle eye on your financial proceedings, as otherwise fraud could cause you to lose a lot of your money. There could also be some legal troubles, but these are not likely to be serious, long-term ones.

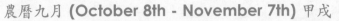

Southeast Sector Main Door

農曆九月 (October 8th - November 7th) 甲戌

Good rewards deservingly await those who have toiled at their work, especially players in the media, travel and courier industries. In particular, females working in the marketing and public relations fields should make use of the energies of the month to excel at work, thereby earning themselves a more enhanced reputation along with extra wealth! As long as there is no natural body of water located in the exterior of this sector, your personal and professional relationships will be harmonious and thriving.

農曆十月 (November 8th - December 6th) 乙亥

Be prepared to have some friction and disagreements with your family members and those whom you live with this month. Domestic issues crop up and demand to be addressed, leaving you with very little peace. However, don't put off addressing these issues, because the sooner you deal with them, the less likely they are to have long-term implications. At the workplace, don't be afraid to step out on a limb and take the initiative as the need arises – your star will glow even brighter, and you'll find yourself swiftly ascending the career ladder as a result!

農曆十一月 (December 7th 2019 - January 5th 2020) 丙子

This is a good room for activities of the metaphysical kind - so if you're a keen student or practitioner of these arts, you may want to continue using this room to further your skills. You'll be able to widen you field of knowledge and find revolutionary and unique ways to use age-old techniques and principles. It's a good room for romance, as well, as couples who use this sector will find their relationship to be sugar and spice and everything nice! You can take your relationship to the next level this month with increased intimacy and tenderness.

農曆十二月 (January 6th - February 3rd 2020) 丁丑

This room will be well used by academics, scholars and researchers this month. You'll be highly inspired and energised where your work is concerned; it will be absolutely satisfying for you to finally publish your writings. As such, your writings will earn you a good amount of recognition and further motivate you to write more. Relationship-wise, you'll be blessed with marital bliss by tapping into the energies of this bedroom during this month, but be forewarned that the presence of too much water in this sector might also result in affairs or sexual scandals.

| Main Door | Southeast | Bedroom Sector | West |

SE	S	SW
7	3	5
6 (E)	**8**	1 (W)
2	4	9
NE	N	NW

農曆正月 (February 4th - March 5th) 丙寅

This month, avoid taking on your rivals directly, as you are sure to come off as second best and this will compound your frustrations. Refrain from getting involved in any office politics and use this month to recapitulate your talents and strengths. Do not engage in casual relationships as these may end up tarnishing your reputation or just causing general problems. What may seem to you to be harmless flirtation could turn out to be anything but! Jealousy could also cause much marital discord to couples using this bedroom. It will be best to address these directly and openly as they come up.

農曆二月 (March 6th - April 4th) 丁卯

Those of you in professional or competitive sports will find this a very good and productive month. This is especially true if you are required to compete or participate in sporting events abroad. Don't refuse any of the opportunities that come up, as it will prove to be very rewarding. You will have plenty of people willing to afford you assistance this month, but you'll need to be a little careful, as there are some people with ill-intentions out to sabotage you. Don't be too trusting of everyone and confide only in a select few.

農曆三月 (April 5th - May 5th) 戊辰

Business owners will be hindered by a lack of progress this month. No matter how much you push and prod, you find yourself not having budged from your current position. Don't be discouraged, as this situation is temporary and soon the winds of change will start to blow. In the meantime, consolidate your position effectively and keep your grander ambitions on hold for the future. Trust is essential between couples using this room; be more open and communicative with each other this month to put any suspicious at bay.

農曆四月 (May 6th - June 5th) 己巳

Romantic relationships start to improve this month, as there is more opportunities to communicate and share experiences. This will forge a closer bond and create a heightened sense of camaraderie and intimacy. Things are looking bright this month for those of you in the construction industry because you will somehow receive media recognition for what you do – increasing your business opportunities and spearheading more profit-making projects. Fame, recognition and publicity will also come to those in the marketing and public relations industry, resulting in increased profits and revenue.

Main Door	Southeast	Bedroom Sector	West

農曆五月 (June 6th - July 6th) 庚午

Any disputes or conflicts that arise this month should be settled in an amicable manner, as otherwise you could find yourself battling out in the law courts – draining you of both your finances and your energy! In fact, people in general need to exercise wisdom and tact to avoid inciting lawsuits, and guard against harmful gossip. Be on your best behaviour this month and try not to step on anyone's toes. Partnerships and new alliances formed recently could become strained for people using this room.

農曆六月 (July 7th - August 7th) 辛未

Expectant mothers should be extra cautious using this bedroom, as possible complications could set in. If possible, use another room in order to avoid any troubles. Those of you who are involved in the real estate business will make a windfall this month. When people seem overly helpful in sharing information with you at this point in time, be sure to put on your skeptic's cloak. Avoid accepting anything at face value, as you seem to be unfortunately surrounded by people who are only looking out for their own interests.

農曆七月 (August 8th - September 7th) 壬申

People in committed relationships should be careful not to get too carried away flirting or doing something that will compromise the integrity of their relationships. In general, it's a good time to do a spring-cleaning of your lives this month, both literally and figuratively! It's the right time to throw out the old and bring in the new. Consider taking up that particularly challenging and ambitious project this month, as you will have the guidance of mentors and experienced elders around you. Their help will give you the confidence to do well, resulting in some very nice financial rewards.

農曆八月 (September 8th - October 7th) 癸酉

It's a good month for married couples to consider going on a holiday together. All you need to do to improve your relationship is to get away from the daily stresses of the 'real world' and find a way to reconnect deeply. If you have been wanting to ask for a promotion, pluck up the courage and go for it! Your superiors have likely recognised your talents and abilities, and will be very inclined to reward you accordingly. Watch out for spine or bladder problems, however, if you are using this room.

農曆九月 (October 8th - November 7th) 甲戌

This is a boom time for those in the printing and media fields, as financial gains are ripe and plentiful this month! Likewise, those in the property sector should close out business deals at this point in time. This is because the terms are likely to be in your favour, so don't hesitate to do it if the timing is right. Spouses may feel a little neglected, as one partner is busy making money and has no time for the other half. Endeavour to pencil in more time together in your schedule, as relationships are like growing plants and also need tending to!

農曆十月 (November 8th - December 6th) 乙亥

It is a good time to travel and go on an adventure if you feel so inclined this month – but do be cautious and take out some form of travel insurance, as there is a slight risk of limb injuries. Your relationships with friends and family take on a sweeter turn, and you'll be able to enjoy increased warmth and intimacy with them. Academics and researchers will be able to market their ideas and commercialise their findings, but you'll need to remove your rose-tinted glasses first, as not everyone is out to help you. Be guarded and vigilant against unscrupulous types who want to take you for a ride, and you should do just fine.

農曆十一月 (December 7th 2019 - January 5th 2020) 丙子

It is time to come out of your shell and brush up on your social skills, because networking is the path to success! Don't shy away from making new contacts with influential people this month, as you are likely to gain financial and professional opportunities through these new connections. However, it will bode well for you to keep both eyes wide open. Although people are generally helpful to you, there are a few who will not think twice to stick a knife in your back, so be smart and discerning about whom you choose to trust.

農曆十二月 (January 6th - February 3rd 2020) 丁丑

For those of you who own a business in the logistics, courier, or travel industries - be prepared for a difficult month ahead. You are likely to face financial challenges that could set you back a bit. That said, having a contingency plan will help to ease the situation and allow you to manoeuvre the transition period well. In general, business owners should avoid embarking on anything ambitious this month, and should instead focus on consolidating their positions and improving their current procedures.

Southeast Sector Main Door

| Main Door | Southeast | Bedroom Sector | Southwest |

SE	S	SW
7	3	5
6	**8**	1
2	4	9

E (left side, middle row) — W (right side, middle row)

NE | N | NW

農曆正月 (February 4th - March 5th) 丙寅

Those living in this room will not have much luck with new romantic affairs this month, as the outcomes will be less than happy and fall far below your expectations. It might be a better idea to concentrate on some other aspect of your life. If you're looking to expand your business, get some advice from mentors or seasoned professionals in your field – otherwise you risk making incorrect choices that will cost you quite a bit, financially.

農曆二月 (March 6th - April 4th) 丁卯

Communicate more openly and honestly with your partner this month, to hedge the possibility of a misunderstanding. You need to be extra sensitive to your partner's feelings, as your relationship will be severely tested this month – and it's really not worth ending a good relationship just because of a temporary rough patch. This month, lawyers may find it harder than usual to put their points across and argue their cases effectively too, no thanks to the energies present in this sector, which bodes ill for all forms of communication.

農曆三月 (April 5th - May 5th) 戊辰

If you are involved in the furniture industry, you will have to work smart this month as merely working hard will not cut it. This is because you'll be battling a lack of support from your bosses and superiors, and you will need to focus on getting your efforts back on track. It will do you well to postpone all investment deals and focus on reigniting employee morale instead. As for those of you working in the political arena, you will gain a lot of support from your friends, family, and acquaintances this month. This will help in pushing your stature further up while at the same time, increasing your visibility.

農曆四月 (May 6th - June 5th) 己巳

This month does not bode well for relationships, so people who use this room should endeavour to exercise more patience and tolerance with their loved ones. You'll be feeling strained and rather emotional, due to the pressure of financial and relationship problems. You should try to find ways in which you can take some time out to recuperate and regain your strength. There are profits to be made from property deals, as long as these are conservative risks and you keep your attention tightly focused.

| Main Door | Southeast | Bedroom Sector | Southwest |

農曆五月 (June 6th - July 6th) 庚午

For those of you who are set to deliver speeches or presentations this month, you might literally find yourself rendered speechless – as a result of impaired vocal abilities. As such, alternative arrangements will have to be made, just in case. Miscommunication will plague most people this month; in addition, those of you working in the telecommunications and IT industries will have to sustain some financial losses. If you are unfortunately mired in legal disputes, it may be better to find a way to delay the case or settle, because the chances of winning are very minimal at this point in time.

農曆六月 (July 7th - August 7th) 辛未

If you are planning to sit for any important examinations this month, you might want to move out of this room temporarily, as it is not very conducive for academic endeavours. Professional sportspeople and those participating in competitive sports events will find this month to be quite challenging and difficult. It will be better not to participate in competitions and to focus on improving your skills instead. Those among you who are required to travel in order to make a living will also find this month very difficult in many respects, especially if you hold positions of authority in your career.

農曆七月 (August 8th - September 7th) 壬申

Rocky relationships become even rockier this month, and you'll have to quell your temper or your inclination to retort with sharp words. To avoid inflicting long-term damage on the relationship, step back from all conflicts and try to maintain a cool head. The situation should revert back to normal soon. Also, this is not a good time to get into any real estate and property transactions, as you might get burned. Business owners are likely to find that everything that can possibly go wrong this month will go wrong, so it will be smart not to begin any new projects at this point.

農曆八月 (September 8th - October 7th) 癸酉

Expectant mothers are advised not to use this bedroom for the month, and to also go for a thorough medical-check up to allay the risk of pregnancy complications or a miscarriage. In fact, those who have been suffering from chronic or persistent health problems should also consult their physicians without delay. Failure to do so could result in dire consequences, such as kidney problems or diabetes. Treat your body with care and nourish it well. Pay special attention while on the road this month, as you risk meeting with an accident.

| Main Door | Southeast | Bedroom Sector | Southwest |

Southeast Sector Main Door

農曆九月 (October 8th - November 7th) 甲戌

This month, the good energies of this room will be helpful for those of you involved in the legal and arbitration fields, so use it to advance your cause and career. Likewise, if you're establishing a new business in the field of property development or real estate, you will attain success relatively quickly. Parents will find that children using this room this month will be a lot more defiant, rebellious and difficult to control – so make sure you take hold of the reigns firmly instead of allowing your children to control you!

農曆十月 (November 8th - December 6th) 乙亥

This is a month to avoid all possible property-related deals and anything that involves an element of risk, as financial losses are very probable. This is especially true for those of you involved in the architecture industry. If you can, avoid using this room this month because it will adversely affect your health; otherwise, you are likely to suffer from gastrointestinal afflictions and diseases. Those of you who hold positions of considerable authority in your career might want to consider investing in property this month, because it is likely to be very beneficial for you.

農曆十一月 (December 7th 2019 - January 5th 2020) 丙子

People who are holding high positions of power and influence such as CEOs, senior officials and the like, will find that applying intelligence and smarts to all their proceedings will lead to greater achievement. By doing so, you're likely to receive further elevation in your status within your organisation and enjoy a greater sense of visibility. There is a very good chance for money to be made through smart investments in spas, fisheries, and information technology companies this month – but bear in mind that the window of opportunity is very small – seize the moment and grab your opportunities quickly.

農曆十二月 (January 6th - February 3rd 2020) 丁丑

You might want to monitor your employees or staff just a little more closely this month, as there's a possibility of disloyal (and overly ambitious) subordinates who will attempt to sabotage you. Additionally, for those of you who have just established new relationships, - be it personal or professional – be sure to give your partner some 'breathing space'; otherwise, you may find the strength of your partnership deteriorating over time. All in all, this looks set to be a trying month, especially for those in authority who are compelled to travel to earn their keep. Stay focused and remember that perseverance is the key to success.

Southeast Sector Main Door

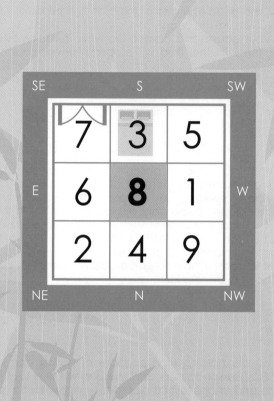

農曆正月 (February 4th - March 5th) 丙寅

If you're a contractor who has been working hard to land that 'deal of a lifetime' that could change your life, then watch out for any potential tenders and throw in your bid accordingly. Don't be overly cautious and miss out on a good opportunity! However, those working on construction sites should prioritize their safety and keep their helmets on at all times while on-site, to minimize the risk of a head injury. Sons living in this room would be rather rebellious and prone to questioning their parents' authority and advice, so it may be wise to temporarily relocate them to another bedroom for this month.

農曆二月 (March 6th - April 4th) 丁卯

This month, all gambling activities should be put to a halt, unless you expect to see only zeroes in your bank account balance! In that same vein, avoid all forms of investment this month because they might go bust and cost you dearly financially. Have any deals vetted and scrutinized by a legal professional before you proceed, if it cannot be avoided. Female inhabitants of this room are advised to go for a thorough medical check-up or mammogram this month, especially if you're previously been diagnosed for breast malignancies.

農曆三月 (April 5th - May 5th) 戊辰

The energies of this room will be detrimental to your health this month. So, those of you who have recently undergone medical procedures should move out of this room temporarily, to avoid the risk of any complications. If you're in the midst of business negotiations with overseas partners, this is the month to close the deal as you're likely to reap huge profits. Be sure to read the fine print on all legal documents, before putting your signature on any of it. There is also the disturbing risk of fraud or theft present this month, either from your staff or from your family members.

農曆四月 (May 6th - June 5th) 己巳

This month, it's all about paying attention to your own personal safety, as there is a strong risk of robbery. This is true if you notice negative external structures or formations outside this sector. It's also important for you to keep your nose out of any disputes and quarrels, as well as avoid participating in any gossip, as legal entanglements are likely to arise out of it. If you're an analyst or scientific researcher, or involved in the IQ-related field, you will find the energies here favourable for your work this month – however, this is dependent on there being a good mountain formation located towards the West.

Main Door	Southeast	Bedroom Sector	South

農曆五月 (June 6th - July 6th) 庚午

This month, romantic relationships will be rocky, due to gossip and miscommunication. Tune out the negative chatter of others and don't allow them to influence your thoughts and emotions, because you know each other best. Exercise fortitude and tolerance, and you'll find that things will improve for you both. In general, you should avoid all forms of gambling and speculative investments this month because it is likely to result in losses. However, if these investments are in real estate, there is a chance that you could see some profits.

農曆六月 (July 7th - August 7th) 辛未

Males looking for a new relationship are likely to meet a compatible new partner this month. The energies of this room bode particularly well for newly-burgeoning romantic relationships! Take advantage of good financial advice given to you by others, especially experts in the field, and invest in research and development. Those working in the media and travel industry will thrive this month. Work hard and you'll attain high achievements and great honour, while enjoying a boost to your reputation.

農曆七月 (August 8th - September 7th) 壬申

This is a challenging month that could result in financial losses, but bear in mind that important lessons can be learned! This will result in positive changes for you, as you'll be able to recoup from any losses and apply the valuable lessons for your future endeavours. Those in the analytical or scientific fields will benefit from the good energies of the sector, and find breakthroughs in their field of work. Do not be drawn into family arguments and squabbles as these could result in major rifts within the family. It is best to remain impartial at all times. Taking sides will only add fuel to the fire and worsen an already explosive situation.

農曆八月 (September 8th - October 7th) 癸酉

This month, you could suffer from financial losses if you jump into new ventures hastily without careful consideration. Do your research before investing, and the results will be in your favour. All you need to do is put in a couple hours of extra legwork now to reap your dividends way into the future. People who are in real estate and property development should invest in clearly thought-out deals in their field of work, as this is a time to make beneficial returns. Those of you who are married should be frank, direct, and open with your spouse this month and discuss all important decisions with each other, as neglecting to do so could lead to stressful relations with your partner.

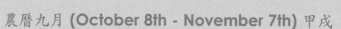

農曆九月 (October 8th - November 7th) 甲戌

Prospects are good for legal professionals, as their persuasive powers and ability to argue constructively will result in positive developments this month. Those of you who are able to articulate your arguments well, should make the most of the positive energies of this room. Travel brings about beneficial outcomes for you and could result in an increase in status this month, especially if you are in the construction or architecture business. In general, all senior personnel should be on their guard against thieves and unscrupulous third parties, who will end up extorting large sums of money from you.

農曆十月 (November 8th - December 6th) 乙亥

You are likely to make good gains this month if you're using this room, and you will know how to protect your interests well enough. However, do bear in mind that there are plenty of swindlers and ill-intentioned people out to spin a pretty tale on you this month. So you will have to be extra cautious of all your recent acquisitions. Those of you who are sitting for examinations will benefit from using this room for doing academic work and studies this month. However, unexpected changes will also crop up, requiring you to be able to adapt swiftly and be flexible.

農曆十一月 (December 7th 2019 - January 5th 2020) 丙子

Young males living in this room, in particular, should be careful so as to avoid sustaining injuries from sharp metal objects and implements. If possible, they should try to limit their usage of these objects for the month. Those of you in the military and involved in strategy, should find this a beneficial month, because you'll be able to plan well for the future. It will also be a good time to accumulate some financial profits from any property investments, especially when using your past experience and superior knowledge to your best advantage.

農曆十二月 (January 6th - February 3rd 2020) 丁丑

The energies prevalent in this bedroom could cause volatile emotions and a turbulent mental state, so don't be too hard on yourself if you run into emotional or psychological problems. Those of you who own or manage a company, will have to be careful of potential fraud or cheating by your employees. As a preventive measure, ensure that all stringent auditing processes are in place. On the other hand, people in the media and marketing industries will find this a generally favourable month, with accolades and recognition easily coming your way.

Northwest Sector
Main Door

Northwest Sector Main Door

Main Door	Northwest	Bedroom Sector	Northwest

This section contains the monthly outlook for all 12 months of the year for different bedroom sectors in a property with a Northwest Main Door.

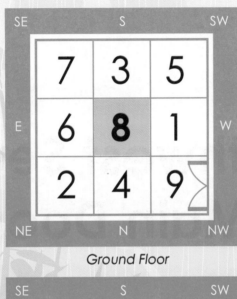

Ground Floor

First Floor

農曆正月 (February 4th - March 5th) 丙寅

It's a good month to feel self-satisfied, because your ability to make money from your investments will benefit you greatly! You also have the uncanny knack of knowing how to invest your gains, so listen to your own counsel this month and proceed without hesitation. However, do beware of potential legal issues. It would be wise to get advice from legal experts before signing any deals.

農曆二月 (March 6th - April 4th) 丁卯

If you're working in the engineering and technical fields, then this is the month to schedule an appointment with your bosses and superiors! If you've been pulling in the late nights and burning the midnight oil and working hard, you will do well to present your case for a promotion, a raise, or both. The likelihood of things working out in your favour is high. You'll also enjoy good romance luck, so this is no time to be a retiring and shy wallflower! Singles should be ready to mingle, and committed couples can enjoy more tenderness and intimacy.

農曆三月 (April 5th - May 5th) 戊辰

Some of that Peach Blossom luck from the previous month will continue to flow into this month as well, enabling you to enjoy harmonious and thriving relationships. Use this amorous month to grow closer to your significant other by doing activities together, such as attending dance classes, playing tennis or taking a vacation together. If you're the academic or scholarly type, you'll find your professional status enjoying quite a boost. On top of that, you can also look forward to a possible promotion!

農曆四月 (May 6th - June 5th) 己巳

Your decision-making capacity is very sharp this month, so make the most of it by trusting yourself to make some good decisions! Your thoughts are lucid and coherent, allowing you to chart a logical path from thought to action that will result in good outcomes. For those in the fashion industry, this is the right time to close some important deals. Travelling may be required to do so, but the financial gains are quite high. This will also be a good room to use for peaceful, contemplative activities like meditation and yoga.

| Main Door | Northwest | Bedroom Sector | Northwest |

農曆五月 (June 6th - July 6th) 庚午

This is a good month for politicians and civil and government servants to enhance their status and positions. It will happen naturally, as you receive due credit for your tireless and unceasing efforts for the improvement of public service. Those in the diplomatic corps will also find this a favourable month as a wave of positive publicity will turn the tide in your favour, garnering you much support and acclaim.

農曆六月 (July 7th - August 7th) 辛未

The temptation to have extra-marital affairs will be strong this month - males who are married should put a check on their roving eyes, lest it leads you down a path of no return. Getting entangled in affairs, no matter how "casual" or meaningless it may be for you, will result in dire consequences for your marriage. So if your spouse is important to you, steer clear of any sort of dangerous situations where you could stray. Business owners might get the chance to enjoy a spot of publicity in the press; capitalise on this opportunity to expand your business further, whether it's through more contacts or revenues.

農曆七月 (August 8th - September 7th) 壬申

Women in the household are particularly prone to eye and heart ailments this month, so be on guard. It is best to get a thorough medical check-up if you have any minor symptoms. This might prove to be a profitable month if you're dabbling in speculative investments in metal trading, or stocks and equities. Try to always stay one step ahead of the rest, and keep abreast of the current trends. This way, you'll be able to swiftly capitalise on any favourable openings that may suddenly crop up.

農曆八月 (September 8th - October 7th) 癸酉

Be extremely cautious in your dealings with money this month, because it is possible that ugly disputes over it can arise. Don't be negligent in whatever it is you have to do. In other ways, as well, you could find yourself feeling extremely agitated and harried, so avoid making any important decisions while in this state. When you're too stressed, your mental faculties will not be working at their optimum best. Nevertheless, you should stay alert to what is going on around you; there could be fraud that is happening right under your nose.

農曆九月 (October 8th - November 7th) 甲戌

Now is an optimum time to expand your business. If you're a business owner, go all out to expand your network of contacts, as you will stand to gain favourably in the financial sense! Make an effort to get in touch with all your old associates, colleagues and friends; you'll never know what these renewed connections could lead to. Get some media coverage, as well, where your business expansion activities are concerned. Good publicity will bring in new business clients. In the domestic realm, do not allow any tension in your relationships to develop into something serious.

農曆十月 (November 8th - December 6th) 乙亥

Legal issues could rear their ugly head this month. If these problems seem overwhelming and insurmountable, there's absolutely no reason for you to suffer in silence. Turn to some of your mentors, or even experienced seniors and helpful people at the workplace, and they just might shine a light on some solutions that you wouldn't have thought of on your own. As far as health goes, there is nothing serious to look out for. Do, however, attend to your minor ailments – because if these are left untreated, then it could develop into something more serious.

農曆十一月 (December 7th 2019 - January 5th 2020) 丙子

For those who're prone to eye problems in general or users of contact lenses, do watch out for potential eye infections. Get it treated immediately to avoid further aggravation. People with existing heart conditions are also advised to seek medical counsel at the first sign of anything being amiss. People using this room will be able to enjoy supreme Peach Blossom luck this month, so expect to find Cupid pointing his arrow in your direction! If you're single, be your most charming self in order to ensnare someone new; while those of you already in relationships can enjoy taking your relationship to a more committed level.

農曆十二月 (January 6th - February 3rd 2020) 丁丑

Academics and scholars will do well to tap into the energies of the sector this month. Use this room for your studies and research, and you'll find plenty of opportunities to be recognized and rewarded, in terms of better perks and a possible promotion at work. What's more, if you are living in this room, you will also find more harmony and closeness in your relationships. Hence, you should use this month to further consolidate your ties with others.

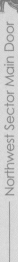

Northwest Sector Main Door

農曆正月 (February 4th - March 5th) 丙寅

If you have children who are sitting for examinations this month, this is the room you want to put them in. The energies here are very conducive for revision and studying; your kids' heightened sense of concentration and clarity of mind will enable them to pass their exams with flying colours! Similarly, academics and scholars will benefit greatly from using this room too.

農曆二月 (March 6th - April 4th) 丁卯

Couples who use this room will generally find their relationships being plagued by quarrels and misunderstandings. Bite your tongue if you must, because giving in to your impulse to say cutting words could lead to greater trouble for your marriage. Make an effort to try to understand what your partner is going through, and don't only focus on your own needs. Business opportunities will be good for those in the publishing and furniture industries.

農曆三月 (April 5th - May 5th) 戊辰

Pregnant ladies are advised to avoid using this room for the month, or it could otherwise lead to unwanted complications. Stay on the safe side, and opt to rearrange your sleeping and living arrangements for a little while. On the other hand, those in the real estate and property industry are likely to enjoy a month of progress and developments. Make the most of the opportunities to further enhance your career prospects.

農曆四月 (May 6th - June 5th) 己巳

Those of you using this room will find the spotlight trained on you this month, bringing you lots of positive publicity and recognition. Don't waste this opportunity due to false modesty! You should use this spotlight to gain more attention for yourself and your business, or even your pet causes. Where health is concerned, elderly individuals should look out for potential kidney problems. If you are involved in the travel, tourism, or even courier and logistics industries, you will be able to enjoy some positive benefits this month as a result of using this room.

Main Door	Northwest	Bedroom Sector	West

農曆五月 (June 6th - July 6th) 庚午

If you are shy and introverted, you must come out of your shell this month, because this is a good month to show off your true talents and capabilities to your superiors! You'll be duly noticed and appreciated, and may even be in line for a possible promotion or career advancement. If you're in the midst of business negotiations or closing a deal, you might find that things will go smoothly in your favour. Students sitting for examinations will also benefit; while, on the romantic front, there is a marked improvement in relationships!

農曆六月 (July 7th - August 7th) 辛未

Good news for you who are single, unattached, and on the prowl - this room bodes well for relationship hookups this month! Turn on that charm and go all out to net yourself a potential romantic mate. People in the construction industry and literary field will benefit from a surfeit of opportunities headed their way. Those of you in the travel and logistics businesses will also gain aplenty from the proliferation of new opportunities. This will be a good time to strike new deals and forge alliances with business partners or associates abroad. In terms of investment opportunities, there is a chance for you to enjoy a good agreement and be able to seal the deal!

農曆七月 (August 8th - September 7th) 壬申

As the saying goes, "curiosity killed the cat." While a little curiosity is not a bad thing at all, being a busybody at the wrong time will certainly land you in hot water this month! This is the month to lay low and avoid poking your nose, even if it's just the tip of it, into other people's affairs. If you go ahead and do it anyway, you must be prepared for the wrath of others – or worse, revenge - that will be directed at you. As long as you keep this in mind, this month in general sees an improvement in your ties with friends and family members.

農曆八月 (September 8th - October 7th) 癸酉

If your relationship has been under considerable strain or pressure recently, don't give up. Things will definitely improve this month, with a little patience and effort to mend ties. This will also be a good room to use if you're going through a divorce or corporate restructuring - as the energies present here can lend an air of agreeableness and cordiality to the proceedings, instead of bringing up resentments and hostilities. Professionally, this is an ideal month to make progress on your career or gain more recognition for your work. It's best to step up and acknowledge credit for what you've done!

農曆九月 (October 8th - November 7th) 甲戌

Couples using this room must make an effort to communicate more with each other, or else suspicion and jealousy will make their unwelcome entrance this month! This could lead to general discord and friction, souring what could otherwise be a sweet connection. So do your best to prevent this from happening. Pregnant women should also avoid using this room for the month to avoid possible complications and miscarriage. It is better to be safe than sorry later.

農曆十月 (November 8th - December 6th) 乙亥

If you're a scholarly or academic type using this room this month, you'll be able to benefit from the energies here. This is especially true for those sitting for important examinations or preparing to write their thesis and dissertations. Use this as a study or bedroom if you want to pass all your papers with an excellent grade! Even if you're unable to use it as a bedroom, it will help nevertheless to do the bulk of your studying and revision here.

農曆十一月 (December 7th 2019 - January 5th 2020) 丙子

Those in the publishing or furniture industries will find this a bumper month of sorts, especially if use this room as a bedroom. You will enjoy a good surge in business opportunities and revenues. It will be good for you to seek out overseas opportunities as well, or offshore deals, as these will likely increase your financial gains tremendously! Unfortunately, couples using this room this month will experience temporary rifts. Discords and arguments will be rife, so both of you must make the utmost effort to be patient.

農曆十二月 (January 6th - February 3rd 2020) 丁丑

This room continues to be a risk for expectant mothers, so where possible, use another room to stay on the safe side. It is worth the trouble to rearrange your sleeping and living arrangements temporarily to avert any complications or miscarriages. If you're in the real estate and property industry, then you're likely to enjoy a month of progress and developments. Make the most of the opportunities to further enhance your career prospects.

| Main Door | Northwest | Bedroom Sector | Southwest |

農曆正月 (February 4th - March 5th) 丙寅

There is a chance to make money from conservative property-related deals. However, people involved in business might find it difficult to leverage off the benefits of their positive investment gains. It will be best to enjoy the gains, then, without hoping that it multiplies into something more. Expectant women are advised against using this room for the month.

農曆二月 (March 6th - April 4th) 丁卯

It's trouble central where relationships are concerned this month. There will be heated arguments and quarrels between you and your partner, leading to a heightened sense of tension between the two of you. Yet the situation is only as bad as you allow it to be. Maintaining a stubborn stance will worsen the situation; conversely, you can salvage your relationship by being more patient and forgiving. Lawyers will find this month somewhat hard-going in terms of effectively conveying your cases. Be more flexible in your approach.

農曆三月 (April 5th - May 5th) 戊辰

Avoid speculative investments this month, as you stand a very strong chance of losing more than you gain! Consider this a month to lay low and keep your wealth close to you. On a more personal note, you might feel lonely and a little down and out while using this room this month. Don't be too overwhelmed by occasionally negative feelings, as this is only temporary and will soon come to pass. Seek enjoyment among good friends and make an effort to do more of the things you love and enjoy.

農曆四月 (May 6th - June 5th) 己巳

There will be signs of thunderstorms and dark clouds, in so far as your relationships are concerned. The trick to maintaining a good relationship is to always seek a solution that is mutually beneficial. Don't be on the warpath, and avoid wanting to antagonize your partner just to win the fight. You may win the argument, but you will have lost a lot more. So try to cool your emotions that threaten to boil over. Professionals in the IT industry will find that the outcome of your work will not be exactly proportionate to the amount of time and effort that you've put in. Also, it would be best to steer clear out of any joint-ventures for the month, as these will likely end in disaster.

Main Door	Northwest	Bedroom Sector	Southwest

農曆五月 (June 6th - July 6th) 庚午

If you've lately profited from any of your recent investments, this is the month to cash-in on your gains! This is not to suggest that you must then spend it all frivolously – but it will be advantageous for you to cash-in now, as the timing is favourable. Do avoid dabbling your cash in the share market, however, because there is a strong chance that you might lose all that you had worked so hard to get! Females using this room will be prone to liver issues; so get medical attention at the first signs of trouble.

農曆六月 (July 7th - August 7th) 辛未

This is a promising month for lawyers and mediators, but maybe not so much if seen from another perspective! There will be plenty of disputes and conflicts requiring your arbitration and litigating skills. You can enjoy a boost in reputation by using your sharp acumen, wit and ingenuity to resolve these matters. There is a higher risk of car accidents this month, so be extra-cautious when you're out and about, and on the move. Those of you with children will be dealing with slightly more rebellious spirits than normal – don't lose your temper too quickly. Instead, surprise them into obedience with tact, understanding and patience!

農曆七月 (August 8th - September 7th) 壬申

Family-run businesses and organisations will be plagued by disputes and internal arguments this month, especially amongst family members. Matters are likely to blow out of proportion and get out of hand, if they are not addressed quickly and nipped in the bud. The situation at the workplace, in general, is not exactly uplifting – possible betrayals are likely among colleagues, so you'll need to watch your back and have your guard up. This is also not a good month for major decision-making, so put off important decisions to another time. Making any major decisions in haste can only bring about negative results.

農曆八月 (September 8th - October 7th) 癸酉

For those people in high positions - CEO's, directors, and people in top management - you will find that your intelligence and aptitude brings about good results for the company. This, naturally, sees your status and authority enjoying a boost within the corporation. Where your health is concerned, kidney stones may pose a problem. Avoid making things more serious by indulging in gambling and drinking, as it will not only adversely affect your health – but will also bring about negative consequences in your life, as well.

農曆九月 (October 8th - November 7th) 甲戌

If you're in the IT industry, you are likely to do quite well this month! Your reputation will spread through good word of mouth from a bevy of satisfied clients, who are happy to recommend your service to others. But health-wise, strokes and internal bleeding pose a serious problem – so people suffering from weak health in general should watch out. Couples using this room will endure a bout of strained relations this month, and the best way to deal with it will be to loosen the strings and give each other more breathing room.

農曆十月 (November 8th - December 6th) 乙亥

Pregnant women will want to avoid using this room, as the risk of complications to your pregnancy is high. To minimise the risk of a potential miscarriage, try to consider using another room for the time being. Couples will experience some turbulence in their relationships this month. The only antidote to counter the extremes of frosty relations or fiery arguments is to exercise more patience, discretion and tact. Politeness and consideration will still go a long way, even among people who have been together for a long time.

農曆十一月 (December 7th 2019 - January 5th 2020) 丙子

For those of you in the legal field, especially lawyers and legal practitioners, this will be a challenging month that will require quite a bit of effort and creative thinking on your part. Otherwise, sticking to your usual tactics might find you having some serious problems in putting all your cases across. Health issues will also come to the forefront this month, so don't neglect your physical wellbeing. In particular, watch out for mouth problems or even speech-related issues. Don't hesitate in getting yourself checked out by a doctor if anything seems wrong.

農曆十二月 (January 6th - February 3rd 2020) 丁丑

Those who use this room will be battling with feelings of loneliness and isolation this month. To compensate, you should seek the company of friends and loved ones, as this is only a temporary feeling which will soon pass. Indeed, individuals who are prone to, or already suffering from depression, are advised not to use this bedroom this month – as the energies present therein will only exacerbate your situation. In terms of money, you'll do well to avoid speculative investments this month.

農曆正月 (February 4th - March 5th) 丙寅

Elderly males who are using this room will be best advised to go for a thorough medical check-up this month to alleviate an increased risk for internal bleeding and injuries. It would be best to eliminate any potential dangers from the outset. Occupants of this room could also be feeling increasingly solitary and cut off from the rest of the world. Try to assuage your loneliness by going out and doing more activities that you enjoy, preferably with your friends, instead of staying in and brooding!

農曆二月 (March 6th - April 4th) 丁卯

Couples using this room must make more of an effort to listen to each other this month, instead of focusing too much on what other people say. Failure to do so will put your relationship in jeopardy. Be open and direct in your communication, but remember to also be tactful and considerate. It goes a long way! Males using this room will still need to be mindful of their health this month, as problems with their livers could crop up. Possible injuries to the limbs are also likely.

農曆三月 (April 5th - May 5th) 戊辰

This month, pay attention to your loved one or spouse, as other people might be trying to encroach into your territory! Your spouse has been feeling neglected lately. While you may have been busy tending to your own issues related to work, it's high time that you now focus on them to make sure they feel well-loved and cared for. Otherwise, they might seek for love and affection elsewhere. If you own a business, be observant of all that your competitors are up to – or you might find the rug being pulled out from under you!

農曆四月 (May 6th - June 5th) 己巳

Those who are using this room this month should drive carefully and practise road safety. Try not to break any laws or take short cuts, as this could affect you adversely. Be on the lookout for potential problematic situations at work, which could develop into more serious problems if left unchecked. Potential robberies and thefts are also likely this month, so upgrade your security measures and install reliable alarm systems.

| Main Door | Northwest | Bedroom Sector | South |

農曆五月 (June 6th - July 6th) 庚午

You'll be glad to know that all forms of speculative investments, especially those in the futures markets, will generate substantial profits for you this month! However, do scrutinise all business deals and contracts carefully, because the slightest oversight will prove to be very costly to you in the future. Any decisions you make that will affect your spouse or partner, needs to be discussed thoroughly. Be sure to pay attention to what he or she has to say, because failing to do so will place a heavy strain on your relationship.

農曆六月 (July 7th - August 7th) 辛未

If you're interested in starting your own business this month, or considering changing careers, then this is the month to do so! All activities of such nature are likely to be favourable and will bring you good results. People who are in public relations, however, will have to brace themselves to face some unforeseen problems or stumbling blocks. You will need to slow down, take stock of your situation, and plan your next move accordingly. Where your health is concerned, take care of yourself and pay extra attention to your liver this month.

農曆七月 (August 8th - September 7th) 壬申

Personal relationships will hit a rocky patch this month. It will be best for you to just play less of an active role and melt into the background for a little while, as giving others some breathing room will allow things to fall into place. Those of you with children will find them inclined to question your authority and being a little defiant! Don't react with anger, you'll only make the situation worse and alienate them. Best to sit down with them and chat, to get to the root of the problem, if there is any – it could be just a phase they're going through!

農曆八月 (September 8th - October 7th) 癸酉

Business owners will need to take your foot off the pedal this month. Don't seek trouble as trouble comes to you uninvited for the most part anyway! Avoid getting into messy disputes and arguments. You won't do much to fall into these, so refrain from willfully attracting it in the first place! Always think before you act or say something, otherwise you risk adding fuel to an already explosive situation. Couples using this room will endure strained relations for the month, so take special care when communicating with each other. Children should be kept away from sharp instruments and implements this month.

農曆九月 (October 8th - November 7th) 甲戌

You may find yourself entangled in a weird power struggle with friends this month, leading to a break-up of ties. In the worst case scenario, this could lead to a legal fallout. Try to see the bigger picture and don't let your emotions get the best of you, as the outcome could be ugly for all involved. If you've recently undergone a serious medical treatment, or some form of surgery, then it's best to avoid using this room or it could prolong what could otherwise be a speedy recovery. Avoid letting more complications come into the picture.

農曆十月 (November 8th - December 6th) 乙亥

This month, employees may be feeling disgruntled and apt to do something about this. So if you're an owner or a simply a manager or a boss, be prepared for some defiant attitude. Sons will be inclined towards friction with their fathers, too, if they're using this room for the month. In general, people using this room will feel a sense of melancholy. Loneliness will prevail, and if it's starting to bother you a little too much, you can either use another room or actively force yourself to get out more and meet up with your friends.

農曆十一月 (December 7th 2019 - January 5th 2020) 丙子

Health will be the primary issue for those of you using this room for the month. Males, in particular, will be prone to liver problems and ulcers. Limb injuries might also be a strong risk. Be extra careful with your body and prioritise your health so that the symptoms don't develop into something more serious. It will not be an ideal month to play around with your money, even if it's in the hopes of gaining some profits! This means you should avoid all forms of speculative investments and gambling, otherwise you risk seeing a big loss.

農曆十二月 (January 6th - February 3rd 2020) 丁丑

Business owners need to be vigilant, and be mindful of what their rivals or competitors could possibly do, to undermine their efforts. Indeed, any underhanded tactics employed by your rivals – including fraud and embezzlement – could well cause you a pretty penny, if you let your guard down. You should also pay more attention to your partner or spouse, as this month brings about the threat of interference from external parties.

Northwest Sector Main Door

Main Door	**Northwest**	Bedroom Sector	Southeast

SE / S / SW: 7 3 5
E / W: 6 **8** 1
NE / N / NW: 2 4 9

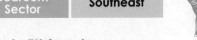

農曆正月 (February 4th - March 5th) 丙寅

This room is auspicious for attempts to enhance your reputation, as your status will increase considerably. In addition, you might get that promotion and pay raise you've been gunning for. Ladies who do business will also find this a profitable month for you, especially if you're closing lots of deals overseas! This room is also conducive for activities related to academics and studies. If you need to mug hard for an exam, this would be the place to do it to ensure you get favourable results!

農曆二月 (March 6th - April 4th) 丁卯

Those of you who were born with an inventive or creative streak - this is the month for you! If you enjoy coming up with new ideas, gadgets, and gimmicks, now's not the time to be a modest wallflower. Put your talents to good use by showcasing your creations when you have the opportunity – an exhibition seems like the best bet. If you own a business, check for potential fire hazards this month.

農曆三月 (April 5th - May 5th) 戊辰

The energies present in this sector bode well for romantic relationships. Those of you who are in long-term committed partnerships and are thinking of taking things a step further – this is the month to do it. If you're thinking of popping the big question, be brave, grab the moment, and go for it! Wealth luck is smiling down upon you this month, so you might want to try your luck in small ways – such as playing the lotto, or entering the sweepstakes. You'll never know just what you might win!

農曆四月 (May 6th - June 5th) 己巳

If you've recently come into some money, well, it will be best to keep that news to yourself this month – or at least, share it only with your nearest and dearest! You'll only be asking for trouble by flaunting your newly-acquired wealth, or spending lavishly. Stay humble and keep your feet firmly planted on the ground, and you'll do just fine. Single men will find that they have a tendency to attract the 'wrong' type of women this month. If so, it would be best to lay low than find yourself living out your own version of 'Fatal Attraction'!

| Main Door | Northwest | Bedroom Sector | Southeast |

農曆五月 (June 6th - July 6th) 庚午

Lawyers and legal practitioners will find yourselves enjoying a good month, as your services become more in demand and your skills and capabilities are up to it! But in general, where work is concerned, stay out of office politics. Walk away from fights that don't involve you, and don't try to be hero. Otherwise, you'll be dragged into messes that will cause further problems, and you don't need any of that. Females, especially elderly ones, will have to battle gallstone issues or stomach problems.

農曆六月 (July 7th - August 7th) 辛未

Salaried employees should be more tactful this month, as miscommunication happens quite easily. While this might seem minor, at this point in time, misplaced words could cause you some financial loss – or worse yet, your job! Even relationships are not spared the bane of miscommunication, so for this month – speak less and listen more. Where you have the option not to say anything – don't! If you're negotiating deals, make sure you look through everything in black and white before you even nod in agreement.

農曆七月 (August 8th - September 7th) 壬申

For those working in the telecommunications industries, you will experience technical glitches this month! Take everything in your stride, as these are only temporary glitches which will be cleared up as soon as the month is out. The green-eyed monster creeps into relationships and causes quite a few upsets. It's vital that both of you remain clear and direct in your communication at all times, as being vague and unresponsive will only lead to worse trouble.

農曆八月 (September 8th - October 7th) 癸酉

If you are feeing lonely and sad, cheer up, because you won't be single and lonely for long! But first, you'll need to engage with your social circle in order to find the romantic partner of your dreams. Who knows, that special someone could come from your existing group of friends and acquaintances. Health concerns will plague you this month, particularly in the form of eye ailments and blood issues. However, this will be a good month in terms of wealth – you'll be able to make some swift investment gains, but you will need to proceed upon gaining some advice from people with some experience and know-how.

農曆九月 (October 8th - November 7th) 甲戌

For those who're professional athletes or involved in sports, you could clinch the gold medal this month when you enter any competitions. Give it your best shot no matter what it is! Doctors and medical service officers will enjoy a good boost to your reputation and professional status, thanks to your tireless efforts in healing your patients. New romantic relationships will be smooth-sailing, as long as you don't expect too much from it. Don't even expect it to develop into something long-term, as it may not, but that doesn't mean that it still can't be enjoyable and good for you.

農曆十月 (November 8th - December 6th) 乙亥

If you're a student or a scholar sitting for examinations pretty soon, you can't go wrong with using this room for your studies. The positive energies of the room will help you gain good results. Female entrepreneurs who have business links and contacts abroad will find this a good month. You stand to enjoy quite a bit of financial profits as a result of your ventures finally pulling in good returns. While you may feel like you want to slack off a little at this point, it's actually the best time to put the pedal to the metal and double your efforts.

農曆十一月 (December 7th 2019 - January 5th 2020) 丙子

It's best to take it easy this month. Stay at home and curl up with a book, or to catch up on those DVDs. Stay away from clubs and places of ill repute – and while you're at it, from shady characters with even shadier motivations and interests! Otherwise, you'll find yourself embroiled in quite a bit of trouble that may be too much for even your reckless streak. Businesses suffer from the risk of a potential fire this month, so ensure that all your fire alarms are in good working condition, and do a thorough spot-check to root out possible oversights than can lead to this risk.

農曆十二月 (January 6th - February 3rd 2020) 丁丑

Why not try your luck at the sweepstakes, or have a go at the lotto this month? Who knows, lady luck might just smile upon you! Don't overdo it and gamble away all your hard-earned cash on such endeavours, though! Also, have your lawyer scrutinise any major deals to mitigate the possibility of running into any legal complications later on. The energies of this room also augur well for relationships this month.

Northwest Sector Main Door

Main Door | Northwest | Bedroom Sector | East

	SE	S	SW	
E	7	3	5	W
	6	**8**	1	
	2	4	9	
	NE	N	NW	

310 Feng Shui for 2019

Northwest Sector Main Door

農曆正月 (February 4th - March 5th) 丙寅

Those of you in relationships will enjoy better and more harmonious relations with your partner this month. This will boost both your spirits, as even your career trajectory is smooth and you're both excelling in your respective jobs. However, you should avoid making significant business deals this month, and wait for a better time in the future. Be wary of potential health ailments too, which will primarily affect your eyes and heart. Respiratory illnesses might bother you this month, as well.

農曆二月 (March 6th - April 4th) 丁卯

If you've been working hard at your job for a while, putting late nights and extra hours – and you know who you are! – then you can expect your efforts to be rewarded this month. It's high time that you receive recognition from your superiors and get that promotion that you've been eyeing. Couples who are on the path to matrimony will find this the ideal month to take the next big step. If you're ready for marriage, then this is the time to make it official. Generally, most people using this room for the month should be prepared for a topsy-turvy emotional landscape.

農曆三月 (April 5th - May 5th) 戊辰

If you're a salaried employee, you'll need to step up your game this month, as competition and rivalry among colleagues starts to intensify and give you some pressure. Instead of bending to the pressure and getting involved in office politics, maintain a low profile while still keeping your guard up. No matter what, you will need to protect your own territory! Just be vigilant while keeping a cool head and stay detached from it all.

農曆四月 (May 6th - June 5th) 己巳

After last month's strenuous situation, this month finds you breathing easier where both your professional and personal lives are concerned. Now that everyone has eased up on trying to beat each other in the rat race, you'll find an opportunity to forge closer ties with your colleagues, as well as your loved ones and friends. However, those of you who manage or direct a company need to be prepared for rebellious employers, while those of you working for others will need to be prepared for hard-to-please superiors! Don't let this get you down, and don't let it hinder you from attempting to make significant financial progress.

| Main Door | Northwest | Bedroom Sector | East |

農曆五月 (June 6th - July 6th) 庚午

You may want to duck from Cupid's arrow, as it will not be an ideal month for love and romantic pursuits. You'd do much better focusing on moving up the career ladder instead. While at work, be careful and considerate in how you handle workplace disagreements and tiffs. Whenever a conflict comes up, keep your cool. Otherwise, you run the risk of jeopardizing your place in the company! Those of you who own businesses need to have eyes on the backs of your heads, as well, to ward off competitors! Possible hostile takeover bids are likely, so keep your guard up and your feelers out.

農曆六月 (July 7th - August 7th) 辛未

Those involved in the academic and literary fields will find this a good month, in terms of increased inspiration and ideas. Go with your gut, and use your ingenuity to develop these new ideas well – as these are likely to bring about financial gains. But bear in mind that you'll have to make it visible to the right people, so choose your audience carefully when you present it. For couples looking to conceive, this room will be ideal to use for the month. People who deal in metals trading and the stock market will be able to derive good profits.

農曆七月 (August 8th - September 7th) 壬申

Elderly people using this room should be extra vigilant of their health this month. Don't neglect any health troubles that crop up, as doing so will only worsen your condition and turn what was minor into something serious. Those of you who are travelling this month should be careful because there is an increased risk of injuries at this point in time, particularly limb injuries. Adolescents using this room will be prone to being rebellious and difficult this month – yes, more so than usual! If it's causing disruptions to your family, then situating them in another room will help.

農曆八月 (September 8th - October 7th) 癸酉

If you've dabbled in property and real-estate investments in the past, then this would be a good time to sell as the chances of earning handsome profits are high. So take good stock of your portfolios and consider this option as a means of attaining extra finances. Those of you in relationships will have harmonious and strong relations with your partner. In general, you'll definitely enjoy improved ties with your loved ones. However, bear in mind that some elderly family members might be prone to kidney and stomach ailments.

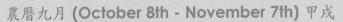

農曆九月 (October 8th - November 7th) 甲戌

New entrepreneurs and those who have recently set up a business, should make full use of the energies present here this month. It will be a favourable start to your ventures. Those of you working in the banking and finance industries will be rewarded this month for your achievements, which could lead to a promotion. Students and scholars preparing for an important examination soon will do well to utilise this room for their learning and revision.

農曆十月 (November 8th - December 6th) 乙亥

Watch out for health issues, as there will be a proliferation of certain ailments this month. This will primarily involve the eyes and heart, as well as the respiratory system. Where business is concerned, make sure you only strike conservative deals – or better yet, bid your time and waiting for another moment to make your move. This will not be the ideal moment to attempt to strike it big or make a play for a major negotiation.

農曆十一月 (December 7th 2019 - January 5th 2020) 丙子

Mood swings and emotional instability will be the blight of your existence this month, as feelings of loneliness and isolation will bother you and bring your spirits down. There is no need for you to suffer alone because that will only set you in a deeper funk. Make an effort to spend more time with your trusted friends and loved ones, as doing so will be a gentle balm to soothe your feelings. Where work is concerned, if you've been working hard all these months, you'll find that you get your just rewards this month.

農曆十二月 (January 6th - February 3rd 2020) 丁丑

This looks set to be a month of intense competition and rivalry, especially at the workplace. Stay out of office politics, at much as you can, because you don't need the added stress. Learn how to maintain a low profile, although this doesn't mean that you should let your guard down. On the contrary, remain vigilant, but keep your cool as well, to prevent any issues from escalating into something more serious. Where possible, don't burn any bridges because you'll never know when you might need those connections.

Northwest Sector Main Door

農曆正月 (February 4th - March 5th) 丙寅

Pregnant women should refrain from occupying this room for the month, or potential serious complications like a miscarriage could occur. Other health issues that are likely to come up include appendicitis, so if any stomach pains seem out of the ordinary, get yourself checked out by a doctor immediately. This month will be a rocky one for relationships. Couples using this particular room should make a special effort to be tolerant and forgiving to each other.

農曆二月 (March 6th - April 4th) 丁卯

You'll need to walk on eggshells this month. It's not a particularly good month for the women in the household, and there is a strong possibility for arguments and conflicts erupting due to words uttered in an angry outburst. If possible, contact between the female members of the household should kept at a minimum in order to prevent them from clashing with each other. Looking on the bright side, this room bodes well for scholarly pursuits, and people sitting for examinations would benefit well from using this room.

農曆三月 (April 5th - May 5th) 戊辰

Your workplace is a battle zone of office politics this month, so you'll be obliged to dodge bullets! Aside from being extremely agile, you'll need to distance yourself from catty arguments and petty gossip by generally being pleasant and agreeable, but in no way biased. Backstabbing will also be rampant, so you will need to have your guard up, or at least don a metaphorical suit of armour! Also, be sure to clear all your outstanding fines, taxes, and summonses – otherwise you just might find the law catching up with you in just the way you have been trying to avoid!

農曆四月 (May 6th - June 5th) 己巳

If you've made a deal or investment in real estate and property lately, then you'll stand to make handsome gains this month. The profits are quite considerable and should leave you smiling! It is not advisable for those of you in frail or weak health to continue using this room. To avoid aggravating your medical health troubles, move to another room until you feel better. As such, doctors and medical practitioners will find their services to be highly sought-after in their work.

Main Door	Northwest	Bedroom Sector	Northeast

農曆五月 (June 6th - July 6th) 庚午

Expectant ladies should go for a full medical-check up this month, because there is a strong possibility that you might run into complications while using this room. It will be best to prevent any untoward incidents than to regret them later. Also, be careful when you're on the road – as car and automobile accidents are likely. Drive cautiously and don't do anything reckless. If you're into competitive or professional sports, you will do well this month, especially if you are required to travel for an event.

農曆六月 (July 7th - August 7th) 辛未

This room is not favourable to pregnant woman for this month, as you might run the risk of miscarrying if you don't pay special attention to your health. Other health problems that you could face include gastrointestinal ailments. If you have stomach trouble, you should make an effort to seek medical treatment at the first sign of something being amiss. Speculative investments in property or equities, as well as stocks, will result in profits for you. However, you will still need to carefully check the fine print before putting pen to paper.

農曆七月 (August 8th - September 7th) 壬申

Parents are likely to find their children being reclusive and solitary, and being unwilling to socialize with others. Try to exercise patience and fortitude in dealing with them, and don't be quick to lose your temper. When you talk patiently to your kids and show that you care, they will reveal their troubles to you. If there is water is located outside of the room, then this could indicate a potential affair for the married ladies – so be on guard. Gastrointestinal illnesses might also plague the people using this room.

農曆八月 (September 8th - October 7th) 癸酉

The potential for good financial gains is very high this month, so you might want to consider taking a small gamble, or buying an affordable lottery ticket to try your luck. But don't be too carried away by the potential dollar signs you see, and remember to only spend what you can certainly afford. Where work is concerned, arguments and jealousy will proliferate. As such, it would be best for women to stay out of these disputes, or otherwise the only outcome would be disaster! Children using this room to prepare for their examinations could run into some obstacles, so it would be best to move them to another room temporarily.

農曆九月 (October 8th - November 7th) 甲戌

Legal practitioners and professionals will likely find their skills in great demand this month. As for those who are involved in business, it would be prudent to not make deals that involve too much capital. Otherwise, the potential for financial losses are immense if the risks are too high. If you're a superior or a boss, take pains to communicate in a more coherent and tactful manner to your subordinates. This is to alleviate the risk of any possible legal complications that could arise.

農曆十月 (November 8th - December 6th) 乙亥

This month will be trying for relationships and requires you to have the patience and fortitude of a saint! You do not have to go out of your way to be self-sacrificial and martyr-like, but do remember that you'll need to be tolerant and patient with each other. Disagreements will crop up, and your primary goal this month is to ensure that these do not get out of hand and blow out of proportion. In terms of business deals or investments, this is not the month to make a play for a big deal because it will not work out in your favour.

農曆十一月 (December 7th 2019 - January 5th 2020) 丙子

This room augurs well for academic and scholarly pursuits, as the positive energies here will boost your mental powers and stamina. If you're sitting for important examinations in the near future, then you should use this room for your revision! In general, this room will bode well for self-cultivation and development pursuits. If you're keen to improve yourself and find new avenues for growth and maturity, you will do well to concentrate on this room.

農曆十二月 (January 6th - February 3rd 2020) 丁丑

Be sure to settle all your outstanding fines, summonses and taxes, if you do not want the long arm of the law to catch up with you. Stay out of office politics as well, more so if you find arguments, gossips and backstabbing to be rampant at the workplace this month. If you're in a relationship, arguments and quarrels are likely to happen. As such, you will do well to give your partner some room to breathe, and be patient with each other.

| Main Door | Northwest | Bedroom Sector | North |

農曆正月 (February 4th - March 5th) 丙寅

In general, you should pay attention to your physical health this month, and don't take anything for granted. If you've been feeling rather under the weather lately, then you should be taking extra precautions. Watch out especially for the risk of lung ailments this month – go see your doctor at the first sign of prolonged wheezing and coughs. Be careful if you have to use sharp metal implements or knives, or an accident of the painful sort could be in order.

農曆二月 (March 6th - April 4th) 丁卯

If you're a politician or a civil servant, or working for the government in some capacity, be careful with any deals or negotiations that involve real estate and property. Try not to let your guard down too soon, because then you could find yourself entangled in serious disputes. Nevertheless, this will be a good month to travel to conclude any business deals. Travelling abroad to wrap things up can only serve to improve your reputation and status, while also increasing financial gains.

農曆三月 (April 5th - May 5th) 戊辰

For those of you knee-deep in property or real estate investments, it's still not too late to pull out and cut your losses. In fact, it's best you do it now rather than later, when the markets take a further plunge! This is not the month to gamble with your finances either, quite literally, so cast all temptations aside and put your cash under lock and key – or somewhere where you can't get at it easily. Women in the household might want to get a medical check-up to rule out possible skin problems or breast malignancies.

農曆四月 (May 6th - June 5th) 己巳

If you have designs on making a name as an artist, then now's not the time to be the shy and retiring type hiding modestly behind your skills! You'll need to let people know of your talent, and what better way than doing it through an exhibition of your works. The time is ripe to do so, and acclaim is likely to follow. Those of you who specialize in selling car and automobile accessories should go all out to target bigger markets aggressively! Couples who are using this room will find this month to be a little difficult, as you'll have to put in more effort than usual to keep your relationship on a smooth and even plane.

Northwest Sector Main Door

| Main Door | Northwest | Bedroom Sector | North |

農曆五月 **(June 6th - July 6th)** 庚午

The tensions that affected couples in the previous month will likely spill over to this one, affecting the female half more so than the males. In this case, both of you should bear in mind that tact and tolerance can go a long way toward soothing ruffled feelings. If you are involved in the literary industry in any way, be wary of unhealthy rivalry and deceit. Watch your back, as backstabbers are aplenty. Travel is particularly beneficial for those in the arts, marketing, and consulting – to negotiate and seal the deal.

農曆六月 **(July 7th - August 7th)** 辛未

Pay special attention to health issues this month. If you're suffering from any ailments affecting your internal organs (particularly your spleen), then take adequate care. Elderly women should also be careful to consult their doctors at the first sign of anything being amiss. If you're in journalism or astronomy, this will be a good month for you in terms of getting funding, or attracting potential sponsors. Use your persuasive charms to the best of your ability!

農曆七月 **(August 8th - September 7th)** 壬申

Those of you who are models or involved in the entertainment industry will be used to the shine of the spotlight. This month, however, you'll be literally basking in the limelight as all things related to you being in the centre of attention will go down favourably. So you should grab this opportunity to go all out on a publicity blitz to promote yourself and your work! Academics and scholars will also enjoy a nice boost to their reputation. Embarking on foreign relations, or merely forging an alliance with partners abroad, will bode well for your business endeavours.

農曆八月 **(September 8th - October 7th)** 癸酉

If you're in the service industry, this will be a good month for you – as long as you stay put, that is! It is best not to travel at this point in time, as any sort of moving about will only reduce your financial gains. If you're looking to conclude and finalise any of your business deals that have been up in air for some time now, then this is the month to push forward and do it.

農曆九月 (October 8th - November 7th) 甲戌

Married people will be at it like cats and dogs this month, so to avoid being at loggerheads at every waking moment, be more careful with each other. This doesn't mean that you have to walk on eggshells, but be more respectful and considerate of each other. A careless word uttered sometimes can be the cause of immense hurt. Elderly people, or those of frail disposition, will be under the risk of a stroke or arterial blockage due to poor blood circulation. It would be best to go for a thorough medical check-up sooner rather than later.

農曆十月 (November 8th - December 6th) 乙亥

Women using this area will have to deal with a lot more disputes and arguments than they thought possible, and if they're not careful, it could lead to a very serious situation. At its worst, it could denigrate into a lawsuit. Be more circumspect with your words, if you're a female, and don't be so quick to anger. Additionally, if your work requires you to come into close contact with sharp instruments and knives on a regular basis, be extremely cautious. It is imperative to prioritise your own safety and not be lackadaisical about it.

農曆十一月 (December 7th 2019 - January 5th 2020) 丙子

Those who are involved in professional sports will want to welcome the chance to travel and compete this month! You'll find that your chances of doing well are better abroad than it is in your home country. Generally, this is a good time to get moving and to satiate that travel bug in you - especially so if it involves work, such as concluding deals abroad. This will bring about handsome profits, as well as cementing your reputation and status.

農曆十二月 (January 6th - February 3rd 2020) 丁丑

If you're involved in speculative investments, especially property or real estate dealings, you should probably pull out before the market takes a plunge, as the forecast isn't too good this month. You should also avoid all gambling activities, unless you wish to end up incurring massive debts by succumbing to your urges. Ladies in the household should go for a medical check-up, as they are more susceptible to skin problems and breast malignancies this month.

JOEY YAP's
QI MEN DUN JIA MASTERY PROGRAM

This is the world's most comprehensive training program on the subject of Qi Men Dun Jia. Joey Yap is the Qi Men Strategist for some of Asia's wealthiest tycoons. This program is modelled after Joey Yap's personal application methods, covering techniques and strategies he applies for his high net worth clients. There is a huge difference between studying the subject as a scholar and learning how to use it successfully as a Qi Men strategist. In this program, Joey Yap shares with you what he personally uses to transform his own life and the lives of million others. In other words, he shares with his students what actually works and not just what looks good in theory with no real practical value. This means that the program covers his personal trade secrets in using the art of Qi Men Dun Jia.

There are five unique programs, with each of them covering one specific application aspect of the Joey Yap's Qi Men Dun Jia system.

Joey Yap's training program focuses on getting results. Theories and formulas are provided in the course workbook so that valuable class time are not wasted dwelling on formulas. Each course comes with its own comprehensive 400-plus pages workbook. Taught once a year exclusively by Joey Yap, seats to these programs are extremely limited.

Getting Whatever You Want from Whatever You've Got™ Spiritual Qi Men™

Qi Men Forecasting Methods™

Qi Men Destiny & Life Transformation™

Qi Men Feng Shui™

Qi Men Strategic Execution™

Qi Men Warcraft™

JOEY YAP CONSULTING GROUP

Pioneering Metaphysics-Centric Personal and Corporate Consultations

Founded in 2002, the Joey Yap Consulting Group is the pioneer in the provision of metaphysics-driven coaching and consultation services for professionals and individuals alike. Under the leadership of the renowned international Chinese Metaphysics consultant, author and trainer, Dato' Joey Yap, it has become a world-class specialised metaphysics consulting firm with a strong presence in four continents, meeting the metaphysics-centric needs of its A-list clientele, ranging from celebrities to multinational corporations.

The Group's core consultation practice areas include Feng Shui, BaZi and Qi Men Dun Jia, which are complemented by ancillary services such as Date Selection, Face Reading and Yi Jing. Its team of highly trained professional consultants, led by its Chief Consultant, Dato' Joey Yap, is well-equipped with unparalleled knowledge and experience to help clients achieve their ultimate potentials in various fields and specialisations. Given its credentials, the Group is certainly the firm of choice across the globe for metaphysics-related consultations.

The Peerless Industry Expert

Benchmarked against the standards of top international consulting firms, our consultants work closely with our clients to achieve the best possible outcomes. The possibilities are infinite as our expertise extends from consultations related to the forces of nature under the subject of Feng Shui, to those related to Destiny Analysis and effective strategising under BaZi and Qi Men Dun Jia respectively.

To date, we have consulted a great diversity of clients, ranging from corporate clients – from various industries such as real estate, finance and telecommunication, amongst others – to the hundreds of thousands of individuals in their key life aspects. Adopting up-to-date and pragmatic approaches, we provide comprehensive services while upholding the importance of clients' priorities and effective outcomes. Recognised as the epitome of Chinese Metaphysics, we possess significant testimonies from worldwide clients as a trusted Brand.

Feng Shui Consultation

Residential Properties
- Initial Land/Property Assessment
- Residential Feng Shui Consultation
- Residential Land Selection
- End-to-End Residential Consultation

Commercial Properties
- Initial Land/Property Assessment
- Commercial Feng Shui Consultation
- Commercial Land Selection
- End-to-End Commercial Consultation

Property Developers
- End-to-End Consultation
- Post-Consultation Advisory Services
- Panel Feng Shui Consultant

Property Investors
- Your Personal Feng Shui Consultant
- Tailor-Made Packages

Memorial Parks & Burial Sites
- Yin House Feng Shui

BaZi Consultation

Personal Destiny Analysis
- Individual BaZi Analysis
- BaZi Analysis for Families

Strategic Analysis for Corporate Organizations
- BaZi Consultations for Corporations
- BaZi Analysis for Human Resource Management

Entrepreneurs and Business Owners
- BaZi Analysis for Entrepreneurs

Career Pursuits
- BaZi Career Analysis

Relationships
- Marriage and Compatibility Analysis
- Partnership Analysis

General Public
- Annual BaZi Forecast
- Your Personal BaZi Coach

Date Selection Consultation

- **Marriage Date Selection**
- **Caesarean Birth Date Selection**
- **House-Moving Date Selection**

- **Renovation and Groundbreaking Dates**
- **Signing of Contracts**
- **O icial Openings**
- **Product Launches**

Qi Men Dun Jia Consultation

Strategic Execution
- Business and Investment Prospects

Forecasting
- Wealth and Life Pursuits
- People and Environmental Matters

Feng Shui
- Residential Properties
- Commercial Properties

Speaking Engagement

Many reputable organisations and institutions have worked closely with Joey Yap Consulting Group to build a synergistic business relationship by engaging our team of consultants, which are led by Joey Yap, as speakers at their corporate events.

We tailor our seminars and talks to suit the anticipated or pertinent group of audience. Be it department subsidiary, your clients or even the entire corporation, we aim to fit your requirements in delivering the intended message(s) across.

CHINESE METAPHYSICS REFERENCE SERIES

The Chinese Metaphysics Reference Series is a collection of reference texts, source material, and educational textbooks to be used as supplementary guides by scholars, students, researchers, teachers and practitioners of Chinese Metaphysics.

These comprehensive and structured books provide fast, easy reference to aid in the study and practice of various Chinese Metaphysics subjects including Feng Shui, BaZi, Yi Jing, Zi Wei, Liu Ren, Ze Ri, Ta Yi, Qi Men Dun Jia and Mian Xiang.

The Chinese Metaphysics Compendium

At over 1,000 pages, the Chinese Metaphysics Compendium is a unique one-volume reference book that compiles ALL the formulas relating to Feng Shui, BaZi (Four Pillars of Destiny), Zi Wei (Purple Star Astrology), Yi Jing (I-Ching), Qi Men (Mystical Doorways), Ze Ri (Date Selection), Mian Xiang (Face Reading) and other sources of Chinese Metaphysics.

It is presented in the form of easy-to-read tables, diagrams and reference charts, all of which are compiled into one handy book. This first-of-its-kind compendium is presented in both English and its original Chinese language, so that none of the meanings and contexts of the technical terminologies are lost.

The only essential and comprehensive reference on Chinese Metaphysics, and an absolute must-have for all students, scholars, and practitioners of Chinese Metaphysics.

The Ten Thousand Year Calendar (Pocket Edition)

The Ten Thousand Year Calendar

Dong Gong Date Selection

The Date Selection Compendium

Plum Blossoms Divination Reference Book

Xuan Kong Da Gua Ten Thousand Year Calendar

San Yuan Dragon Gate Eight Formations Water Method

BaZi Hour Pillar Useful Gods - Wood

BaZi Hour Pillar Useful Gods - Fire

BaZi Hour Pillar Useful Gods - Earth

BaZi Hour Pillar Useful Gods - Metal

BaZi Hour Pillar Useful Gods - Water

Xuan Kong Da Gua Structures Reference Book

Xuan Kong Da Gua 64 Gua Transformation Analysis

BaZi Structures and Structural Useful Gods - Wood

BaZi Structures and Structural Useful Gods - Fire

BaZi Structures and Structural Useful Gods - Earth

BaZi Structures and Structural Useful Gods - Metal

BaZi Structures and Structural Useful Gods - Water

Earth Study Discern Truth Second Edition

Eight Mansions Bright Mirror

Secret of Xuan Kong

Ode to Flying Stars

Xuan Kong Purple White Script

Ode to Mysticism

The Yin House Handbook

Water Water Everywhere

Xuan Kong Da Gua Not Exactly For Dummies

SAN YUAN QI MEN XUAN KONG DA GUA
Reference Series

San Yuan Qi Men
Xuan Kong Da Gua
Compendium

San Yuan Qi Men
Xuan Kong Da Gua
**540 Yang
Structure**

San Yuan Qi Men
Xuan Kong Da Gua
**540 Yin
Structure**

Xuan Kong
Flying Star
**Secrets Of The
81 Combinations**

Xuan Kong Da Gua
Fixed Yao Method

Xuan Kong Da Gua
Flying Yao Method

Xuan Kong Da Gua
**6 Relationships
Method**

Xuan Kong
Flying Star
**Purple White Script's
Advanced Star Charts**

The **San Yuan Qi Men Xuan Kong Da Gua Series** is written for the advanced learners in mind. Unlock the secrets to this highly exclusive art and seamlessly integrate both Qi Men Dun Jia and the Xuan Kong Da Gua 64 Hexagrams into one unified practice for effective applications.

This collection is an excellent companion for genuine enthusiasts, students and professional practitioners of the San Yuan Qi Men Xuan Kong Da Gua studies.

Xuan Kong Collection

Xuan Kong Flying Stars

This book is an essential introductory book to the subject of Xuan Kong Fei Xing, a well-known and popular system of Feng Shui. Learn 'tricks of the trade' and 'trade secrets' to enhance and maximise Qi in your home or office.

Xuan Kong Nine Life Star Series (Available in English & Chinese versions)

Joey Yap's Feng Shui Essentials - The Xuan Kong Nine Life Star Series of books comprises of nine individual titles that provide detailed information about each individual Life Star.

Based on the complex and highly-evolved Xuan Kong Feng Shui system, each book focuses on a particular Life Star and provides you with a detailed Feng Shui guide.

Joey Yap's BaZi Profiling System

Three Levels of BaZi Profiling (English & Chinese versions)

In BaZi Profiling, there are three levels that reflect three different stages of a person's personal nature and character structure.

Level 1 – The Day Master

The Day Master in a nutshell is the basic you. The inborn personality. It is your essential character. It answers the basic question "who am I". There are ten basic personality profiles – the ten Day Masters – each with its unique set of personality traits, likes and dislikes.

Level 2 – The Structure

The Structure is your behavior and attitude – in other words, it is about how you use your personality. It expands on the Day Master (Level 1). The structure reveals your natural tendencies in life – are you a controller, creator, supporter, thinker or connector? Each of the Ten Day Masters express themselves differently through the five Structures. Why do we do the things we do? Why do we like the things we like? The answers are in our BaZi Structure.

Level 3 – The Profile

The Profile depicts your role in your life. There are ten roles (Ten BaZi Profiles) related to us. As to each to his or her own - the roles we play are different from one another and it is unique to each Profile.

What success means to you, for instance, differs from your friends – this is similar to your sense of achievement or whatever you think of your purpose in life is.

Through the BaZi Profile, you will learn the deeper level of your personality. It helps you become aware of your personal strengths and works as a trigger for you to make all the positive changes to be a better version of you.

Keep in mind, only through awareness that you will be able to maximise your natural talents, abilities and skills. Only then, ultimately, you will get to enter into what we refer as 'flow' of life – a state where you have the powerful force to naturally succeed in life.

www.BaZiprofiling.com

THE BaZi
60 PILLARS SERIES

The BaZi 60 Pillars Series is a collection of ten volumes focusing on each of the Pillars or Jia Zi in BaZi Astrology. Learn how to see BaZi Chart in a new light through the Pictorial Method of BaZi analysis and elevate your proficiency in BaZi studies through this new understanding. Joey Yap's 60 Pillars Life Analysis Method is a refined and enhanced technique that is based on the fundamentals set by the true masters of olden times, and modified to fit to the sophistication of current times.

   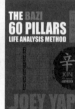 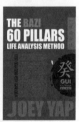

BaZi Collection

With these books, leading Chinese Astrology Master Trainer Joey Yap makes it easy to learn how to unlock your Destiny through your BaZi. BaZi or Four Pillars of Destiny is an ancient Chinese science which enables individuals to understand their personality, hidden talents and abilities, as well as their luck cycle - by examining the information contained within their birth data.

Understand and learn more about this accurate ancient science with this BaZi Collection.

BOOK 1   BOOK 2   BOOK 3   BOOK 4   BOOK 5   The 10 Gods

(Available in English & Chinese)

Design Your Legacy

Design Your Legacy is Joey Yap's first book on the profound subject of Yin House Feng Shui, which is the study Feng Shui for burials and tombs. Although it is still pretty much a hidden practice that is largely unexplored by modern literature, the significance of Yin House Feng Shui has permeated through the centuries – from the creation of the imperial lineage of emperors in ancient times to the iconic leaders who founded modern China.

This book unveils the true essence of Yin House Feng Shui with its significant applications that are unlike the myths and superstition which have for years, overshadowed the genuine practice itself. Discover how Yin House Feng Shui – the true precursor to all modern Feng Shui practice, can be used to safeguard the future of your descendants and create a lasting legacy.

Must-Haves for Property Analysis!

For homeowners, those looking to build their own home or even investors who are looking to apply Feng Shui to their homes, these series of books provides valuable information from the classical Feng Shui therioes and applications.

In his trademark straight-to-the-point manner, Joey shares with you the Feng Shui do's and dont's when it comes to finding a property with favorable Feng Shui, which is condusive for home living.

Stories and Lessons on Feng Shui Series

All in all, this series is a delightful chronicle of Joey's articles, thoughts and vast experience - as a professional Feng Shui consultant and instructor - that have been purposely refined, edited and expanded upon to make for a light-hearted, interesting yet educational read. And with Feng Shui, BaZi, Mian Xiang and Yi Jing all thrown into this one dish, there's something for everyone.

(Available in English & Chinese)

Pure Feng Shui

Pure Feng Shui is Joey Yap's debut with an international publisher, CICO Books. It is a refreshing and elegant look at the intricacies of Classical Feng Shui - now compiled in a useful manner for modern day readers. This book is a comprehensive introduction to all the important precepts and techniques of Feng Shui practices.

Your Aquarium Here

This book is the first in Fengshuilogy Series, which is a series of matter-of-fact and useful Feng Shui books designed for the person who wants to do a fuss-free Feng Shui.

More Titles under Joey Yap Books

Walking the Dragons

Compiled in one book for the first time from Joey Yap's Feng Shui Mastery Excursion Series, the book highlights China's extensive, vibrant history with astute observations on the Feng Shui of important sites and places. Learn the landform formations of Yin Houses (tombs and burial places), as well as mountains, temples, castles and villages.

Walking the Dragons : Taiwan Excursion

A Guide to Classical Landform Feng Shui of Taiwan

From China to Tibet, Joey Yap turns his analytical eye towards Taiwan in this extensive Walking the Dragons series. Combined with beautiful images and detailed information about an island once known as Formosa, or "Beautiful Island" in Portuguese, this compelling series of essays highlights the colourful history and wonders of Taiwan. It also provides readers with fascinating insights into the living science of Feng Shui.

The Art of Date Selection: Personal Date Selection (Available in English & Chinese)

With the Art of Date Selection: Personal Date Selection, you can learn simple, practical methods to select not just good dates, but personalised good dates as well. Whether it is a personal activity such as a marriage or professional endeavour, such as launching a business - signing a contract or even acquiring assets, this book will show you how to pick the good dates and tailor them to suit the activity in question, and to avoid the negative ones too!

Your Head Here

Your Head Here is the first book by Sherwin Ng. She is an accomplished student of Joey Yap, and an experienced Feng Shui consultant and instructor with Joey Yap Consulting Group and Mastery Academy respectively. It is the second book under the Fengshuilogy series, which focuses on Bedroom Feng Shui, a specific topic dedicated to optimum bed location and placement.

If the Shoe Fits

This book is for those who want to make the effort to enhance their relationship.

In her debut release, Jessie Lee humbly shares with you the classical BaZi method of the Ten Day Masters and the combination of a new profiling system developed by Joey Yap, to understand and deal with the people around you.

Being Happy and Successful at Work and in your Career

Have you ever wondered why some of us are so successful in our careers while others are dragging their feet to work or switching from one job to another? Janet Yung hopes to answer this question by helping others through the knowledge and application of BaZi and Chinese Astrology. In her debut release, she shares with the readers the right way of using BaZi to understand themselves: their inborn talents, motivations, skills, and passions, to find their own place in the path of professional development.

Being Happy & Successful - Managing Yourself & Others

Manage Your Talent & Have Effective Relationships at the Workplace

While many strive for efficiency in the workplace, it is vital to know how to utilize your talents. In this book, Janet Yung will take you further on how to use the BaZi profiling system as a tool to assess your personality and understanding your approach to the job. From ways in communicating with your colleagues to understanding your boss, you will be astounded by what this ancient system can reveal about you and the people in your life. Tips and guidance will also be given in this book so that you will make better decisions for your next step in advancing in your career.

The BaZi Road to Success

The BaZi Road to Success explains your journey in life through a chart that is obtained just from looking at the date you were born and its connection with key BaZi elements.

Your Day Pillar, Hour Pillar, Luck Pillar and Annual Pillar all come together to paint a BaZi chart that churns out a combination of different elements, which the book helps interpret. From relationships, career advice, future plans and possibility of wealth accumulation - this book covers it all!

Face Reading Collection

The Chinese Art of Face Reading: The Book of Moles

The Book of Moles by Joey Yap delves into the inner meanings of moles and what they reveal about the personality and destiny of an individual. Complemented by fascinating illustrations and Joey Yap's easy-to-understand commentaries and guides, this book takes a deeper focus into a Face Reading subject, which can be used for everyday decisions – from personal relationships to professional dealings and many others.

Discover Face Reading (Available in English & Chinese)

This is a comprehensive book on all areas of Face Reading, covering some of the most important facial features, including the forehead, mouth, ears and even philtrum above your lips. This book will help you analyse not just your Destiny but also help you achieve your full potential and achieve life fulfillment.

Joey Yap's Art of Face Reading

The Art of Face Reading is Joey Yap's second effort with CICO Books, and it takes a lighter, more practical approach to Face Reading. This book does not focus on the individual features as it does on reading the entire face. It is about identifying common personality types and characters.

Faces of Fortune 2

We don't need to go far to look for entrepreneurs with the X-Factor. Malaysia produces some of the best entrepreneurs in the world. In this book, we will tell you the rags -to-riches stories of 9 ordinary people who has no special privileges, and how they made it on their own.

Easy Guide on Face Reading (Available in English & Chinese)

The Face Reading Essentials series of books comprises of five individual books on the key features of the face – the Eyes, the Eyebrows, the Ears, the Nose, and the Mouth. Each book provides a detailed illustration and a simple yet descriptive explanation on the individual types of the features.

The books are equally useful and effective for beginners, enthusiasts and those who are curious. The series is designed to enable people who are new to Face Reading to make the most out of first impressions and learn to apply Face Reading skills to understand the personality and character of their friends, family, co-workers and business associates.

2019 Annual Releases

| Chinese Astrology for 2019 | Feng Shui for 2019 | Tong Shu Desktop Calendar 2019 | Qi Men Desktop Calendar 2019 | Professional Tong Shu Diary 2019 | Tong Shu Monthly Planner 2019 | Weekly Tong Shu Diary 2019 |

Cultural Series

Discover the True Significance of the Ancient Art of Lion Dance

The Lion has long been a symbol of power and strength. That powerful symbol has evolved into an incredible display of a mixture of martial arts and ritualism that is the Lion Dance. Throughout ancient and modern times, the Lion Dance has stamped itself as a popular part of culture, but is there a meaning lost behind this magnificent spectacle?

The Art of Lion Dance written by the world's number one man in Chinese Metaphysics, Dato' Joey Yap, explains the history and origins of the art and its connection to Qi Men Dun Jia. By creating that bridge with Qi Men, the Lion Dance is able to ritualise any type of ceremony, celebrations and mourning alike.

The book is the perfect companion to the modern interpretation of the art as it reveals the significance behind each part of the Lion costume, as well as rituals that are put in place to bring the costume and its spectacle to life.

Chinese Traditions & Practices

China has a long, rich history spanning centuries. As Chinese culture has evolved over the centuries, so have the country's many customs and traditions. Today, there's a Chinese custom for just about every important event in a person's life – from cradle to the grave.

Although many China's customs have survived to the present day, some have been all but forgotten: rendered obsolete by modern day technology. This book explores the history of Chinese traditions and cultural practices, their purpose, and the differences between the traditions of the past and their modern incarnations.

If you are a westerner or less informed about Chinese culture, you may find this book particularly useful, especially when it comes to doing business with the Chinese – whether it be in China itself or some other country with a considerable Chinese population. If anything, it will allow you to have a better casual understanding of the culture and traditions of your Chinese friends or acquaintances. An understanding of Chinese traditions leads to a more informed, richer appreciation of Chinese culture and China itself.

Educational Tools and Software

Joey Yap's Feng Shui Template Set

Directions are the cornerstone of any successful Feng Shui audit or application. The Joey Yap Feng Shui Template Set is a set of three templates to simplify the process of taking directions and determining locations and positions, whether it is for a building, a house, or an open area such as a plot of land - all of it done with just a floor plan or area map.

The Set comprises three basic templates: The Basic Feng Shui Template, Eight Mansions Feng Shui Template, and the Flying Stars Feng Shui Template.

Mini Feng Shui Compass

The Mini Feng Shui Compass is a self-aligning compass that is not only light at 100gms but also built sturdily to ensure it will be convenient to use anywhere. The rings on the Mini Feng Shui Compass are bilingual and incorporate the 24 Mountain Rings that is used in your traditional Luo Pan.

The comprehensive booklet included with this, will guide you in applying the 24 Mountain Directions on your Mini Feng Shui Compass effectively and the Eight Mansions Feng Shui to locate the most auspicious locations within your home, office and surroundings. You can also use the Mini Feng Shui Compass when measuring the direction of your property for the purpose of applying Flying Stars Feng Shui.

MASTERY ACADEMY
OF CHINESE METAPHYSICS
Your **Preferred** Choice to the Art & Science of
Classical Chinese Metaphysics Studies

Bringing **innovative** techniques and **creative** teaching methods to an ancient study.

Mastery Academy of Chinese Metaphysics was established by Joey Yap to play the role of disseminating this Eastern knowledge to the modern world with the belief that this valuable knowledge should be accessible to everyone and everywhere.

Its goal is to enrich people's lives through accurate, professional teaching and practice of Chinese Metaphysics knowledge globally. It is the first academic institution of its kind in the world to adopt the tradition of Western institutions of higher learning - where students are encouraged to explore, question and challenge themselves, as well as to respect different fields and branches of studies. This is done together with the appreciation and respect of classical ideas and applications that have stood the test of time.

The Art and Science of Chinese Metaphysics – be it Feng Shui, BaZi (Astrology), Qi Men Dun Jia, Mian Xiang (Face Reading), ZeRi (Date Selection) or Yi Jing – is no longer a field shrouded with mystery and superstition. In light of new technology, fresher interpretations and innovative methods, as well as modern teaching tools like the Internet, interactive learning, e-learning and distance learning, anyone from virtually any corner of the globe, who is keen to master these disciplines can do so with ease and confidence under the guidance and support of the Academy.

It has indeed proven to be a centre of educational excellence for thousands of students from over thirty countries across the world; many of whom have moved on to practice classical Chinese Metaphysics professionally in their home countries.

At the Academy, we believe in enriching people's lives by empowering their destinies through the disciplines of Chinese Metaphysics. Learning is not an option - it is a way of life!

MASTERY ACADEMY
OF CHINESE METAPHYSICS™

MALAYSIA
19-3, The Boulevard, Mid Valley City, 59200 Kuala Lumpur, Malaysia
Tel : +6(03)-2284 8080 | Fax : +6(03)-2284 1218
Email   : info@masteryacademy.com
Website : www.masteryacademy.com

Australia, Austria, Canada, China, Croatia, Cyprus, Czech Republic, Denmark, France, Germany, Greece, Hungary, India, Italy, Kazakhstan, Malaysia, Netherlands (Holland), New Zealand, Philippines, Poland, Russian Federation, Singapore, Slovenia, South Africa, Switzerland, Turkey, United States of America, Ukraine, United Kingdom

The Mastery Academy around the world!

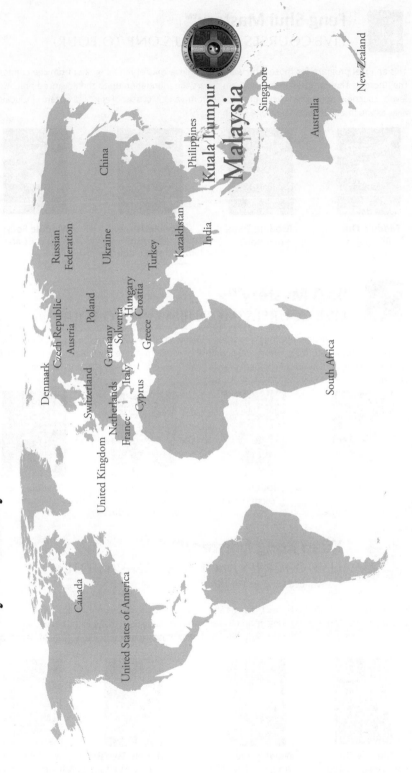

Feng Shui Mastery™
LIVE COURSES (MODULES ONE TO FOUR)

This an ideal program for those who wants to achieve mastery in Feng Shui from the comfort of their homes. This comprehensive program covers the foundation up to the advanced practitioner levels, touching upon the important theories from various classical Feng Shui systems including Ba Zhai, San Yuan, San He and Xuan Kong.

Module One:	**Module Two:**	**Module Three:**	**Module Four:**
Beginners Course	Practitioners Course	Advanced Practitioners Course	Master Course

BaZi Mastery™
LIVE COURSES (MODULES ONE TO FOUR)

This lesson-based program brings a thorough introduction to BaZi and guides the student step-by-step, all the way to the professional practitioner level. From the theories to the practical, BaZi students along with serious Feng Shui practitioners, can master its application with accuracy and confidence.

Module One:	**Module Two:**	**Module Three:**	**Module Four:**
Intensive Foundation Course	Practitioners Course	Advanced Practitioners Course	Master Course in BaZi

Xuan Kong Mastery™
LIVE COURSES (MODULES ONE TO THREE)
* Advanced Courses For Master Practitioners

Xuan Kong is a sophisticated branch of Feng Shui, replete with many techniques and formulae, which encompass numerology, symbology and the science of the Ba Gua, along with the mathematics of time. This program is ideal for practitioners looking to bring their practice to a more in-depth level.

Module One:	**Module Two A:**	**Module Two B:**	**Module Three:**
Advanced Foundation Course	Advanced Xuan Kong Methodologies	Purple White	Advanced Xuan Kong Da Gua

Mian Xiang Mastery™
LIVE COURSES (MODULES ONE AND TWO)

This program comprises of two modules, each carefully developed to allow students to familiarise with the fundamentals of Mian Xiang or Face Reading and the intricacies of its theories and principles. With lessons guided by video lectures, presentations and notes, students are able to understand and practice Mian Xiang with greater depth.

Module One:
Basic Face
Reading

Module Two:
Practical Face
Reading

Yi Jing Mastery™
LIVE COURSES (MODULES ONE AND TWO)

Whether you are a casual or serious Yi Jing enthusiast, this lesson-based program contains two modules that brings students deeper into the Chinese science of divination. The lessons will guide students on the mastery of its sophisticated formulas and calculations to derive answers to questions we pose.

Module One:
Traditional Yi Jing

Module Two:
Plum Blossom
Numerology

Ze Ri Mastery™
LIVE COURSES (MODULES ONE AND TWO)

In two modules, students will undergo a thorough instruction on the fundamentals of ZeRi or Date Selection. The comprehensive program covers Date Selection for both Personal and Feng Shui purposes to Xuan Kong Da Gua Date Selection.

Module One:
Personal and
Feng Shui Date
Selection

Module Two:
Xuan Kong
Da Gua Date
Selection

Joey Yap's
SAN YUAN QI MEN XUAN KONG DA GUA™

This is an advanced level program which can be summed up as the Integral Vision of San Yuan studies – an integration of the ancient potent discipline of Qi Men Dun Jia and the highly popular Xuan Kong 64 Hexagrams. Often regarded as two independent systems, San Yuan Qi Men and San Yuan Xuan Kong Da Gua can trace their origins to the same source and were actually used together in ancient times by great Chinese sages.

This method enables practitioners to harness the Qi of time and space, and predict the outcomes through a highly-detailed analysis of landforms, places and sites.

BaZi 10X

Emphasising on the practical aspects of BaZi, this programme is rich with numerous applications and techniques pertaining to the pursuit of wealth, health, relationship and career, all of which constitute the formula of success. This programme is designed for all levels of practitioners and is supplemented with innovative learning materials to enable easy learning. Discover the different layers of BaZi from a brand new perspective with BaZi 10X.

Feng Shui for Life

This is an entry-level five-day course designed for the Feng Shui beginner to learn the application of practical Feng Shui in day-to-day living. Lessons include quick tips on analysing the BaZi chart, simple Feng Shui solutions for the home, basic Date Selection, useful Face Reading techniques and practical Water formulas. A great introduction course on Chinese Metaphysics studies for beginners.

Joey Yap's
Design Your Destiny

This is a three-day life transformation program designed to inspire awareness and action for you to create a better quality of life. It introduces the DRT™ (Decision Referential Technology) method, which utilises the BaZi Personality Profiling system to determine the right version of you, and serves as a tool to help you make better decisions and achieve a better life in the least resistant way possible, based on your Personality Profile Type.

Millionaire Feng Shui Secrets Programme

This program is geared towards maximising your financial goals and dreams through the use of Feng Shui. Focusing mainly on the execution of Wealth Feng Shui techniques such as Luo Shu sectors and more, it is perfect for boosting careers, businesses and investment opportunities.

Grow Rich With BaZi Programme

This comprehensive programme covers the foundation of BaZi studies and presents information from the career, wealth and business standpoint. This course is ideal for those who want to maximise their wealth potential and live the life they deserve. Knowledge gained in this course will be used as driving factors to encourage personal development towards a better future.

Walk the Mountains!
Learn Feng Shui in a Practical and Hands-on Program

 ## Feng Shui Mastery Excursion™

Learn landform (Luan Tou) Feng Shui by walking the mountains and chasing the Dragon's vein in China. This program takes the students in a study tour to examine notable Feng Shui landmarks, mountains, hills, valleys, ancient palaces, famous mansions, houses and tombs in China. The excursion is a practical hands-on course where students are shown to perform readings using the formulas they have learnt and to recognise and read Feng Shui Landform (Luan Tou) formations.

Read about the China Excursion here:
http://www.fengshuiexcursion.com

Mastery Academy courses are conducted around the world. Find out when will Joey Yap be in your area by visiting
www.masteryacademy.com
or call our offices at **+6(03)-2284 8080**.

Online Home Study Courses

Gain Valuable Knowledge from the Comfort of Your Home

Now, armed with your trusty computer or laptop and Internet access, the knowledge of Chinese Metaphysics is just a click away!

3 Easy Steps to Activate Your Home Study Course:

Step 1:
Go to the URL as indicated on the Activation Card and key in your Activation Code

Step 2:
At the Registration page, fill in the details accordingly to enable us to generate your Student Identification (Student ID).

Step 3:
Upon successful registration, you may begin your lessons immediately.

Joey Yap's Feng Shui Mastery HomeStudy Course

Module 1: Empowering Your Home
Module 2: Master Practitioner Program

Learn how easy it is to harness the power of the environment to promote health, wealth and prosperity in your life. The knowledge and applications of Feng Shui will not be a mystery but a valuable tool you can master on your own.

Joey Yap's BaZi Mastery HomeStudy Course

Module 1: Mapping Your Life
Module 2: Mastering Your Future

Discover your path of least resistance to success with insights about your personality and capabilities, and what strengths you can tap on to maximise your potential for success and happiness by mastering BaZi (Chinese Astrology). This course will teach you all the essentials you need to interpret a BaZi chart and more.

Joey Yap's Mian Xiang Mastery HomeStudy Course

Module 1: Face Reading
Module 2: Advanced Face Reading

A face can reveal so much about a person. Now, you can learn the Art and Science of Mian Xiang (Chinese Face Reading) to understand a person's character based on his or her facial features, with ease and confidence.